Foster Placements

Supporting Parents

Series edited by David Quinton,
Professor of Psychosocial Development, University of Bristol
Consultant editors: Carolyn Davies and Caroline Thomas,
Department for Education and Skills and Department of Health

This important series is the result of an extensive government-funded research
initiative into how we can best support parents and carers as part of an integrated
service for children. Underpinning current policy directives including the Children's
National Service Framework, the titles in the series are essential reading for
practitioners, policy makers and academics working in child care.

Foster Placements

Why They Succeed and Why They Fail

Ian Sinclair, Kate Wilson and Ian Gibbs

Jessica Kingsley Publishers
London and Philadelphia

First published in 2005
by Jessica Kingsley Publishers
116 Pentonville Road
London N1 9JB, UK
and
400 Market Street, Suite 400
Philadelphia, PA 19106, USA

www.jkp.com

Copyright © Ian Sinclair, Kate Wilson and Ian Gibbs 2005

Library of Congress Cataloging in Publication Data
Sinclair, Ian, 1938-
    Foster placements : why they succeed and why they fail / Ian Sinclair, Kate Wilson and Ian Gibbs.
        p. cm.
    Includes bibliographical references and index.
    ISBN 1-84310-173-4 (pbk.)
    1. Foster home care--Great Britain. 2. Foster children--Great Britain. I. Wilson, Kate, 1943-
II. Gibbs, Ian. III. Title.
    HV887.G7S56 2005
    362.73'3'0941--dc22

                                                                        200402299

British Library Cataloguing in Publication Data
A CIP catalogue record for this book is available from the British Library

ISBN-13: 978 1 84310 173 4
ISBN-10: 1 84310 173 4

Printed and Bound in Great Britain by
Athenaeum Press, Gateshead, Tyne and Wear

Contents

Acknowledgements

As always this has been a team effort. Our work in preparing the book has been greatly aided by the efforts of Helen Jacobs and Dawn Rowley. Claire Baker took part in the subsequent research on the programme but has played a key role in checking this earlier work.

Throughout the project we have benefited from the wise counsel of an advisory group composed of Professor Jane Aldgate, Jane Allberry, Dr Carolyn Davies, Helen Jones, Gerri McAndrew, Professor David Quinton, Caroline Thomas and Professor John Triseliotis.

Our thanks must also go to those who, for reasons of confidentiality, we cannot name: the managers and liaison officers in the seven local authorities who were prepared to participate in, and support, a project that made great demands on their time, especially in completing the Census of Registered Foster Carers at two points of time.

Our main thanks are reserved for the foster carers and foster children who took part in our study. Without them this book would not have been possible. We hope it does justice to their concerns.

Ian Sinclair
Kate Wilson
Ian Gibbs

Chapter One

Background and Introduction

Introduction

> In the UK, on any one day, over 75,000 children are looked after by local
> authorities. Numerically the most important form of provision for these
> looked after children is foster care. This caters for about 60 per cent of those
> looked after at any one point in time. (Wilson *et al.* 2004, p.1)

This book is about foster children, their placements and what makes these
placements work.

Foster care itself is a highly diverse activity. Families of different culture,
composition, commitment and skills deliver it to children and young people
who vary widely in age, temperament, background and willingness to be
fostered. The purposes for which placements are set up vary too. And so does
the context – the legal basis for the placement, the attitude of the birth
families, the support provided by social workers and others such as teachers to
the placement, the way in which it was set up and much else besides. Against
this background it is not surprising that there is uncertainty over which of the
various possibly relevant factors lead, either on their own or in combination,
to success.

In practice success in this field is not easy to define. Some foster placements clearly succeed: the foster children do well and are happy, they are loved
in a way which does not threaten their relationships with their families, their
behaviour improves, they get glowing reports from school. Other placements
just as clearly fail: behaviour gets worse, the child truants from school, the
carer asks for the child to be removed. Between these two extremes many
placements get by or do as well as could be expected. This book sets out to
contribute to the understanding of placement success by identifying from the

research factors which seemed to make placements go well or badly. It also sets the scene for this analysis by discussing what counts as success and a description of the foster children. In our final chapter, we draw on our understanding of what has brought about these outcomes to make some suggestions as to what could be done to improve them.

The book itself forms part of a set of three complementary titles. These draw on the findings of three linked studies of foster care which we undertook over a six-year period in seven local authorities in England. The first book, *Foster Carers: Why They Stay and Why They Leave*, is, as its title suggests, primarily about foster carers: who they are, what diminishes or increases the stresses they feel and what makes them find foster care fulfilling and want to continue (Sinclair, Gibbs and Wilson 2004). As already described this, the second book, focuses by and large on foster placements, the children in them and what makes the placements go well or founder. The third book provides a detailed account and analysis of these same children (n=596) as we charted their care careers over a period of two years.

Inevitably some of the discussion in the three books overlaps: for example, in this book we say a good deal about foster carers and whether they have identifiable skills which can contribute to placement success. The third book also discusses what contributes to things going well, but it concentrates more on case success, i.e. what has been achieved for the child in the longer term, rather than as here focusing on the outcome of a particular placement. Although the books form a set we have written each so that it can be read independently of the others.

Locating the study within the literature

The questions we examine are not new. Our study can be seen as part of a long tradition of research concerned with foster care and adoption. The aims of this tradition have been to describe the characteristics of foster children, to track their progress through the care system, and to identify the factors which lead to success. The criteria for success have included ratings of the degree to which placements have met their varied aims (Cliffe with Berridge 1991; Rowe, Hundleby and Garnett 1989). Many studies have used 'breakdown', 'disruption' or 'not lasting as long as needed' as a measure of failure (Berridge and Cleaver 1987; Borland, O'Hara and Triseliotis 1991; Cleaver 2000; Farmer, Moyers and Lipscombe 2004; Fratter *et al.* 1991; George 1970; Parker 1966; Quinton *et al.* 1998; Rowe *et al.* 1989; Rushton and Treseder 1995; Thoburn, Norford and Rashid 2000; Trasler 1960; Walker, Hill and

Triseliotis 2002). Less commonly they have included measures of changes in children's educational performance or psychological status (Aldgate *et al.* 1992; Lambert, Essen and Head 1977). Whatever the measure of outcome, a common desire of all researchers has been to determine what makes for success or lack of it.

Taken as a whole, the body of work broadly supports Berridge and Cleaver's (1987) view that the reasons for breakdown have to do with the child, the characteristics of the placement or both. First, there is consistent evidence that breakdowns are more likely when the child is older, or when he or she is, on a variety of criteria, 'more difficult'. Second, there is agreement in the literature on the kinds of foster carers who are seen as most likely to succeed. Third, there is agreement that 'matching' is important, particularly in relation to the age gap between foster children and the other children in the foster family (for reviews of the evidence on these points see Berridge 1997; Sellick and Thoburn 1996).

Research on the factors which lead to success is complemented by some work on the process by which it takes place and which uses qualitative methods such as case studies (e.g. Beek and Schofield 2004; Berridge and Cleaver 1987; Bullock, Little and Millham 1993; Millham *et al.* 1986; Schofield *et al.* 2000) and interviews with carers and current or former foster children (e.g. Triseliotis 1980). Two sets of case studies (Aldgate and Hawley 1986; Berridge and Cleaver 1987) suggest that breakdowns come about through a series of events building up to a final incident which may act as the 'last straw' rather than itself being the sole cause.

Much of this work is of very high quality. However, although telling, the results are not conclusive. Some of the studies are small; some are so dated that it is unclear whether or not the conclusions are still relevant to current policy and practice. In some there is a danger of circularity (lack of commitment is found to lead to breakdowns but a family which had asked for a child to be removed would hardly been seen as committed to the placement). The results are not always consistent. In two areas in particular, those relating to the less easily measured characteristics of carers (warmth, for example, and skill) and the interactions between carer and child, there is (with the honourable exceptions of Farmer and her colleagues in 2004 and Quinton and his in 1998) rather little statistical evidence.

In building on this evidence, and beginning to address the gaps in it, we needed to understand what counted as success or, in current parlance, a good outcome. This meant that we needed to understand what placements were intended to achieve, what foster children wanted from them and what foster carers and others counted as success.

Second, we needed to describe the foster children, their needs and the characteristics that make them more or less likely to succeed. Only in this way could we tell if any aspects of the placement made a child more likely to succeed than he or she would have been without them.

Third, we became concerned with identifying the potential impact of a wide range of factors which might contribute to the success of placements. Our key focus was on the qualities and skills of the foster carers themselves. However, we also considered direct interventions with the young people – their contacts with social workers, psychologists and psychiatrists and so on, in addition to qualities and skills of the foster carers themselves and other issues concerning the context in which the placement occurred, such as relationships with the birth family and the impact of school. In this way we have effectively mounted a large study of what makes for success in foster care.

The study

Our evidence comes from a study which, as originally planned, set out to look at support for foster carers. The study was carried out in seven local authorities: two London boroughs, a metropolitan district council, two shire counties and two unitary authorities. To judge from national statistics, the local authorities were, taken as a whole, highly representative. They had almost exactly the national proportion of children looked after per 10,000 of the population, and the national proportions of those fostered, in children's homes, or placed for adoption.

Our data is based on a cross-sectional sample of foster children of all ages placed with foster carers within these authorities. We sent out questionnaires on 596 individual children to foster carers who had agreed to take part in the study, the children's social workers and the foster carers' family placement social workers. The carers were those who had responded to our General Questionnaire (the findings of which form the focus of our first book – Sinclair *et al.* 2004) and agreed to take part in a further exercise focused on an individual child. We followed the children up 14 months later, seeking the same information from the same three sources.

The basic data at Time 1 were as follows:

- *The first questionnaire to foster carers* (n=495) – collected information and views from foster carers on the characteristics of the foster child, their own approach and that of their family, the support they receive for the placement from social workers and other sources, how well the placement was going (e.g. progress of child).

- *The child's social worker postal questionnaire* (n=416) – collected information and views from social workers on the characteristics of the foster child, the approach taken by the foster carers, the support provided and how well the placement was going.
- *The family placement worker postal questionnaire* (n=492) – collected information and views from family placement workers (sometimes known as link workers) on the approach taken by foster carers, their own characteristics (e.g. if trained), and outcome.

Information at Time 2 came from the same three sources and yielded 504 questionnaires (from foster carers), 337 questionnaires (social workers) and 462 questionnaires (family placement social workers). Each of these questionnaires dealt with the outcome as perceived by the respondent and – to varying extents – with the factors that might lead to this outcome.

We had two additional sources of information. First, we sent 250 questionnaires to children aged five or over whose carers and social workers agreed we could do so. We received 150 usable replies. We used these to describe what children wanted from placements, to compare these wants (for example, for a placement that lasts till 18) with what happened, and to develop our understanding of what was likely to make a placement go well.

Second, we carried out 24 detailed case studies, 13 selected to represent cases which had 'gone well' and 11 representing cases which had gone less well. We selected the cases in pairs and matched them as closely as possible in terms of age, sex, and length of time in placement. Some cases selected as 'successes' were undergoing difficulties when the case studies were carried out and others selected as 'less successful' were going better. Nevertheless it was still possible to use the contrast between cases to derive hypotheses on what made placements more or less successful.

Like any study within this tradition, our research has its distinctive characteristics which bring both strengths and limitations. These relate to:

- *date* – compared to the classic work of, for example, Parker (1966) or Trasler (1960), this is a recent study, and even Berridge and Cleaver's important study (1987) is now more than 16 years old
- *sample* – our study focuses on children placed with foster carers other than with a view to adoption or respite at a particular point

in time, and this distinguishes it from studies which have followed children from the moment they entered the care system

- *data collected* – our study has collected an unusually wide range of data, some of it (like ratings of parenting) of a 'soft' kind; it is unusual (although not unique) in seeking to collect this kind of data in a study of this size and in combining multi-variate analysis with case studies.

These differences do not make it better or worse than earlier or contemporary work – merely different. Being different has, we believe, an important contribution to make.

The main limitations of the study arise first from the fact that we did not follow up the children from the moment they entered the care system or even before this point. Descriptive information (e.g. on the proportion of children who go home after a certain length of time) is accurate in relation to the sample we have. A sample of children entering the system could well have rather different characteristics. An additional difficulty in this kind of cross-sectional sample is that we may underestimate the degree to which the care system can achieve change (as seen later, we have some evidence that children change psychologically more at the beginning of a placement than they do later on).

Second, there may also be problems of interpretation. For example, it may be difficult to decide whether the foster carer's parenting reflects their characteristics or the behaviour elicited from them by the child. In our case this difficulty was lessened, although not fully overcome, by the fact that we followed our children up. We could therefore see whether future success was more likely with certain kinds of foster carers after allowing for the earlier behaviour of their foster children.

These disadvantages need to be balanced against strengths. The sample describes the population in foster care at a particular point in time. This population will contain many more longer-staying foster children than a sample of entrants. These are the children who take up the major part of the resources devoted to foster care and for whom the system bears the most awesome responsibility. It is also possible to study them at all periods in their career. A study of entrants is unlikely to have much to say about the progress of its charges six years later, while a cross-sectional survey will have children who have been in the system for very varying lengths of time *and* will include more long-stay children than a sample of entrants.

Overall, the potential strengths of the study lie in its recent date and its combination of size, success in collecting follow-up information on a large number of children, the range of information collected, and the combination of qualitative and quantitative approaches.

Sources of information

The fact that our information came from a variety of sources has a number of advantages. In particular we were able to:

- seek information from those most likely to be in a position to provide it (for example, foster carers were in a better position than social workers to provide details of the children's daily behaviour)

- compensate for missing information from one source (e.g. on a child's subsequent destination) by supplying it from another

- check the reliability of 'soft' information (i.e. answers based on respondents' opinions and judgements, sometimes in response to open-ended questions) by comparing ratings given by one source with ratings given by another.

Less positively, the use of multiple sources of information could make it harder for the reader to know which sample is being used at which point. If the sample was restricted to those for whom all sources of information were available, it would shrink considerably in size. In practice the size of the samples depends on the kinds of analysis we are doing.

- Where we are describing the sample we use the maximum information available (for example, if the information comes from the social worker questionnaire we use it, irrespective of whether the children also attracted replies from carers).

- Where we are relating information from a questionnaire collected at Time 1 to our main outcome variables at Time 2 we were again able to use almost all the replies from the questionnaire (we had measures of all three outcome variables for over 96% of the sample).

- Where the analysis involves relating information from one questionnaire to that in another the analysis is restricted to those on whom both sets of information are available.

The last condition can decrease the numbers in the sample quite sharply. This is particularly so if the measure is not available on all the children. For example, the numbers on whom we had questionnaires from foster carers at both points in time was 444 (75% of the potential sample). The numbers on whom we had both a social work questionnaire and a Time 1 foster carer questionnaire was 361 (61% of the potential sample). A number of our measures were only suitable for children aged three and over or children of school age. This obviously shrinks both the potential sample and the numbers included in any analysis.

These complications make it important to check for bias in our samples. We need to know how the various samples differ from each other and how far the core sample appears to be represent foster children in England as a whole. These issues are considered in Chapter 2 and – in much more detail – in Appendix 1. The general conclusion is that in many ways our sample is highly representative of foster children in the care system in England at any particular moment in time. Detailed consideration suggests some particular biases. We do not, however, think it at all likely that these invalidate our conclusions.

Approach to analysis

Our analysis proceeds in three steps. First, we describe the characteristics of the placement (notably the characteristics of the foster child and details of the way the placement was made).

Second, we try to build an analytic account or model of what counts as success and what leads to it. We base this on qualitative material – what the children, carers, social workers and family placement workers said to us.

Third, we explore this model statistically by relating the variables (or, more strictly speaking, groups of variables) in which we are interested to various measures of outcome. This allows us to assess the impact of support on outcomes after allowing for the characteristics of the child, the foster carer and the interaction between the two.

The relationship between the qualitative and quantitative models is, in fact, rather more complicated than implied above. The qualitative model specifies certain conditions and processes which foster success. We later try to measure these and see if they are statistically associated with good outcomes. In this way we try to 'test' our hypotheses through what is called 'triangulation'. At the same time the qualitative model contains suggestions, and, in our view, insights which go beyond the statistical data, although they are compatible with it. These insights are, we believe, particularly relevant to practice.

One further qualification should be made at this point. Our interest is in the success of the placement. For us this involves how well the foster child settles in, how happy he or she is there, how he or she gets on with the foster carers and so on. Placement success tends to be a prerequisite for case success – in the sense that the long-term outcome is good – but the two things are not synonymous. From time to time we will talk about case success. Usually such an outcome would be seen as 'final' – something to which this particular placement has contributed. These final outcomes are not the focus of the book.

Statistical tests

The book is intended to be accessible to the interested reader. He or she may or may not be familiar with statistical techniques.

The need for these techniques arises because the study focuses on a sample, rather than on all foster children. The assumption is that the process of drawing a sample of foster children is essentially the same as that of drawing a number of cards from a shuffled pack. In the case of a pack of cards it is obvious that from time to time a sample of cards drawn from it will be misleading. For example, it is logically possible that if one draws four cards all will turn out to be aces, even though the parent pack only had four aces out of 52 cards. Equally it could be that on drawing 12 cards one would find that all the court cards drawn were spades and all the others were hearts. Nevertheless these results are clearly unlikely.

The essential purpose of most of the tests in this book is to show how likely or unlikely a particular association is. If a result should occur by chance less than one in twenty times this is shown by writing '$p<0.05$'. The more unlikely it is that a particular finding would occur by chance the more confidence we can have that it would be repeated in another sample. We have tried to write the text in such a way that a reader who is not interested in these niceties can skip the symbols and still understand what is being said. Occasionally it is necessary to explain some more complicated piece of analysis, as it is central to the argument. Where we believe this to be so we shall do so.

Structure of the book

The structure of the book follows the basic approach outlined above.

In our first three chapters, we set the context for the study, describing the basic characteristics of the sample, the purposes of the placements, what the children who replied to our questionnaires said they wanted from foster care, and what had happened to the sample when we followed them up.

Our next four chapters use our qualitative material to discuss the meaning of 'success' in different kinds of foster care, and the accounts given by foster carers and social workers of what leads to it. These foster carer and social worker accounts are complemented by two chapters giving the analysis suggested by our case studies. Taken together, this yields a 'model' of what produces success in foster care.

Our remaining chapters, apart from our conclusion, are concerned with testing this model. They deal respectively with the relationship between two measures of success and:

- the child's placement history
- the child's characteristics
- contacts with the birth family
- the approach and characteristics of the foster carers
- the support provided by social workers
- other forms of support, in particular support from school.

Our penultimate chapter is particularly concerned with psychological change among those children who remained in the placement at follow-up.

Characteristics of the book

In presenting these results we emphasise that they represent only part of the account of research on foster care that took six years to complete. It would have been very difficult to write one volume covering all aspects of the research. Instead we have written three books that each, while complementary, tell their own story.

As already described our present book concentrates on placements. It is only part of a longer story that we pick up again in our next book. That said, what happens within placements is crucially important to all those involved. This is what this book is about.

Chapter Two

The Sample: Characteristics and Reasons for Placement

Introduction

One aim of this project was to describe a large sample of foster children and foster placements. This was seen as of interest in itself. There is no recent large-scale study of children in foster care at a particular point in time. It is also an essential preliminary to any study of the impact of support on outcomes. It is only after describing these characteristics and their association with outcome that we can try to tease out the additional impact of support.

This chapter begins the task of description. It provides information on the age, sex, ethnicity and legal status of the children in the sample, their previous careers in the care system, and the reasons for their current placement. This information helps to identify the broad kinds of fostering experienced by the sample – for example, whether their placements were short- or long-term. It also gives information relevant to some of the key concerns about the system – for example, about the degree of choice available when placements are made.

Basic variables

Table 2.1 gives the age distribution of children in the sample. As can be seen, half are aged under 11, and half are 11 or over. These figures are in keeping with what is known from official statistics at the time of our study, where 45 per cent of foster children were aged under 10 (Department of Health 1999). As 5 per cent of our sample are aged 10, the two figures are effectively the same.

Table 2.1 Age distribution of foster children

Age group	n	%
Under 5	126	24
5–10	138	26
11–15	134	25
16 and over	135	25
Total	533	100

Sources: Social worker and foster carer questionnaires at Time 1.

Interestingly, the figures conceal a highly significant degree of variation between authorities (chi square=44.19, df=18, $p<0.001$). This was mainly evident at the extremes. In one authority, only 13 per cent of those in the sample were aged under five, whereas the comparable figure in two other authorities was 36 per cent. In one authority, only 9 per cent of the sample were aged 16 or over, whereas the comparable figure in the other authorities lay between 19 per cent and 32 per cent. It is unclear whether a low proportion in a particular age group is desirable or undesirable. On the face of it, however, an authority which has a very low proportion of its foster children aged 16 or over is not providing a particularly permanent form of care.

Overall, 46 per cent of the sample were female and 54 per cent were male. The latest official statistics do not give the comparable proportions of females and males in foster care. However, the figures for this sample are close to the national figures for children who are looked after, 45 per cent of whom are said to be female. In this respect, there were no differences in the proportions by authority.

Eighty-four per cent of the children were said by the foster carers to be English, Welsh, Irish or Scots. Of the remainder, the largest number (9%) were 'dual heritage' children, a group which researchers have consistently found to be over-represented in the care system (Bebbington and Miles 1990; Fratter *et al.* 1991; Rowe *et al.* 1989). Other groups included children of West Indian origin (1.7%), African origin (1.9%), or a variety of Asian (1.8%) or European origins (1.2%).

These figures can be compared with those provided by Bebbington and Miles (1990), who studied a large sample of children admitted to the care system. They report a slightly smaller proportion from ethnic minorities (12% as against 17%), which included a smaller proportion whose origins were mixed (6% as against 9%). Our figure was also higher than the 6 per cent reported by Cleaver (2000) in her study of foster care placements lasting at least three months in two authorities. By contrast, the proportion from ethnic minorities in our study equalled the 17 per cent of admissions reported by Rowe and her colleagues (1989).

Our figure is likely to reflect the nature of the sample (current cases, not admissions as in the other studies), and – most crucially – the local authorities included in the study. As might be expected, there was a very large variation by local authority. Carers in three authorities reported very low proportions of children from ethnic minorities (4% to 8%). In two authorities the figures were 14 per cent and 20 per cent. Carers for the two London boroughs reported proportions of 69 per cent and 79 per cent. Given this variation, a national figure for proportions of ethnic minority children is not particularly meaningful, and different studies are likely to show very different proportions.

In terms of legal status, 60 per cent were on some form of care order. This compares with national figures for 31 March 1998 of 60 per cent. There was a similarly close correspondence on the proportion accommodated (33% in this study as against 36% nationally). Again, there were variations between authorities, with the proportions on a care order varying from 86 per cent to 46 per cent.

Career variables: placements and episodes of care

'Career variables' are, in our terms, those which have to do with the sequence, length and number of placements in a child's career in the care system. Previous studies which have covered careers have used the material to raise three major concerns about the foster care system. First, there is the problem that children may 'drift' in care, neither returning home nor entering a permanent and secure placement, a concern which in Britain goes back to work by Rowe and Lambert (1973). Second, a natural reluctance to face the inevitable may mean that children remain at home or oscillate between home and foster care when there is no realistic prospect that their family is viable for them (Bullock *et al.* 1993). Third, the child may experience a highly unstable career in care, moving from placement to placement and finding no permanent home (e.g. Stein and Carey 1986; Marsh and Triseliotis 1993).

Much of the argument around these issues is based on 'first principles'. Children, it is naturally believed, need a permanent family (Maluccio, Fein and Olmstead 1986). It can hardly be good for them either to remain in a dangerous and abusive home (Goldstein 1973), or to move from place to place, failing to acquire a sense of identity, suffering repeated disruptions to their education, and feeling that there is no one who cares for them. There is evidence that young people who have had unstable careers in the care system do worse on leaving it than others (Biehal *et al.* 1992; Garnett 1992). There is also some empirical evidence that young children at least are more likely to thrive and achieve reasonable adjustment if they remain in the care system than if they return to their homes (Hensey, Williams and Rosenbloom 1983; King and Taitz 1985) – a finding which agrees with the generally favourable evidence on the impact of infant adoptions. Studies of the outcomes of long-stay foster care similarly suggest that length of stay in foster care corre-lates positively with outcomes (Minty 1999; Minty and Ashcroft 1987; Zimmerman 1982).

The new *Quality Protects* initiative has been influenced by these consider-ations. It seeks to ensure that children in the community are appropriately assessed, that the number of moves in the care system is kept to a minimum, and that adoption is considered whenever appropriate. What, then, is our evidence on the frequency of such placement changes?

Care episodes, age at admission and number of placements

In exploring careers, we looked first at the age at which the children first entered the care system. Half had had their first experience of being looked after when they were less than six and roughly a third when they were between six and ten. Only a fifth had their first experience when they were 11 or over. Even among those who were aged 11 or over, 59 per cent had first been looked after when aged under ten and just under a quarter when they were aged less than five. Clearly, a sizeable number of children are having a great deal of contact with the care system. As we shall see this may or may not involve prolonged stays in care.

In practice, the efforts to return children home meant that fewer children had lengthy continuous periods in the care system than their age at first contact with the system would suggest. Figures on the length of the current episode were only available for 304 children. These suggested that around a quarter (29%) (national figures 30% for 31 March 1998) had been away from home for less than a year, but more than three-quarters (84%) for less than five years (national figures 78%). At the other end of the spectrum, one child had been continuously in the care system for nearly 18 years. The length of time in the current placement was obviously no greater and often considerably less than this. According to the foster carers, one third of these children had been in placement for eight months or less. A further third (35%) had been in the placement for between 9 and 21 months. The remainder had spent longer than this.

The impression that children were experiencing 'serial parenting' was naturally greater among those who were older and had had more time to go in and out of the care system. In Table 2.2, an episode is defined as a distinct period during which the child lived away from her or his parents and was 'looked after'. The small numbers of children in the sample who were first admitted before the age of six and who were still being looked after at 16 had experienced, on average, nearly four distinct admissions. Even children who were still under five had experienced an average of one-and-a-half admissions.

Table 2.2 Mean number of episodes by age group and age at first admission

| Age group | Age at first admission | | | |
	0–5	6–10	11–14	15+
Under 5	1.5 (92)	–	–	–
5–10	2.5 (60)	1.6 (39)	–	–
11–15	2.9 (30)	2.3 (60)	1.7 (39)	2 (2)
16+	3.5 (16)	2.7 (15)	2.0 (35)	2 (7)
Total numbers	198	114	74	9

Source: Social worker questionnaire at Time 1.
Note: Numbers in brackets represent the base from which the averages are calculated. Some averages are underestimates since 5 or more was treated as 5.

Table 2.2 also brings out the paradoxical extent to which instability in the care system represents an attempt to provide permanence. Re-admissions generally represent the failure of an attempt to provide the child with a permanent home with her or his family. In this way, attempts at providing permanence at home run the risk of producing the instability which is notoriously one of the reasons for wishing to avoid the care system in the first place.

In considering this point, it is worth noting the degree to which a small number of children accounted for a relatively high number of episodes. Forty-two per cent had had no more than one episode including the present one, while nearly three-quarters had had no more than two. At the other end of the spectrum, 10 per cent had had five or more episodes.

A similarly skewed distribution was found when we counted the number of placements in foster or residential care experienced by the sample. Just over a quarter had only one, and around three-quarters no more than three. Sixteen per cent, however, had experienced five or more. This figure is also related to age, so that among those aged 11 or over, more than a quarter (27%) had experienced five or more placements.

It is tempting to regard the number of placements as an index of the child's difficulty, with children with many problems going through placements like a knife through butter. As we will see later, more difficult children are more likely to have placement breakdowns and hence a somewhat higher number of placements. However, a multi-variate analysis which included indices of the child's difficulty showed that by far the strongest predictor of number of placements was number of returns home, followed by age. A policy which aimed above all at permanent placements would therefore probably reduce the number of times a child returned to her or his family. This morally fraught approach would increase the amount of time children spend being looked after and thus the number of foster carers required.

A somewhat disturbing aspect of the number of placements was the proportion of them which involved a breakdown. Table 2.3 gives the distribution of various kinds of breakdown among those children for whom we had a questionnaire from their social worker.

Table 2.3 Proportion of children noted as having experienced different kinds of disruption

Nature of disruption	% (n=416)
Child's behaviour/relationship with carers	36
Reasons connected with carers' circumstances	22
Reasons connected with birth family	18
Other reasons	11
At least one of above	62

Source: Social worker questionnaire at Time 1.
Note: Percentages do not add up to 100 as respondents could indicate more than one form of disruption.

The placement: reasons behind it, matching and plans

The circumstances surrounding the current placement are likely to be at least as influential as the child's previous 'care career'. There is evidence, for example, that placements made 'in a rush' are likely to be less successful than others (Berridge and Cleaver 1987; Farmer *et al.* 2004), and also that those made for short-term purposes such as assessment are likely to be perceived as more successful (Rowe *et al.* 1989). There is certainly a widespread belief (reflected in social workers' responses to our questionnaires) that satisfactory matching is crucial to placement success. In this section, we concentrate on the reasons for which placements were made, the degree to which they were planned or made in an emergency, whether they were from the community or from within the care system, whether they were seen as a satisfactory placement at the time, and the plans for them in the future. Other information on the placement (particularly the quality of the information provided to the carer) is considered elsewhere.

The circumstances

We asked the social workers to describe the circumstances which led to the child being looked after. As might be expected, the reasons were varied. Some reflected neglect or abuse:

> Parent a Class A drug user. Child not being supervised and fed adequately.

> All the child's siblings were taken into local authority care when it became obvious that the three eldest had all been sexually assaulted.

Some involved the breakdown of relationships which previously had more or less managed to provide the child with care, or the introduction of new dangerous adults into the child's family:

> Child had been in care of father who commenced relationship with Schedule 1 offender. Child moved to natural mother who found she could not cope. Child lost weight dramatically.

> Father admitted to psychiatric unit and mother unable to care for child without father's support.

Others involved rejection by one or more of the parents or by the child:

> Child's wishes – refused to return home. Combined with evidence of abuse and neglect.

Father in drink and unable to care for child. Mother separated from father and unwilling to care for daughter.

And there were other reasons – stress on the parents, parental requests for respite, unsatisfactory private fosterings which broke down, the decision by the local authority to remove the child at birth, abandonment and the death of all those who might provide care. The events themselves seemed to take place against a backcloth of adults joining and leaving the family, poverty, stress, psychiatric ill-health, and sometimes drink, drugs and criminality.

Against this background, we asked the social workers to characterise the main reason for which the child was accepted as someone who needed looking after. We gave them a list of six options derived from similar lists developed by Berridge and Cleaver (1987) and Millham and his colleagues (1986). The most commonly chosen was 'abuse' (40%), closely followed by 'neglect' (23%). The next most popular category was 'breakdown in relationship between child and parents' (21%). 'Family illness/housing problem' and 'other' each accounted for 7 per cent and 'child's behaviour' for 3 per cent.

As might be expected, the frequency with which these explanations were given depended on the age at which the children were first looked after. Nearly half those first entering when aged ten or over did so because of a perceived breakdown of relationships at home. This explanation was only given for one in eight of those first entering when under five. By contrast hardly any of those entering when over ten did so for reasons of neglect – a reason given for around a third of those first entering when less than five.

According to the social workers, the majority of the placements resulted from some kind of emergency – a third because of the breakdown of a placement and a further fifth because of some kind of 'crisis' in the community. A further third were planned placements – a quarter from within the care system and one in ten from the community. The final 10 per cent were categorised as 'other' – either because their placement could not properly be described as from the community or the care system (e.g. the child was in some kind of hospital) or because it could not properly be described as planned or emergency. Two points, however, are clear. First, only a minority of placements were planned. Second, the majority of placements were made from within the care system (see Table 2.4, where figures differ slightly because of omission of 'don't know').

Table 2.4 Characteristics of placement at time it was made

In social workers' view was the placement:	n*	Yes (%)	Other (%)
Planned (or otherwise)	305	36	64
Result of choice between placements (or otherwise)	227	26	74
Thought suitable (or otherwise)	292	74	26

Source: Social worker questionnaire at Time 1.
*Numbers do not include the 'don't knows'.

Emergencies, matching and choice

As others have found (Farmer *et al.* 2004), this situation allowed for rather little choice. In half the cases, the social workers said there was no choice of placements and the child had the only one available. In one in five cases they said that were was some choice. In 30 per cent of the cases they did not know whether there was choice or not.

We had expected that choice would be less likely when the child had been a teenager at entry – in one study, 70 per cent of local authorities reported placement shortage for this group (Waterhouse 1997). Our data failed to confirm this hypothesis.

Unsurprisingly, however, the existence of a perceived emergency made choice less likely. In such cases, social workers who had the relevant information said that there had been the possibility of choice in less than one in five cases. They were twice as likely to consider there had been some choice in four out of ten cases where the placement had been planned.

Again unsurprisingly, the degree of choice was related to whether the placement was seen at the time as satisfactory. In seven out of ten cases this was said to be so. In just over a fifth (22%) it was said that this was more or less so, and in only 4 per cent of cases that the placement was thought unsatisfactory. (In the remaining 4% of cases, the social worker did not know. In calculating these percentages, we have excluded cases where the social worker did not know if there was choice.) Only 9 per cent of cases where there was choice were apparently not felt to be fully satisfactory. By contrast, this was true of 39 per cent of those where there was no choice.

We asked the social workers to say why the placement was or was not considered satisfactory. Their answers suggested six main groups of reasons.

These related to:

- *culture* – social workers wanted placements which were as far as possible matched in terms of ethnicity, culture and language
- *foster carer skills* – some foster carers were seen as experienced with and having a proven track record with certain kinds of children – teenagers, babies, disabled children, and traumatised children were all mentioned
- *willingness to work with the care plan* – social workers wanted foster carers who were willing and able to work with birth parents when appropriate and who did not, for example, want a long-term placement when the plan was preparation for adoption
- *family characteristics* – issues of space, whether the child would have to share a bedroom, whether the child needed to be with other children or on their own, whether it would be possible to take the child's siblings, and whether the carer would be at home during the day were all important, although not always valued in the same way
- *geographical location* – social workers sometimes wanted placements where the child could continue to go to the same school or see her or his birth parents frequently
- *choice and commitment* – in a surprisingly large number of cases the placement seemed to build on choices made by the child. Sometimes the carers were relatives, sometimes they were friends of previous foster carers, sometimes they were foster carers with whom the child had had short-term placements, and sometimes placements made for short-term purposes had forged a bond which had led to more permanent plans.

This convincing but potentially demanding list of characteristics makes it surprising that as many as seven out of ten placements were seen as satisfactory.

Initial purposes

We asked the social workers and foster carers about the purposes for which the placements were initially made. Table 2.5 gives the results which reflect answers to closed questions originally developed by Rowe and her colleagues (1989). We asked similar questions of social workers and foster carers and so were able to compare the results.

Table 2.5 Purposes for which original placement was made

Reasons	n	%
An emergency place (roof over head)	62	20
Help in assessing child's needs	27	9
Rehabilitation*	27	9
A home (long-term placement)	117	38
Preparation for adoption	33	11
Preparation for another placement	6	2
Preparation for independent living	7	2
Help foster child to change (treatment)	5	2
Give birth parents a break	4	1
Other	20	6
Don't know	1	0
Total	309	100

Source: Social worker questionnaire at Time 1.
*Defined as 'helping in getting child and her/his parents back together again'.

According to the social workers, around three in ten of the placements involved relatively short-term goals. The child was to be held while an emergency was sorted out, or his or her needs could be assessed. In around half the cases, the aim was a long-term placement – most commonly (38%) in the same foster home, but in a substantial minority of cases (11%) through adoption. Rehabilitation home was a goal for a further 9 per cent (although as seen later, more were expected to return home at some stage). Other goals – for example, 'treatment' (2%) – were rarely envisaged.

According to the carers, the situation was rather different. As can be seen, the questions were not worded in precisely the same way. Nevertheless, they suggest that as the foster carers saw it, short-term goals were in mind for around four in ten of the children (as against 30% according to the social workers). Social workers and carers recorded the same purpose for a given placement more often than would have been expected by chance, but the match was certainly far from exact. The figures suggested that social workers were more likely to see current plans (e.g. for adoption or long-term placement) as having been there from the beginning: a fact that may reflect turnover among social workers, with some not knowing what the original plans were, or a failure at the time of the placement to communicate these plans to the carer. In some cases, it may involve an inadvertent rewriting of history, with plans that preceded placements longer than envisaged being redefined as having been for long-term care all along.

Table 2.6   Carers' views of what social workers had most in mind for placement

Reasons	n	%
Short-term place while things were sorted out	167	34
Help in getting child and her or his parents back together	41	8
A period of assessment	39	8
A long-term home	131	27
Preparation for another placement	25	5
Preparation for independent living	14	3
Help foster child to change in some way	6	1
Give parents a break	9	2
No clear plan	27	5
Other	31	6
Don't know	3	1
Total	493	100

Source: Foster carer questionnaire at Time 1.

A rather striking feature was the rarity with which social workers saw the purpose of placement as being for 'treatment' or foster carers saw it as being to bring about some kind of change. As we have glimpsed in this chapter, and will see in more detail when we follow the children up, foster care does not offer its charges much hope of a permanent placement. So its charges need to be well-equipped if they are to cope with an uncertain world. Traditionally foster care has provided ordinary 'upbringing' with the more ambitious goal of 'treatment' reserved for residential care or outside intervention. This view may underestimate its potential for addressing children's problems and helping them develop life skills.

Conclusion

Our study contains the only recent large-scale survey of children currently in the foster care system. The first aim of this chapter was to see how far the children resembled the picture that would be expected from national statistics or – in the case of ethnicity – those suggested by samples entering the system or moving into, out of, or within it. In terms of age, sex, ethnicity, legal status, and length of time in the care system following last entry to it, our sample is almost identical with what would have been expected.

More substantively, the results illustrate some perennial problems of the foster care system.

First, by seeking to return children to their families, social services almost inevitably involve some of them in serial parenting. The problem is exacerbated by the number of breakdowns which children experience, and the fact that the foster care system does not supply care after 18 or, apparently in the case of one of our authorities, much after 16.

Second, the wide variety of foster children, the number of criteria against which they need to be matched with carers, and the number of emergency placements, means that immediate close matches are very unlikely to take place. The only way of ensuring them would be to ensure a very large pool of vacancies indeed. This would be very expensive.

Third, carers and social workers often differed in their views about what the plan for a placement was. This may betoken difficulties in communication, the difficulty of formulating, let alone communicating, plans in an emergency situation, or a tendency for children in care to 'drift'.

Fourth, there seems to be little conscious intention of using the foster care system to enable children to change.

The danger therefore is that the foster care system may fall between two stools. It provides few children with a long-term, stable, carefully matched alternative to living at home. Conversely it may not form part of a system where there is a conscious coherent attempt to enable both child and family to change so that the child can return home. We foreshadow this dilemma here. We return to it with further evidence in our third book.

Chapter Three

Placements and Destinations

Introduction

Our second chapter concentrated on the basic characteristics of the children and the circumstances and purposes surrounding the placement. The present one takes up the story from the time the child was placed. We give some basic details on the placement and on where we found the children a year later and we discuss how far these outcomes were expected, wanted and planned.

The chapter is particularly concerned with how far the foster care system provides its children with a permanent base. We also look at three related topics – the degree to which children are adopted by their carers or by others, the degree to which carers stayed in touch with children after they had left, and the degree to which some young people stayed on with their carers after the age of 18 when they were officially out of the care system. We place these outcomes in the context of what the carers and children told us they expected and wanted.

Current lengths of stay, plans, expectations and wants

Foster care is family care with a difference. Members of a family generally feel they have right to be there. By contrast, foster children are with carers in a sense 'on sufferance'. As we will see in the next chapter, some children were preoccupied with the insecurities that flow from this position. How far did the children's lengths of stay justify these insecurities, and how far did what was planned for them correspond to what they and their carers wanted and expected?

Lengths of stay

Overall, a quarter of the sample had spent six months or less in their current placement, and approaching a half (43%) had spent less than a year. Sixty-eight per cent had spent less than two years and 82 per cent less than three. The remaining 18 per cent had spent longer and included six young people who had spent nine years or more.

As we will see later, the lack of very long-stay placements partly reflects the sizeable chance that a child will leave a placement even after he or she has been there for some considerable time. The preponderance of placements under one and two years also reflects the community care policies on which we commented in the last chapter.

In relation to the second of these two points, we compared the length of time the young people had been in their current placement with the length of time they were said to have been in the care system since their last 'admission'. Those who had been in the system for five years or more had spent, on average, 50 months in their latest placement. Of those said to have been in the system for three years or more, only 13 per cent were said to have been in their current placement for less than a year. So, short lengths of stay in the current placement reflect recent entries to the care system. As we saw earlier many of these recent entries involved children returning to the care system after being tried at home.

Current plans

We asked the social workers to give us their current plans for where the child would go on leaving the placement – a question for which we provided them with a possible list. In around a quarter of the cases they had no plans for this as yet (many of these were expected to remain looked after, so detailed plans may not have been appropriate). In just under a fifth, the aim was rehabilitation home, almost invariably to the child's own birth parent(s) but occasionally to other relatives. In just over a quarter, the aim was another long-stay placement – long-stay fostering (8%), adoption with contact (6%) and adoption without contact (13%). In just over a fifth, the aim was independent living (see Table 3.1).

Table 3.1 Where foster child expected to go on leaving this placement

	n	%
No plans made as yet	83	27
Return to birth family	46	15
Return to other relatives	8	3
Other long-term foster care	23	8
Adoption with contact	19	6
Adoption without contact	38	13
Some form of independent living	65	21
Something else	20	7
Total	302	100

Source: Social worker questionnaire at Time 1.

This classification of plans was, as might be expected, related to the age of the children and provides a rough and ready way of grouping the placements:

- *No plans* – the average age of children for whom there were not yet plans for their destination on leaving was 10.5. Nearly nine out of ten of them were expected to stay for more than three years or 'the foreseeable future'. It was, presumably, early days to think what should happen when the child left.

- *Plans for rehabilitation* – the average age for children where rehabilitation was planned was 8.1 (somewhat younger if the relative involved was not a parent and slightly older if it was a parent). In nearly 70 per cent of the cases, the aim was to achieve this within six months or the child had already returned.

- *Other long-term placement* – the average age of the children destined for other long-term placements varied with the placement in mind. The relevant ages were: adoption without contact 2.9, adoption with contact 4.6, fostering 9.3. Expectations for lengths of stay varied and presumably depended on whether there was a firm placement in the offing. Around half (46%) of the current placements were expected to have ended within six months.

- *Independent living* – the average age of children destined for independent living was 15.2, but this varied with the type of accommodation envisaged, ranging from 13.8 (hostels), through 14.9 (supported lodgings) to 16.0 (flats). Such moves were rarely seen as likely to occur in the near future and the timing was obviously related to the age of the child.

- *Other* – this was a small group that seemed similar to those for whom no plans were made. Their average age was 11.8 and 70 per cent were expected to stay long-term.

One striking feature of this analysis is the relatively small proportion of children who were expected to return to a birth family (around one in six) or in a small proportion of cases (around 3%) other relatives. As Rowe and her colleagues (1989) have pointed out, the 'bread and butter' business of foster care is, in a sense, work with young children placed as a result of some temporary emergency and expected to return quickly to their parents. This generalisation is no longer quite so true as when it was first made (Wilson *et al.* 2004). Nevertheless a sizeable proportion of the placements which are made are still of this kind. By contrast, in a high proportion of the placements in existence at any particular point in time the children are not expected to go home. These are the placements surveyed in a cross-sectional study such as ours. For them, the care system has to provide whatever sense of permanency they are going to get.

Plans and expectations

We examined how far the foster carers and foster children saw the placements as aiming at 'permanency' in the sense that it should last till at least the age of 18. In four out of ten cases, the foster carers had, at the time of the first survey, expected the placement to finish before the child was 18. In around a quarter of cases, they said the plan was not fixed. In around one in seven cases, they said the plan was that the child should leave when he or she was 18, and in one in five after that date. So in around a third of cases they expected the child to stay until 18 or beyond (see Table 3.2).

Table 3.2 Age when foster child expected to leave current placement

	n	%
Before they are 18	195	41
When they are 18	70	15
After they are 18	91	19
Don't know	116	25
Total	472	100

Source: Foster carer questionnaire at Time 1.

The children who replied to our questionnaire were not usually at the beginning of their placement and they were, on average, older than the sample as a whole. Probably for these reasons their carers expected them to stay somewhat longer than the figures just given would suggest, with a third expecting the child to leave at 18 and a further sixth expecting them to leave after this (a combined total of 50%). Where carer and child had definite expectations, the correspondence between them was quite close. Overall a quarter of the children expected to stay until they were 18 and a third expected to stay longer than this (a combined total of nearly 60% expecting to stay to 18 or over). Only one in seven expected to leave before this, while just over a quarter did not know.

Plans and wishes

Expectations are not necessarily the same as wishes. We therefore asked the carers to say whether the child was there 'for the foreseeable future' and, if so, whether they would ideally like to have some other arrangement such as adoption or a residence order or to continue with long-stay fostering. In a quarter of cases, they said that the child was there for short-term purposes and the question was therefore not applicable. In half the cases they preferred the *status quo* of long-stay fostering. In 13 per cent of cases they would have liked to adopt the child themselves, generally without contact with the birth parents. In 3 per cent they would have liked a residence order, and in 8 per cent they were uncertain what arrangement they would prefer.

The children who replied to our questionnaire seemed, like the carers, to be looking for a long-term outcome. In 44 per cent of cases (out of 150 who answered this question) they wanted to stay until they were over 18 or 'for ever'. In a quarter of cases they wanted to stay until they were 18. In a fifth of cases they were unsure, and in around one in ten cases they wanted to leave within a 'year or two' or earlier. The main point is that more than two-thirds of the children wanted to stay until they were 18 or beyond.

Some caution is needed in assessing these figures. The replies from the children do not represent an unbiased sample. They are older than non-respondents – we did not approach those under five, although four did in fact send in completed questionnaires. Even among those over five, those replying were significantly more likely to be with their carers a year later (64% as against 44%), to be female (53% as against 42%), and to be white rather than black or Asian (92% as against 83%).

Despite these caveats there seems little doubt that a high proportion of children do want to stay until they are 18 or over, and that this is so even among groups which are under-represented in our sample. For example, this was apparently true of 70 per cent of those found in the same placement a year later but also of 40 per cent of those who had moved. It was as true of females as of males. It was somewhat less true of dual heritage or black and Asian children, although the numbers were too small for this difference to be statistically significant. Nevertheless, 50 per cent of this small group also did not want to leave before 18.

More detailed examination of the children who responded to our questionnaire confirms a considerable mismatch between what the children said they wanted and what was planned for them. Among those under 17 and answering the questionnaire, half of those who were expected by the social workers to leave within the year (admittedly a small number: n=14) wanted to stay until they were 18 or over. Among the rather larger group who answered and were expected by carers to leave before 18 (n=29), half still said they wanted to stay until 18 or over. So did 68 per cent of those where the carer was uncertain what the plans were. In many cases, what is planned for children offers a shorter period with their carers than they say.

Where the children were at follow-up

So much for what was planned for the children. What actually happened? We asked all our respondents in the follow-up survey where the children now were. Table 3.3 gives these outcomes.

Table 3.3 Sample outcomes

	n	%
Stayed with same foster carer	250	44
Other foster carer	85	15
Residential care	29	5
Adoption	54	10
Birth family/relatives	76	13
Independent living	41	7
Other	36	6
Total	571	100

Sources: Family placement worker, social worker and foster carer questionaires at Time 2.

As can be seen, the most common outcome was that the child remained where he or she was.

The next two most common destinations involved a move to another foster placement or a return to the birth family or relatives. Adoption (or at least a move to a placement with a view to adoption), independent living and 'other' were the next most common. A move to residential care was the least likely.

As might be expected, stability was related to length of time in placement. Moves were most likely among those who had spent a year or less in the placement. Sixty-nine per cent of this group were no longer there a year later. The comparable figure for those who had been in placement for between one and two years was 50 per cent. Thereafter, it remained steady at around 34 per cent.

As might also be expected, the children's destinations were related to their ages:

- Where the child was under five, more strenuous attempts seemed to be made to provide a permanent base with her or his family or through adoption. Overall, 31 per cent remained in the same placement. Nine per cent moved to another placement. A third (34%) were placed outside the placement for adoption and 18 per cent returned home.

- Where the child was aged between five and ten, long-stay fostering was seen as a more suitable option – 56 per cent were still in the same placement on follow-up. Twenty-one per cent were in another foster home. Only 5 per cent went to adoption and only 10 per cent went home. As can be seen three-quarters remained within the foster care system.

- Where the child was aged between 11 and 15, 53 per cent remained in the same placement. A further 19 per cent moved to another foster home. Almost all the remainder were evenly split between family (12%) and residential care (12%). Overall, 72 per cent remained within the foster care system.

- When the child (or, more properly, young person) was aged over 16, only 32 per cent were in the same placement at follow-up. Forty-eight per cent went to independent living, 11 per cent to their birth family and 5 per cent to another foster carer. Overall, 37 per cent remained within the foster care system.

So a key feature of the system lies in its ability to 'export' children. Forty per cent of those in the system when we first contacted them were not there a year later. In the younger age groups they had gone to adoption and birth families.

Among those aged 10 to 15, they had gone to residential care and birth families. Among the 16 to 18-year-olds, they had largely gone to independent living. Without this exodus the pressure on the foster care system would be considerably greater than it is.

Wishes, plans and outcomes

We examined how far the wishes and expectations that a child would stay until aged 18 were borne out, in the limited sense that he or she was still there at follow-up just over a year later. In making this analysis, we omitted young people who were aged 17 or over at the time of the first survey. All those included could therefore have remained.

In general, those who were expected or wanted to stay were much more likely to be in the same placement at follow-up. For example, around seven out of ten of those who were expected by the social worker to remain in the same placement for over a year were still there at follow-up. The corresponding proportion for those expected to stay for less than a year was just over two out of ten.

That said, neither wishes nor expectations were invariably borne out. We looked particularly at groups for whom issues of permanence were clearly salient. Very nearly six out of ten (57%) of those for whom the placement had initially been intended (as the carers saw it) to provide a long-term home were still there. Three out of ten of the children who wished to remain until 18 or over were gone on follow-up, as were a quarter of those who expected to remain until 18. Similarly, just under a third of those expected by their carers to stay until 18 or over had left, as had four out of ten of those whose placement was hoped by the carers to be long-term.

Plans could fail because the child remained, as well as because the child moved. Five out of ten (48%) of those who had been supposed to return home were still in the same placement. So too were five out of ten (50%) of those for whom there were no clear plans at that point, and four out of ten (41%) of those whose initial stay was supposed to be for assessment or emergency purposes only.

More recent plans had also, in some cases, not been borne out. As noted above, one in five of those who, according to the social workers, had been expected to leave the placement within 12 months were still there. Two-thirds (65%) of those whose plans envisaged a return home had indeed done so, but a third had not, and of these roughly half were no longer in the original placement.

Of those who had been definitely expected by their social workers to spend more than a year in placement more than a quarter (27%) were no longer in the same placement on follow-up. This 'impermanence' was basically a characteristic of children and young people aged 11 or over. Almost all those under this age were there on follow-up. By contrast just over half of those aged 11 or over and expected to stay in the same placement for a year or more were no longer there on follow-up. This suggests that before the age of 11 'permanence' or the lack of it predominantly reflects the plans of adults, particularly social workers. Among those over 11 other factors come to influence the likelihood of lengthy stays. As we will see, these include the views and behaviour of the young people themselves.

Special issues: adoption, independence, staying in touch

As we have seen, our sample was likely to spend a considerable period of time in the care system. Carers and (as far as our evidence goes) children seemed to have adapted to this situation, in most cases both expecting and wanting the placement to last to at least 18. In practice, however, this seems to have been unlikely to occur. This 'impermanence' could potentially be mitigated by adoption, by the child remaining in placement after he or she was 18, and by the carer staying in touch with the child after he or she had left. We look at these issues in the remainder of this chapter.

Adoptions

In relation to adoption we had 91 cases (just under one in five of the sample) where adoption seemed a possibility at the time of the first survey. In these cases, either the carer said that they would want to adopt the child if he or she remained with them, or the social worker expected the child to go to adoptive parents on leaving.

On following up these cases, we found that in roughly four out of ten of them the child had moved to an adoptive placement. In a further four out of ten they remained with the carers, and in half these cases (20% of the total) their status had changed, almost always because they had been adopted by the carer. In the remaining 20 per cent of cases, the child had gone elsewhere.

We looked for differences between those who were adopted outside the placement and those who remained. In 90 per cent of the cases where the child had remained and changed status, the carer had expressed an interest in adoption at the time of the first survey. However, this was also true of two-thirds of the cases where the child had remained without a change of status, and just over two-thirds of those where the child had been adopted outside the placement. Unsurprisingly, the carer's expressed wish to adopt was more or less a necessary condition for a subsequent adoption of the child by the carer. It was far from ensuring that this occurred.

We need to be careful about interpreting the apparent lack of influence of carer wishes on outcome. Our question asked: 'If the child is to stay with you for the foreseeable future, would you prefer the arrangement to be for adoption…'. It would be consistent to answer this question in favour of adoption but to be happy to let the child go to satisfactory adoptive parents. For this reason, we also asked a more direct question at follow-up as to where, ideally, the carer would like the child to be. At this stage, 1 in 11 (9%) said that their ideal option was a residence order (2%) or adoption by themselves (7%).

At this stage, the carers' perception was that 8 per cent of their foster children would have liked to have a residence order and a further 15 per cent would have liked adoption by themselves. Foster carers wished to adopt (and sometimes already had adopted) a third of the children whom they saw as wanting to be adopted by themselves. In a third of the remainder they said that their preferences would have been different if more support or better allowances had been available. So our evidence suggests that more foster children wish to be adopted by carers than their carers wished to adopt, but that some of this gap might be bridged through enhanced adoption allowances and support.

A key influence on whether and by whom the child was adopted seemed to be the social worker's views (or the authority's views as relayed by the social worker). In four out of ten cases where the child had remained in the placement without a change of status, the social worker had been uncertain at the first survey about what the plans should be, or had planned something other than adoption. This was true for only two cases where the child had remained with a changed status, and for no case where the child had been adopted outside the placement.

The social worker's plans for family contact were also related to whether the child was adopted inside or outside the placement. In 85 per cent of cases where the child was adopted outside the placement, the worker was planning for no contact with birth parents. This was true of only half of those for whom they planned adoption and who remained with the foster carers (chi square with continuity correction=3.71, $p=0.054$).

To our surprise, the age of the child was not related to whether the social worker thought the child should be adopted with or without contact. Age was, however, related to whether the child was adopted by the carers or outside the placement. Those adopted outside the placement were, on average, just over three years old, those where adoption was a possibility and who remained in the placement were aged almost exactly four years, and those who remained in the placement with a change of status were aged, on average, seven years.

Wittingly or otherwise, the local authorities seemed to have pursued a policy adapted to the market and to their need to husband their own resources of foster carers. In this sample traditional adoptions (young children placed without a view to contact with birth families) were made outside the placement. In-placement adoptions were made for older children and children where contact was planned and for whom outside adoptions might be more difficult to find.

Independent living

A group of particular interest comprises those who were aged 16 or 17 at the time of the first survey. We wanted to know how many were discharged when aged less than 18 to independent living. Conversely, we wanted to know how many stayed on with their carers after reaching the age of 18. The reason for these interests was a desire to see how far long-stay fostering approximated to adoption with its implications of support for 'a family for life'.

Fifty-three young people were aged 16 at the time of the first survey and of these, ten were discharged to independent living by the time of the second survey before they were aged 18. The existence of these 'early discharges' is in keeping with the picture provided by Garnett (1992) and Biehal et al. (1992) and may partly represent the wish of social workers to get the young person settled in accommodation before their statutory contact with social services stops.

Only five young people remained with their foster carers after reaching 18 (20% of those who might have done so – a figure in keeping with the 21% reported by Biehal et al. (1995), although higher than that suggested by Fry (1992)). This outcome seems sometimes to have been contrary to what was expected. In half the cases (12 out of 25), the carer said at the first survey that 'it was planned' that the young person would remain after the age of 18. In all but one of the five cases where the young person did stay this was the case. However, in two-thirds of the cases where this was planned, the hope of a continuing stay was not borne out. In almost all of these cases, the young person moved into the community.

As to the wishes of the young people in the 16 to 17 age group we had replies from only 27 of them – a response rate of 51 per cent. Of these, nearly half (44%) said that they hoped to remain in the placement after 18 or 'for ever'. A further 30 per cent hedged their bets and said they did not know. Very nearly all the remainder said that they wished to remain until 18.

As it turned out, 7 of the 12 who wished to remain in the placement after the age of 18 were still there when followed up. Only one of these, however, had been aged 17 at the time of the first survey, and thus in a position to have stayed beyond 18 at the time of the second one. There seems no doubt that more young people would like to stay on with their foster carers than actually do so.

Contacts with foster carers after placement

The length of time for which the young people had been in placement suggested that they would form important relationships with their carers. How far did these outlast departure? Like others, we were interested in the degree to which the children and young people saw their carers after leaving them.

In practice, most carers had some contact, but this was rarely frequent enough to count as 'ongoing support'. In 5 per cent of cases, the children saw the carers at least as often as once a week. In a further 9 per cent of cases, contact was said to be 'every two or three weeks'. More common patterns were 'in occasional bursts' (22%) and 'less frequently but contact by phone or letter' (27%). In 36 per cent of cases there was no contact at all.

The likelihood of further contact depended in part on where the child went. No contact was most common when the child went to another placement (adoption 77%, residential care 66%, and foster care 63%). Conversely, reasonably regular contact (every two to three weeks) was most commonly reported when the child or young person went to independent living (31%, a figure close to the figures for foster carer support reported by others – Fry 1992; Wade 1997), birth family (19%) and 'other destinations' (20%). Four children in residential care (around a fifth of those placed there) were also said to keep in reasonably regular touch with their carers.

So there arises a question over whether this low level of contact is for the best. In some cases no doubt this is the case. In others it may represent a loss of emotional capital – the disappearance of someone who might have counted in a sense as part of an extended family – and a reinforcement of the experience that relationships are haphazard, casual encounters that start and stop for reasons beyond the child's control and have no predictable or enduring life (cf. Fisher *et al.* 1986).

Conclusion

The key aim of this chapter was to provide evidence on the working of the foster care system with particular reference to the degree to which it provided 'permanence'. The main conclusion is that it rarely does.

On the face of it, most of the children could have reasonably expected to remain in the foster care system, if not permanently, at least for a substantial period of time. A high proportion had entered the system because of abuse, but most had nevertheless been returned home on at least one occasion. Rehabilitation had therefore usually been tried. Only a minority were now expected to return home on leaving the placement. On follow-up a year later, only around one in seven were with their birth families. Most were past the age at which adoption outside the placement was likely (the average age of those adopted was around three). The majority of carers and the great majority of children who replied to our questionnaire both wanted and expected the placement to last until at least 18.

On the other hand, the system contained a great deal of impermanence. Forty per cent of the children were in placements which, according to the carers, had originally been intended to be short-term. More than half were no longer in the placement on follow-up. Movements were particularly likely among those who had spent less than two years in placement. Even after this, however, around a third of those in placement were no longer there a year later. The figures for those who were placed 'long-term' and those who wanted to stay till at least 18 were similar (around 30% in both cases).

A major influence on 'impermanence' was age. Children aged less than 11 who were expected to remain for a year were almost always in the same placement on follow-up. Only half the adolescents subject to a similar expectation were there when we followed them up. These figures suggest that the chance of very long-term placements is low. Only 6 per cent of the sample had been in the same placement for six years or more.

One difficulty with tackling this problem is that 'impermanence' is in certain respects both desirable and inevitable. Much of it arises because of the efforts to return children to their homes. If this is done almost as a matter of routine, it is inevitable that some will break down at home and return to the care system. Those whose rehabilitation fails and who then remain in the system on a longer-term basis therefore represent the inevitable result of an approved and intentionally benign policy of community care. At the same time, the foster care system could not cope with the demands placed on it unless it routinely 'exported' a high proportion of the children in it at any one time (on our figures, about 40% over a year).

Our evidence on what might be done about these problems is obviously limited. We do not, for example, examine how adoptions outside the placement turned out or about the extent of support available if the child goes home. However, our findings suggest that a number of options might be considered.

First, the adoption of young children outside the placement is a very important way in which strains on the system are relieved. It is also a plausible response to the problem of impermanence in the care system. On these grounds, the policy of encouraging adoption has much to recommend it.

Second, the adoption of slightly older children by their carers might be expected to provide a more permanent placement – albeit at the cost of losing carers. This seems to be an option that needs evaluation, although some research already suggests that such adoptions are more likely than others to succeed (Barth and Berry 1988; Borland *et al.* 1991; Lahti 1982). Evidence from this study suggests that this option and the related one of residence orders or the new 'special guardianship' might be encouraged through better support and allowances for carers, but that, even so, more children would wish to be adopted by their carers than their carers wished to adopt. At the minimum, there needs to be a 'level playing field' so that these difficult decisions are taken on the basis of needs, rights and wants rather than on the basis of their financial implications.

Third, very long-stay placements are clearly exceptional – a fact which supports the need to keep family relationships in some state of repair if possible, and the need to develop children's skills through education so that they will be able to survive in the relatively unprotected world for which many of them seem destined. In this respect, the very small number of placements which were intended to provide any form of treatment seems surprising. A rather different method of responding to inevitable turnover would be to utilise the relationships which children had formed with carers by encouraging contact in appropriate cases after the children had left.

Fourth, attempts need to be made to increase the permanence of places which are provided. Long-stay fostering is, as far as we can see, here to stay. Most of the children in this study did not apparently wish to be adopted and most were not going home in the foreseeable future. In part, greater permanence for this group might be achieved by encouraging children to 'stay on' after 18 – something which carers and children seem to want much more often than it occurs – and encouraging contacts after the children have left. In part, it depends on efforts to minimise breakdowns – a possibility which is a focus of much of the rest of this book. It also probably depends on more strenuous attempts to create a sense of permanence among foster children as they become older.

A necessary consequence of success in increasing the permanence offered by foster care would be that additional foster carers would need to be recruited.

Chapter Four

A Kind of Loving: The Children's Accounts

Introduction

So far we have described, as it were, the bare bones of fostering – the basic characteristics of the sample, the plans made for them and so on. For the rest of the book we will be concerned with outcomes and with what might be done to improve them – in short, with support as broadly defined.

In order to assess the effects of support we needed to understand what would have happened if it had not been offered. This required us to list the factors which might affect outcome, and develop hypotheses on the way these would operate. We could then test the resulting model statistically.

We based our model on four main sources: the literature on foster care, ideas thrown up by our preliminary analysis, the questionnaires returned by the foster children and the accounts of carers and social workers. This chapter deals with the material from the children's questionnaires.[1]

Our focus is on the written material provided by children in these questionnaires. We have two main questions. First, what are the aspects of foster care that the children emphasise? Second, what would they like to see happen – what recommendations do they make?

Answers to these questions bear on the model we are trying to create. The aspects of foster care which the children chose to describe both help to define what counts as an outcome and to identify what leads to it. For example, if children emphasise the degree to which the carers are able to convey they love them, this, at least for some children, is a key 'outcome' of foster care. It is also likely to influence the way they behave and for this reason too needs to be taken into account. Their recommendations may also suggest the mechanisms that in their view influence outcomes. Things may therefore go better if this or that variable was changed.

As will be seen, our treatment of the material is qualitative and impressionistic. This approach was made necessary by the brevity and variety of the children's replies and the difficulty of interpreting them. We chose to present this material towards the beginning of the book because we believe in its importance rather than because of the certainty of the conclusions we draw. To enable the reader to understand both points we begin with a brief discussion of the replies from four children, one of whom is placed with a relative.

Four brief examples

The children whose answers we have chosen to illustrate our method and problems are simply the first four in our system for numbering. We have called them Abel, Bella, Charles and Dennis. In presenting their replies we have omitted those from our warm-up page whose aim was to illustrate the kind of questions we asked (e.g. children were asked to complete sentences: 'The Spice Girls are...' and 'Manchester United is...'. Occasionally we have changed details to avoid any possibility of identification.

The first open-ended question which referred to the placement simply asked the children to complete the sentence: 'What I like about the placement is...' Their replies were as follows:

I get treated like everybody else. (Abel)

It has a caring, friendly atmosphere. (Bella)

I get treats. (Charles)

They're kind, generous and funny. (Dennis)

These replies suggest that the children want what anybody would surely want: a place where they are cared for by kind people, given things they like and feel they belong. There are implicitly three references to caring (i.e. to 'kindness', to 'caring' itself, and to the negative feature of 'not being picked on'). There are two references to generosity (i.e. to 'treats' and to 'generosity' itself).

At the same time the replies are hard to interpret in their brevity. Are 'treats' a symbol of love or a substitute for it? Is the 'caring, friendly atmosphere' a conventional description or a heartfelt one presented in rather formal terms to reflect its author's wish (as apparent from later in the questionnaire) to become a journalist? We are reasonably sure that we are tapping the terms in which the children evaluate the placement (e.g. whether or not it is caring). We are uncertain how they in fact experience it (e.g. whether Bella feels this is a caring placement).

A further question invited the children to complete the sentence: 'One thing I do not like about the placement is…' Their replies were as follows:

[No comments.] (Abel)

Nothing. (Bella)

Nothing. (Charles)

My uncle is very strict. (Dennis)

This set of answers is less illuminating. As we will see later 'strictness' is one of the features in a placement to which a number of children rightly or wrongly object. The blank and 'nothing' answers may mean that the children were completely satisfied with their placements or that for one reason or another they did not like to voice any dissatisfactions they had.

Our next question asked: 'The main difference between me and this family is…' Their answers were:

I am the youngest. (Abel)

I can't think of any because it doesn't exist. (If this is a reference to the fact of me being in care, I feel no different as they treat me the same as their own family.) (Bella)

[No comment.] (Charles)

I am mixed parentage and the family are white. (Dennis)

These replies are tantalising. Abel gives a difference which is in a sense no difference. Every family has a youngest member. Bella chooses this question to emphasise what Abel emphasised in the answer to the first – to wit that she is treated as a family member. Her loyalty to the family is further emphasised by her fear that this is a trick question, something designed to get her to emphasise an undeniable feature of her situation – that she is a child in care – but to distort the meaning the situation has to those involved. Only Dennis mentions a difference which, as is apparent below, is important to him.

Our next question was: 'What I feel about this difference is…'. The replies were:

[No comments.] (Abel, Bella, Charles)

Nothing, it does not matter, but sometimes my uncle goes against black people. (Dennis)

The blanks from Abel and Bella are not surprising. They have already conveyed the fact that it is important to them that they are part of the family and that they feel treated as such. Charles remains cagey. Dennis says that the difference does not matter. However, he instances not only racism but also racism that has a particular twist since he is placed with his uncle. Family feelings are involved. Whereas current policy suggests that family placements should always be considered, this example suggests that they are not always without problems As we will see later, other data suggest that these problems are common.

Our next question asked for two wishes for the future. Abel did not answer it. The other answers were:

To be successful in my career in media: be happy and caring to others. (Bella)

Be with my mummy and daddy when they get a new house: live close to [foster carers]. (Charles)

Stay with all my friends: do well at school and get a good job. (Dennis)

Charles' answer contains perhaps a clue to his caginess. He wants to be with his family, but this is dependent on something which has not yet happened. In the meantime, indeed for the foreseeable future, he wants to keep his relationship with his foster carers. Bella and Dennis are more concerned with their personal future.

These wishes all seem normal and admirable. As will be seen, most of those answering the questionnaire answered in a similarly 'normal' way. For the wishes to be met, a reasonable proportion of children must return to their families, they must gain the education necessary to fulfil their ambitions, and there must be some continuity of contact with carers after the placements ends.

Our next question bore on the question of movement, continuity of schooling and so on. We asked whether there was anything the social workers had done that the children liked:

No. (Abel)

My current social worker (Jim Swanton) helped me out of an unhappy situation with my old foster parents. Without him I do not know what would have happened. (Bella)

She has liked seeing what I have been doing. I have liked showing her things. (Charles)

No. (Dennis)

The meaning of these questions is illumined by the answers to the next. 'Is there anything social workers have done for you that you disliked?'

Arrange a meeting with my mum and on the day cancel it. (Abel)

My previous social workers ignored the situation despite the knowledge they had of it. (Bella)

No. (Charles)

No. (Dennis)

So the children evaluated the social workers in three respects – for their personal characteristics (for example, showing an interest and reliability), for their role in the movements that children make (e.g. by removing or failing to remove a child from a placement) and for their part in contacts.

Asked if they had any advice for social services, the replies were as follows:

No. (Abel)

Listen to the children for they are your main priority. (Bella)

[No comments.] (Charles)

More money provided for foster parents and for social services to take less time sorting out a situation. (Dennis)

Bella's comment needs to be related to her view that she should have been removed earlier from her previous placement. It is policy to discourage moves. Bella felt that this policy is not always in the children's best interests. The second part of Dennis' comment also probably relates to the process of movement; i.e. to the time before decisive action is taken and the child is, in a sense, in limbo.

These four cases, selected on no better grounds than they came up first in our system of numbering questionnaires, illustrate well the limitations and potential of this material. On the negative side, it is patchy (questions are quite often left blank); it lacks context (we do not know why Bella wished to leave her previous placement, or how realistic is Charles' wish to return home); and for these and other reasons its meaning is sometimes ambiguous. That said, the children make some strong points (e.g. on the need to be careful in framing blanket policies about the undesirability of moves) and they make clear, if not necessarily in the same questions, some of the key dimensions along which they evaluate social services. We will argue later that these dimensions are the same as those which are selected by the others who responded to the questionnaire. Before making this claim we need to look at the remainder of the material.

The children's accounts

As just described, the children's questionnaire contained a small number of open-ended questions. These covered what they liked and did not like about foster care, whether they saw themselves as different from their foster family, and if so what they felt about this, what they liked and did not like about what social workers had done for them, what they hoped for themselves in the future, and what advice they would give to social services. Their replies were typically short. Sometimes they were obscure, depending for their interpretation on a knowledge of named individuals, which we lacked. Commonly they were pithy and revealing.

To judge from these replies, the salient features of being in foster care are those apparent from its title. A key feature is that it is, in many respects, like being in a family. A further key feature is that it is not the child's family. Yet another feature is that the child is away from its own family. A final feature is that the child is, in a sense, at the mercy of others who may move children from places where they are happy, leave them in places where they are unhappy, or leave them in uncertainty as to whether or when they are to be moved at all.

Good and bad points of family life with foster families

From the point of view of the child, foster families can resemble ordinary families in both their good and bad points. Good points are that they can provide support. At its best, this means that the child can feel loved and cared for: 'everyone here loves me'. More neutrally, the carers may be seen as 'nice' or as 'liking me'. They may be valued because they listen ('I have a woman to talk over my problems with which I did not have before') and are 'understanding' and 'I always get attention'. They may provide a sense of belonging, either to quasi-parents ('having a mum and dad') or to a group ('there is a good sense of belonging and there are lots of people around'). There are also material goods which may be valued: 'a room of my own', 'bunk beds', 'food', 'pocket money', 'toys', 'swimming baths', 'outings'. These various provisions may merge in the child's eyes ('lots of food and money and love') and leads to a sense that the child is 'treated as one of the family' and gets 'the love and support I need'.

Unfortunately, as the children see it families also had their negative aspects. Discipline could be a sore point. So some children complained of 'strict rules', 'going to bed early', 'having to wash and dry up', 'losing points', 'being told off' and 'moaning on about your music and room'. Some accepted this:

> We have different expectations about what time I should be in etc. – [I feel] unhappy about this but it is one of the sacrifices I have to accept.

Some even acknowledged that it only happened when they were 'naughty'. Others were less understanding:

> I think I should be able to hang around with who I want to and be able to choose my own boyfriends.

Troubles over discipline shaded into other difficulties of family life, antagonism and arguments:

> ...being accused of something when you haven't done it...
> ...when everybody is shouting...

times when:

> ...you could cut the atmosphere with a knife...

and quarrels with other foster children or with birth children in the house:

> I get tormented by another lad.
> I don't like to argue with James.
> I'm not very keen on the mum and dad.

Others described themselves as quieter and more withdrawn:

> They don't talk to me and I don't talk to them...

or complained of loneliness or (more commonly) boredom:

> It is not a lot of fun.

Being with a family that is not your own

These problems interacted with the second salient characteristic of foster family life – the fact that the foster family is not the child's own. This salient fact was emphasised by the difference in surnames. 'Their surname is Austen and mine is Dickens' – something that a number emphasised and which might require explanation to friends at school. Attitudes to this difference differed. One thought that children who had been adopted should be able to keep their own names. One was grateful to her social worker because:

> ...she took me to court to change my adoptive name back to my mum's name.

Others wished their names could be changed to that of their carers, even though they were still fostered. Others felt that the situation was all right because they were going to be adopted or they felt that they were nevertheless part of the family.

The lack of normality suggested by differences in surname was emphasised by other features – the number of people who called at the house to discuss the children's futures ('too many people involved in my life, i.e. social services'), meetings and the numbers at them, and the need for clearance by social services for overnight stays, trips and so on. These bureaucratic intrusions were sometimes seen as accompanied by a bureaucratic style of family life within the placement itself. One child commented negatively on a contract which had been drawn up:

> Made a stupid contract and made me sign it. A contract of house rules! It's stupid to have to sign it.

Another commented negatively on the parenting style of the carers:

> It is not a family. It is a staff team.

Even sympathetic responses could arouse unease:

> I don't like the way people treat me specially (friends, teachers) when they know I'm in care. They are sympathetic and treat me differently.

Perhaps an even more important source of tension lay in differences between the children's own family culture and that of the new foster family. Each family has its own distinctive style – customs about television, what happens at weekends, the use of space, in-jokes, implicit and explicit rules. And the nature of these taken-for-granted arrangements may only be apparent when newcomers join. There could be differences in ethnicity ('they are blacker'), in religion ('they are Christian'), and in food. They could live in different towns and the carer's children could support different football teams. There could be differences in personality:

> I'm more or less opposite to everybody…

in social habits:

> They like to go out to meet new people, I don't…

and in discipline:

> They are used to rules in the house where I am not.

Much was summed up in the reflection that:

> I was brought up in a different way.

As illustrated earlier, many children seemed to feel that there were no such differences:

> They treat me the same as their own family.

Others said that any differences were of little importance:

> The son supports Sheffield Wens football club. They are a rubbish team (sorry if you support them) but really there are not any differences that I can think of. We all get on together very well.

Others felt that the carer's concern more than compensated for such differences as there were ('They love me so much'). As a result, some felt that they were indeed part of the family:

> I love it here, I fit in a lot.

One commented:

> I am being adopted so we are all one big happy family.

Others, however, were not being adopted and did not wish to be. Some found that things were difficult at first but got used to it:

> We come from different backgrounds. At first it was hard to accept but now it doesn't bother me.

And others said that their carers could tolerate difference:

> They can sometimes have very different opinions to me…but everyone is entitled to their own opinion and they realise that – no real problems occur.

As we saw earlier, a much more serious difference of opinion was noted by a child of mixed parentage living with a white family:

> I am of mixed parentage and the family are white.

[What do you feel about it?]

> Nothing. It does not matter but sometimes my uncle goes against black people.

So for some children, at least at first, entering such an alien environment was 'scary'. They felt that 'it's not my home', that it was:

> …somebody else's house so I just have to stick with it…

that:

> I am the odd one out because all the rest is family.

One child found some of the 'rules strange' adding that:

> …it is a bit stupid sometimes and I have to act in a different way in order to fit in sometimes.

This tactic of diplomatic concealment was also adopted by another child who said that the carers did not understand her but added:

> I'd rather they didn't anyway, they might get a shock.

Such an experience may leave the child feeling 'lonely', 'sad', 'mixed up and confused', 'out of place', 'unable to tell them things that upset me' – all words or phrases used by different children to describe their situation. A balanced, sad and thoughtful comment was that the child felt like:

> …an outsider – when I say this I mean that I feel like part of the family but it's not like being with my birth family.

Being away from your real family

Asked to give two wishes for their future, just over a quarter gave a wish that involved seeing more of, or getting back together with, their family. Even children who were apparently happy in the placement could nevertheless wish they were home:

> I like it [here] but I don't really want to be here. I want to be with my parents, but I like everyone here.

The children explained this preference in various ways. The foster placement could seem in a sense wrong simply because it was a foster placement:

> I should be with my mummy and brother and sisters.

Some children were homesick:

> I miss my mum and family.

Some wished that things at home were different:

> I wish my mum and dad had some nice friends so I could go back home.

Others knew that such wishes were unrealistic:

> I'd rather be with my mum but I know it is not possible.

Nor did they necessarily blame the foster home:

> I can't see my mum but that's not to do with the foster home, just with being in care.

Others felt that they had traded a family for empty promises:

> They got involved in my life and now they won't leave me alone. I feel very bitter towards social services. They have been in my life for nine years now. I know they are only trying to help but all I can see is they are interfering.

Others, however, were glad not to be at home, and appreciative of the foster home, not least because of the contrast with what went before:

> It was the best thing that could have happened to me. It stops a lot of suicides (I know it did with me). It's not like most kids say. I enjoyed being in foster care. I had a foster sister whom I got on well with most of the time, although we did have fallouts.

Another complained that social workers were:

> …trying to push me back home.
> I would like to stay with my mum and dad foster carer.
> Leave me where I am.

Their gratitude to social services was commensurate:

> Keep on with the good work.

There were similar divisions over visiting. One commented:

> I think all children should see lots of their natural family even if they are in care.

Another asked social services:

> ...to respect my decision not to see my family.

Another complained that:

> ...she said that I had to see my sister in Scotland every month.

One complained about social workers:

> ...stopping me seeing my mum alone.

Another complained that social workers:

> ...left me at my mum's on my own all day.

A key point was that some children wanted to see (or live with) some members of their families but not others, and they envisaged varying roles for their carers in these arrangements. At the extreme one wanted to:

> ...to be with my mother, to kill my father.

Another was quite discriminating:

> Let me see Richard and Jean (step-mother). I would like to see Gran and Grandad (mum's side) or speak on phone with any family.

In general, the replies revealed a great variety of wishes – for example, children who wished to change their name to that of their foster families but see their mother and siblings, children who wished to live with their father or their brother, children who wished their mother was with them but who also wanted a 'new mum'.

Not being in control

Foster families might not be seen as offering real security. Foster carers are not bound to children by ties of blood ('they are not my real family') and are theoretically free to wash their hands of them. Some children believe, according to one foster child, that difficult behaviour might get them returned to their own families:

> When I meet other foster children and we talk about being in care, they and I always say when we first came into care we thought if we were bad we could go home.

Moving on is almost an essential feature of the situation ('I can't live at my foster family for ever'). Children change schools and have to make new friends. They have to get used to new families, and new and perhaps alien family cultures. Many children have experienced a number of moves:

> When I first arrived in care I was moved from one home to another.

When the child was not happy in a placement a move could be welcome – as we saw earlier, one, for example, thanked her current social worker for moving her but complained that her previous ones had paid no attention. Another's advice to social services was:

> ...can you move me soon please.

Another appreciated her social workers because:

> ...they have tried so hard to get me the right family every time I did not like my placement.

However, when the child was happy in the placement, thoughts about moves could be unwelcome. One child advised her social worker:

> ...not to come too often and *not* to keep asking if I am happy where I am. If I were not happy, I could phone them any time. My foster parents love me and I love it here.

Another concurred:

> Social workers have not done anything I liked. Up to now they have moved me around a lot, specially from different schools with change of addresses. And it's hard to keep making new friends and fitting in. The social worker should not call so much at my home and stop asking me the same things over and over again, specially about my past. I want to forget all that. I would like my foster carer to adopt me. No one asks me about that!

Children's recommendations

The children's recommendations stemmed naturally from the dimensions along which they appeared to assess the placement.

First, they made a number of financial and practical suggestions – some perhaps motivated by financial self-interest, but others reflecting a desire to 'normalise' the placement. Pocket money should be increased. They should 'pay for the things we do', or even:

> ...they should let us borrow a seven seated mini bus so we could fit more people in it and pay for the places we go like Wacky Warehouse and super club.

They should give:

> ...more responsibility for foster carers e.g. hair cuts, ear piercing, trips, sleepovers, general requests from foster carers

– an administrative change that might expose carers to more pressure from children but deal with some of the delay in getting decisions, of which other children complained. They should:

> ...not tell teenagers of 14 what to do and what not to do when their foster carers can tell them.

They should stop having meetings during school lunch breaks.

Second, they were concerned to improve the quality of the fostering and the fit between foster children and the families with which they were placed.

> They should make sure they are placing the child in the correct environment they should be in. Sometimes foster carers are not as good as they should be...(this is not advice from personal experience though).

This might be partly a matter of ensuring better foster carers:

> [I advise social services] to put foster children with people who have raised their own families.

It might be partly a matter of ensuring choice for both sides:

> Children should always meet their carers before they move into a placement.

It might be partly a matter of exercising some supervision. So social workers were urged by some (certainly not by all, as we have seen) to visit more frequently and (quite frequent advice) not to believe all they were told by foster carers. And as we have seen, some grateful children were keen that foster carers should be better rewarded financially.

Third, they should be more sensitive to children's feelings in relation to their family. And as we saw earlier, this would mean respecting the differences among them – some wanted contact, some did not, and some wanted face-to-face contact with some, telephone contact with others, and no contact at all with others. It would also, in the view of some children, mean getting them back home to a particular member of their family, while in the view of others it would mean remaining with their carers, and in the view of others it would mean adoption.

Fourth, there should be steps to reduce the insecurity which hangs over fostering. This would mean tackling delays and doing what was promised. It might mean being more organised:

> To be more organised, to get their act together, example, review and planning meetings. Not having these means I don't know where I am going to be.

It might mean, as discussed earlier, moving children less or, if a move did not turn out well, being prepared to move them again (a way of reducing a different kind of insecurity – the fear of a bad placement). In a rather different sense it might mean being more open with children about information which they felt they would only learn when they were 18:

> To let people know more than they just pretend to know and let us read things they don't want us to read.

Conclusion

The foster children who answered our questionnaire did not all want the same things. Nevertheless they had some common needs.

Some of these related to a *need for a normal family life*. Foster care is family care. Some children and young people wanted to be part of the family more than others. Some, for example, wanted to take their foster family name but others did not. However, typical 'wants' were for:

- the care, concern and encouragement others get from their families
- to feel they belonged and were not the 'odd one out'
- fair treatment – not to be picked on or treated too strictly
- to get on with all in the placement including other children
- not to have their family or school turned into a branch office of social services
- as much pocket money etc. as other children
- to be able to ask their foster carers for permission to stay with friends
- some say in who their carers were to be.

Foster children do not always see things as the foster family do. They wanted *respect for their individuality*. This meant that:

- their different values and culture were recognised
- adults listened to their particular concerns.

Another key issue related to *contact with their own families*. Wants, however, varied a great deal. Most wanted:

- contact with their families (from none to a lot)
- choice in the kind of contact provided (e.g. some wanted telephone contact)
- contact with the family members they selected (not necessarily everyone)
- choice over the amount of support provided when contact occurred (from none to a lot)
- as few conflicts of loyalty between carers and family as possible.

Foster children are placed and moved by others. This can lead to feelings of insecurity and of being powerless. So most wanted *a say in their careers in care*. This involved:

- respect for their wishes over their status (e.g. to be adopted, fostered, or return home)
- a say in who fostered them

- less frequent moves
- moves when placements were not working out
- ability to stay after 18 if they wanted this
- efficient planning and review
- good information on plans for their future and on their own past
- regular contact with social workers on their own (not all wanted this).

As far as we know, none of what we report here is out of keeping with the views expressed by children in other studies. Even more important perhaps is the fact that what they want can be seen as flowing naturally from the basic characteristics of the children's situation. Being cared for in someone else's family raises, predictably, issues about the quality of this care, about how the child fits into the family, about the degree of security and sense of belonging he or she feels, and about the relationships with the child's own family and with professionals. It is also natural that within these broad preoccupations they should want differing things – some, for example, will want to return home while others will not. The children's views, then, begin to help us identify factors in foster care which may contribute to outcomes, and to build our model of how these factors would operate. We take this further in the next chapter.

Note

1. The chapter itself is reproduced with a few changes from an article in *Adoption and Fostering* (Sinclair, Wilson and Gibbs 2001) and we are grateful to the journal for permission to reproduce it here.

Chapter Five

Outcomes

Introduction

The concerns of the young people focused on process rather than outcomes. They were clear about how they wanted to be treated; they said little – and we did not ask them – about the outcomes this might achieve. In our follow-up questionnaires, however, we asked the carers, social workers, and family placement social workers to rate the success of the placement. We also asked them to give the grounds for making the ratings and to say why they thought things had turned out this way. The next two chapters are based on what they said.

In considering the outcomes, we will examine five main groups of case, distinguishing between those where the child:

- returns home
- is adopted
- goes to independent living
- moves within the care system and
- remains in long-stay care.

In each of these categories we will try to identify, in very broad outline, some of the key determinants of placement success – a topic which we consider in more detail in the remainder of the report.

Method

Our method relies on our two 'open-ended' questions about the reasons for judging a placement as a success or otherwise, and about how success or the lack of it might be explained. We coded the resulting accounts using very broad and overlapping categories (for example, as relating to the child, the child's family, the foster carer) and grouped them using the qualitative data analysis package *WinMax*. We studied the quotations within each grouping and identified key themes. This method has a number of difficulties.

First, our questions allowed great scope for carers to decide on the kinds of explanation which were relevant. In any given case, many different factors are likely to have affected the outcome and carers chose which ones to emphasise. So factors such as a child's jealousy may be mentioned when its presence leads to obvious failure or success. However, when the opposite applies (e.g. a child is not jealous) this may be passed over (the phenomenon of the 'dog which did not bark in the night'). Similarly, one carer may attribute success to personal qualities (e.g. commitment or persistence), whereas another describing a very similar situation may emphasise the stability of a placement and not mention the persistence which produced it.

Second, the accounts are likely to depend on the standpoint and assumptions of the respondent. For example, carers who experience different children may see differences between children as the source of outcomes, while social workers who experience different carers may be more likely to explain outcomes in terms of the carers' qualities. Moreover, there are considerations of loyalty and self-respect which may influence the kind of factor which is mentioned. And there may be common assumptions deriving from training or from the media which render some accounts plausible to the respondent, while other, perhaps more valid, explanations are ignored.

Despite these qualifications, the carers and social workers in our study had accumulated a vast store of hard-won experience and wisdom. Their ability to do their jobs depends on their skill in analysing the situations which arise. It would have been foolish not to make as much use of social work and carer judgements as possible.

In summarising their replies we have emphasised explanations which are (to us) plausible and which seem to underlie a variety of diverse responses. For example, as will be clear in the next chapter, the carers laid great store by 'persistence', 'stability' and 'commitment'. Fundamentally, they seemed to see these factors as providing security for children who had not had much in their lives. We found this explanation plausible as an account of what might help the children. We also saw it as a theme which underlay a great deal of what the carers wrote. Inevitably, there is a large element of judgement in this kind of research approach. We believe that the statistical approach adopted in most of the rest of the report provides an appropriate methodological check to the inevitable subjectivity.

Essentially we are using these accounts to generate hypotheses. What ideas did they suggest?

Cases involving return home

A successful return home seemed to involve a situation whose basic features were amenable to change. Sometimes these factors involved the birth family – a father was in prison and would return, a mother was mentally ill but could be treated – and sometimes the child, who, for example, might be seen as temporarily 'out of control'. Given such a situation, further requirements were that all concerned should be working towards a return, the children should 'do well' in foster care, the return should be carefully planned and, in some cases, there should be some ongoing support from carer to family (e.g. through respite care). A number of these features were described by Mrs Arthur:

> This placement was a success because it accomplished the desired outcome with minimal upset and damage to the children. James and John came straight to me. We bonded well straight away. They stayed with me until their mother had undergone therapy and then had a gradual planned return home. They came as weak sick children and left as fit, strong, healthy boys and have remained so back with birth parents. [Things worked out this way] firstly because they came to one carer and stayed. If they had been moved or passed around the system James (especially) would have been damaged and ill and not thrived. He had asthma (which was caused by emotional stress). This cleared up with stability. Secondly because the mother admitted to needing therapy and worked hard to improve. She really wanted to see her boys back and to be a good mother. Thirdly because I never tried to take the mother's place but kept their love and respect aimed at her.

This heartening account was broadly confirmed by the children's social worker, who also pointed out that the outcome was not achieved without difficulty:

> The placement went through very stressful times, the carer was inexperienced as a foster carer, the placement lasted 18 months rather than the original few weeks [that were intended], the carer faced great personal stress as well. There were also difficulties with birth parent who constantly complained about carer or social worker. Clearly the carer was a strong personality who was able to remain in touch with the children's needs, and was able to be honest in working with professionals and to learn from the series of

difficult situations. Alongside this it was vital to have good communication, between social worker and carer, carer and support worker, carer, support worker and social worker. This involved time…[also clarity of role for all involved] but the end result of the placement was excellent.

A less encouraging account of a return home was given by Mrs Noble:

> When Cherie was with us she attended high school on a regular basis and although her behaviour was not good at school, she did start and make an effort. Within the foster home Cherie was polite and well-mannered and caused us no trouble at all. She was really good with the younger children in the home. Once back home with mum (who has a severe drinking problem) Cherie went back to her old ways. Lack of supervision from her parents has enabled her to do whatever she pleases, drinking, shoplifting etc. She no longer attends school…I know she would have liked to return to us but with eight children already and the size of the house it would have been impossible.

Implicitly at least, the social worker went along with some of this analysis. She agreed that things had not worked out very well and thought that for the moment at least Cherie would be better off fostered – a further foster placement was tried. Her conclusion was that shortage of foster placements had made it impossible to create the conditions in which a successful accommodation between fostering and birth family was possible:

> There is little choice of placements. Child had a second brief placement. As with the first it was too far from her home and school and there was no chance to match.

So key differences from the first case were perhaps that the basic problems were more intractable – the 'mental illness' responded to treatment, the drinking problem did not change – and that there was less clarity about what was intended – in the first case, carer and social worker were agreed that return home was the best outcome, in the second they were not sure. Perhaps for these reasons, the first case fits the criterion that the outcome was perceived as good and as having a logical relationship to the way the case was handled. The second case does not.

On the face of it, placement success has much to do with the child and the carer. For example, the success of the first placement seems to have had something to do with Mrs Arthur's strong character and that of the second to Cherie's willingness to make an effort. However, the placement takes place within a context where other variables – the availability of suitable placements and the characteristics of the child's family – are also very important. Arguably, these influence the placement itself (for example, the first might not have been a success if the children had been moved around before entering it), and they certainly have an influence on the outcome of the case as a whole (for example, through the behaviour of the mothers involved).

Cases involving adoption

Permanency could be sought through adoption as well as through return home. This could be with the foster carers or with outside adopters. In contrast to other kinds of case, it was difficult to locate any adoptions which had occurred after we drew the sample and which were seen as unsuccessful. (That not all adoptions were likely to turn out well was illustrated by the number of failed adoptions represented in the sample, but time was required for such problems to become apparent.) Comments, however, on the 'successful adoptions' did illustrate the difficulties that could occur.

An example of a smooth and 'uncomplicated' adoption was provided by Mrs Dunwoody:

> Baby Leo was with us for four and a half months from birth. His placement with suitable adoptive parents was extremely smooth. The plan for handing over was well thought out and in stages, staggered over a week. The adoptive parents met birth mum and were very sympathetic. They were also sensitive to the fact that baby started life with a foster family so want us to continue as part of his life.

The social worker concurred with this assessment:

> This was a relatively straightforward adoption at the request of the birth family who visited the baby in the foster home. It was an appropriate and positive placement...the introduction to the prospective adopters went well. There was close liaison between all professionals, service users and foster carers throughout and procedures were made very clear.

An account of a rather more complicated but ultimately successful adoption was provided by Mrs Clwyd:

> Because the child settled so well, our family soon loved her. Birth mother gave consent to adoption provided she was adopted by us (whom she had grown to trust over the years the child was fostered by us). Social services were very supportive over the adoption providing an allowance to enable it to go ahead.

The social worker broadly concurred with this, but pointed also to some difficulties:

> As foster placement this was ideal. As foster carers couple were very child centred, openly and actively encouraging birth parents' involvement. Promoted child's understanding of care/life history. When intention to adopt was made by carers with ongoing contact arrangements this was initially accepted by birth parents but they later withdrew co-operation re contact, causing confusion and level of upset to child. There were issues around collaboration between professionals in maintaining the best deal for the child but due to staff changes and shortages much of the ultimate adoptive placement preparation was left with carers.

Although these adoption cases were seen as successful, there were problems. Often, adoptions seemed to take 'for ever', and this could lead to changes of heart on the part of birth parents and to attachments forming between carers and child so that it was hard for them to leave each other.

A rather different set of issues surrounded adoption by carers. This sometimes occurred when attempts to find outside adoptions had failed. In contrast to the above example, they were sometimes resisted by the authority – possibly because they were reluctant to lose carers or felt that the wish to adopt, on the part of carers, was 'unprofessional'.

There seemed to be varied views about the degree to which, and the circumstances in which, foster carers should adopt. In some cases carers, social worker and family placement social worker were all agreed that a carer adoption was the best course. Even, then, however, there could be references to resistance to the idea of carer adoptions:

> Although foster carers are generally discouraged from adopting foster children in their care, I feel this situation is in the best interests of the child – both carer and child have bonded so well. The child fits into the family and he looks very much like the foster carer, although this was not a planned match there could not have been a better one. (Family placement social worker)

> We got attached to her and her to us. It would have been too distressing for all of us had she moved on to another family. (Foster carer)

> Common sense won and the child was adopted where he had bonded, where he was loved. (Social worker)

In cases of adoption, the characteristics of the children seemed less important than in the case of return home – perhaps because they were mainly quite young. Success was perceived as depending on the availability of satisfactory adopters, the quality and timeliness of the handover, and – as a prerequisite of these – the decisiveness and skill of the social workers, 'generosity' of the foster carers, and dispatch of the courts and local authority. It was a bonus in these cases if initially weak and frightened children visibly thrived under the care of the foster carers and were handed over happy and healthy to their new families.

Moves to independent living

Adoption was an option for younger children. At the other end of the age range, some young people left fostering for independent living. The issues were those of timeliness (was the young person ready to move on and did they want to?), career (did the young person have a job or place at college?), accommodation (was it adequate and appropriate?) and support (could young person turn to carer or family for support?).

As described by Mrs Kelleher, Karen's move met a number of these conditions:

> When Karen joined us both our children had left home and married. We gave Karen all the attention she required. We helped her develop into a young adult, being strong when required and treated her as a daughter. As we socialised we took her with us and took her around on holidays. We gave her a stable lifestyle when she was with us and will continue to support her and always will... She was given support and encouragement in all her activities both at home and at college.

The social worker concurred and amplified these conclusions:

> Karen was unusually mature and clear sighted. She chose this placement herself when a former placement became unsatisfactory due to the behaviour of another young person. Foster parents were parents of a friend. They were assessed and approved for Karen and the placement was very successful providing both support and independence. Karen was able to avoid projecting her emotional problems onto the foster parents with the help of psychotherapy. Eventually she made her own arrangements for independence while continuing further education.

Unfortunately, such promising beginnings can falter:

The young person was supported in his wish to join the army. Prior to this he had a job, friends and a good relationship with us and our adult children. He left the army during training, living first with his own family and then came back to us for a short time. (Not fostered by us as by now he was over 18) and got his old job back – grants and support from agency. We helped and supported him to obtain a flat. He refused help once he was in the flat both from us and the support agency. Refused to return loans (money and items) despite receiving grants for these things. We later heard from landlord that he had left owing rent, having lost his job for non-attendance. We really regret this outcome.

In this case there was no obvious initial gap in what was provided. Nor did the young person follow the pattern of others where difficult behaviour in the placement was followed by difficulties in independent living. So we do not know why the young person behaved as he did. We had no questionnaire at the time of the follow-up (presumably he had by then no social worker). What could explain this turn of events? A drug problem? Depression? And if so, was this at the failure of his hopes in the army, or because his return to his family had not turned out as expected, or because he could not then stay on with his foster family? Something else?

Whatever the explanation, the example illustrates the persistent vulnerability of many young people, and their need for more than simple practical support. The broad framework we have suggested again seems to work. Placement success is influenced by child and the carer and their family. Longer-term success probably depends quite heavily on contextual factors.

Moves within the care system

Many moves within the care system were unplanned and therefore seen almost by definition as the result of less than fully successful placements. As with the situations discussed above, success was seen as reflecting the timeliness of the move, the degree to which it had been possible to find an appropriate 'match', and the degree to which all concerned had been working to the same end. In order to achieve this result, the appropriate placements had to be available, those concerned had to attend to the views of the child, and there was a need, on occasion, for flexibility when the original plans did not turn out to be appropriate.

A number of these conditions seemed to be satisfied in the example given by Mrs Appleby:

We spent six months with the children and the social worker and ourselves thought the best place for the family would be their home town, so they would be near their birth parents. We were only registered for short-term placements so they decided to place them in Holby with carers who had more room.

The social worker commented on the new situation that:

Hard work on structuring contact and defining expectations is bearing fruit.

The family placement social worker also felt that the move had been right but gave rather fuller comments on the difficulties in the initial situation:

This was initially an emergency placement – keeping the children together was stated as the priority. The match was not good in terms of area, numbers, accommodation and stress on the carers working full-time. The placement almost disrupted on two occasions. Relationship between carers and me and family social worker became difficult and I found it almost impossible to ease communication between them. If another resource had not been found this would have disrupted.

Disruption was not avoided in the case of Jack. From the point of view of the carers, things went wrong suddenly:

The child placed with us had a lot of emotional problems from very early in life, some of which we felt he had yet to face up to and cope with. This had resulted in ongoing disruptive behaviour, causing the breakdown of a six year placement. Having been on his best behaviour for such a long spell when it surfaced again he seemed to lose control completely.

The social worker felt that Jack's subsequent placement in residential care had not been good for him, and consequently deplored the fact that he had not been contained in his previous foster placement:

More quality carers should be recruited and maintained but things must change considerably if this is to be achieved… I feel foster carers (or at least a corps of specialist carers) should be paid employees of the authority, receiving equivalent pay to residential staff. Until this is considered, preparation, collaboration etc. is a luxury which means little to many young people.

The family placement worker had a simple but terse comment:

Adolescents who display difficult behaviour should not be placed with those caring for elderly relatives. There was no planning or preparation (an emergency placement). A match was unavailable.

The difficulty of matching suggested to some that when placements were working, there was a case for not moving the child, even when this had originally been intended:

> The young person knew we liked her and she felt comfortable and safe. She made contact with birth family for first time in five years. Never stayed out late (always on time) and never ran off (she had been running since the age of 12). I believe she felt safe and secure with us. We gave her back control over her life and allowed her to make choices. She said she felt free here but didn't need to run off as she did two weeks into her next placement.

There was no questionnaire from the social worker but the family placement worker concurred:

> She had friends in London and often used to run off, sometimes sleeping rough. Very needy immature girl who should never have left long-term carers.

So, the general issues of movement were those of ensuring that a child did not outstay her or his welcome, of finding appropriate matches, and of maximising the benefits of matches when they occurred. As will be seen later, careful matching was almost universally seen to be an unusual luxury, and longer stays than envisaged were common. A rather special set of issues arose for the small number of children who, for reason of learning or physical impairments, were not able to look after themselves after the age of 18. At this stage, young people who had been with carers provided and supported by children's services became the responsibility of others, and were in consequence sometimes moved.

In these cases, contextual factors (the social worker and the availability of placements) seemed directly important in influencing success. If further appropriate placements were not available, existing placements might fail, when they could have been ended with honour and reasonable good will on all sides. In other respects, examination of these cases suggests again that much depends on the child, the carer and the fit between the two.

Long-stay foster care

As we have seen, a sizeable proportion of the children in the sample were fostered long-term or for the foreseeable future. Impressionistically, these placements were of very different kinds. They included long-term, peaceful 'quasi-adoptions' but also a number which were hanging on by the skin of their teeth ('the success is that after three years he's still here – he's had 35 previous placements – we will never give up on him'). There were placements with relatives, placements with foster carers with ongoing contact with birth families, and placements where all contact with the birth family had virtually ceased. And these differences cut across other equally obvious distinctions in terms of the age, sex and personality of the child, the characteristics of the foster family and so on.

Those we asked to judge the success of the long-term placements seemed to do so in terms of two related but distinct sets of criteria. First, there was the question of how well the placement was working – whether it was stable, whether the child was happy and settled, and whether the child was developing normally, doing well at school, coming to terms with his or her psychological problems and so on. Second, there was the question of how far issues relating to the child's family and hence 'identity' and long-term future had been resolved.

These concerns were very similar to those we identified in the children's responses – to wit the need to feel welcome in a family, to feel that one's identity and difference are respected, and to maintain the kind of contact with one's family that one wants to maintain. The issues were also related to the first set of criteria, inasmuch as it was likely that a failure to resolve questions related to the child's family would impinge on the stability of the placement, either immediately or in the future. Issues of identity were seen as having importance in their own right so that, for example, a failure to ensure that a child was in an ethnically appropriate placement could be seen as regrettable, irrespective of its wider effects.

A number of these issues were raised by the example of Ricky. Ricky's foster carers were in no doubt the placement was working:

> He is part of our family and we are happy with him and he is with us. We have a bond. He is treated like any other child in the family.

The social worker agreed that the child was progressing well but nevertheless had doubts about the placement's appropriateness:

The child was placed with this family as a short-term measure. During this time it was clear he would not return home. Now he may stay there permanently but he is a mixed parentage child (white-Caribbean) living with an African family. Is this then a 'trans-racial placement'? The child has had white carers before entering care. He has made great progress in this placement but it has also raised issues for him about his place in the family, his identity and his feelings for his birth family.

These thoughts were clearly some way from those of the carers. The gap disturbed the family placement worker who commented:

[The lessons are] listen to children/young person, agency to have clear plans for child, carers to be consulted when plans are being discussed at every stage and not just at the end, link worker's experience and knowledge of child to be sought and acted on more readily, agency to be more creative in areas of financial expenditure, professionals to move beyond the us and them, 'we do this, you do this' position.

Conclusion

This chapter emphasises the important difference between placement outcome and case outcome; either can be successful when the other is not. In general, however, placement success is desirable in itself and makes case success more likely. As explained in the first chapter, we are more often concerned with placement than case success.

The chapter suggests a broad framework for explaining these outcomes. This framework is compatible with, but different from, that suggested by the children's responses. Unsurprisingly, social workers and foster carers lay much more stress than the children on *the part the children play* in bringing about different outcomes. Children, carers and social workers are equally likely to stress the importance of *carers*, the interaction between carer and child, sometimes described as the *'match'*, and the influence of relationships with *birth families*. Like the children, carers and social workers stress the influence of movement and stability, but they give a rather more elaborate account of the *contextual factors* that give these moves and their timing the arbitrary character of which the children complain.

Chapter Six

Explanations: Social Worker and Carer Accounts

Introduction

Our last two chapters suggest that placement, as opposed to case, outcomes in foster care are likely to depend primarily on the child and foster carer. However, the relationship between these two parties may also be influenced by the context in which it takes place. Key elements in this context are the child's family, other members of the carer's family and the social worker. This chapter again uses qualitative material, this time from the carers and social workers to look in more detail at the variables which may be involved.

The child's contribution

The descriptions by the carer and social workers fell into three broad categories: according to them, the foster children varied in:

- their attractiveness (at least to the carer)
- their motivation to make the placement work and
- the difficulties they presented.

These broad areas covered considerable variations in behaviour and personality which were held to make success or failure more likely.

Attractiveness

The attractiveness of a child sometimes stemmed from the obvious extent of the child's needs, sometimes from the gratification carers felt from being able to meet those needs, and sometimes from the children's winning ways and personality. So a carer might respond to:

> ...a delightful baby who was being beaten, starved and neglected...

and feel justifiable pleasure when a child became:

> ...so different from the frightened person who moved in with us.

A placement might work:

> ...because of her lovely ways and her need of love, security and stability...

and was reinforced when children learnt to use a knife and fork or told their teachers how happy they were with their new foster mum. Such children were variously referred to as 'fit, healthy, happy, loving', 'very easy to please', 'loveable' and 'lovely'.

Attractive characteristics included an ability to display affection, the ability to succeed at school, and resilience. Loving children aroused love and were consequently 'easy to care for'. Children who did well aroused pride:

> ...she's a beautiful child and she's the sort anyone would be proud to say she's their daughter.

Resilience commanded respect:

> ...he has overcome a lot of things in his life.

Such qualities could make them in the carers' eyes 'special'.

These positive qualities could compensate for others which were less endearing:

> This kid is a darling, very affectionate and we get lots of laughs and good times – has given an awful lot back to this family, he has given his love and he makes us laugh most days. This makes up for the times he makes us scream.

Motivation

Children who wanted the placement were commonly seen as 'work(ing) hard to make this work' and as 'meeting us half-way'. A motivated child 'understood reason for placement and accepted it' with the result that 'she's been happy and made herself one of us'. This acceptance was related to the child's view of her or his birth family:

He realises his birth family could not have looked after him.

Such acceptance led children to:

> ...want a new home where he could be loved or brought up...

or, more specifically, 'adoption' or a 'new start':

> Although not wanting to be fostered it was an understandable opportunity to her and one (at age 14/15) she was prepared to grasp. She knew that living with her birth parents was depriving her of opportunities. (Social worker)

Motivation was reinforced if the child had chosen specific foster carers. Choice could reflect prior experience:

> ...they both expected and wanted to come back to us...

or a reaction to the current situation:

> ...has stated he loves us and wants to live here.

The fact that the placement involved relatives, or acquaintance with the carers for other reasons, or the existence of siblings in the placement could obviously make such specific choices more likely:

> ...still wants to remain with us, he is our grandson and wants to stay with us forever. (Foster carer)

> ...knew foster carers previous to move...therefore she felt that she was included in the choice. (Social worker)

The reasons why placements did not work out well were also seen as related to motivation:

> He actually stated on numerous occasions he did not want to live with anyone.

> There are some kids you can help and want help and some kids you can't and don't want help.

Such a lack of motivation was sometimes related to the young person's wish for a certain kind of placement. These comments generally seemed to relate to teenagers:

> He didn't want to make things work, he always wanted to be in a children's home because he wouldn't have to make any commitments and be a free agent. (Foster carer)

> Young teenagers sometimes don't want to be part of family, having to engage in family activities. (Social worker)

More commonly, however, the reason for the lack of enthusiasm for fostering was related to the child's wish to be with her or his family. The reasons for preferring family to foster care varied. They included missing particular people, feeling the odd one out in the family, and divided loyalties. So the progress of a placement might be explained on the grounds that a child:

> ...just wanted to be with his mum...

or because:

> ...his two sisters remained at home while he had to go into care...

or because he:

> ...liked being here but couldn't cope with divided loyalties.

Changes in the family were sometimes seen as provoking changes in the progress of the placement:

> We knew when mum was found she would want to go and live with her but not as quick as she did. (Foster carer)

> She was settled and happy until hearing about her mother going to court to apply for a residence order. Since then her feelings have been muddled. She likes the idea of going back to her mum but I think she is fearful of what might happen if she does. I don't think she will settle down again until a decision has been made about her future. (Foster carer)

The degree to which a child's wish to leave the placement influenced outcomes probably varied with age. Young people had more power to end a placement than children under five:

> If a young person decides they want a placement to end they are able to disrupt. (Social worker)

> Her placement disrupted (engineered by her). (Foster carer)

Difficulty of child

Some foster children, particularly very young ones, were seen as 'easy'. Even an older child might be seen as:

> ...obedient, helpful, got along with other family members.

However, others presented:

> ...severe behaviour problems that could not be coped with in a family environment.

> This placement was not successful because of his behaviour towards family members and property. (Foster carer)

> All her other placements and her family home had broken down, this placement was difficult – most placements broke down after a violent argument and this is what happened here. Having coped with a lot of outbursts the final one proved too much for me. (Foster carer)

In a minority of cases, difficulties related to the child's medical condition or learning impairment:

> Because of the Down's syndrome needs 24 hour care. (Foster carer)

> At eight months old he began to have fits, every three or four weeks we would be in hospital.

These problems must have brought with them the strains faced by carers of disabled children, for example, additional physical labour, the need to contain risk, challenging behaviour and (as illustrated above) the need to provide continuous care:

> The diagnosis of epilepsy has made his behaviour worse. (Foster carer)

> Leaving consumables in front of fires, he became a liability so we had to make a choice. (Foster carer)

Some children with special needs presented behavioural problems. More commonly, however, these were not seen as having their origin in an identifiable medical condition. The problems presented included lying, stealing and aggression:

> This child made up lies about us to the psychologist. (Foster carer)

> He stole whatever he could take including Christmas presents bought for others. (Foster carer)

Some carers reported 'sexualised behaviour' which, although apparently a common response to previous abuse (Farmer and Pollock 1998), is nevertheless difficult for the carers. At the minimum it was embarrassing:

> Over-sexualised behaviour which caused a lot of problems with friends and family.

At the worst it was dangerous:

> Young person abusing brother and grandchildren of carer. (Social worker)

> Sexualised behaviour with carer's own child. (Social worker)

As the children grew older, the carers were more likely to report problems relating to attitude, to the behaviour of the young person outside the home, and to the young person's involvement in activities such as drinking, drug-taking, overdosing and sexually risky behaviour for which younger children seemed to lack the opportunities and inclination. Such young people were variously described as bored, demanding, violent, paying inadequate attention to hygiene, and needing to manipulate the situation so that they were rejected:

> No interest in her schooling, attitude to her brothers and sisters one of indifference, friendships with the wrong kinds of people, can be promiscuous. (Foster carer)

> The young person has found the delights of being an older teenager (i.e. going out drinking etc.) and this has caused some problems. (Social worker)

Some of these problems were attributed to the young person's rebelliousness and general attitude:

> Did not like rules – always wanted her own way and had a very up and down relationship with her parents.

Other problems seemed to be more a response to deprivation. Having experienced little that was positive from others, the foster children seemed determined to test the limits of what was on offer or, alternatively, to ask for nothing at all:

> She demands more than is possible.

> She feels the only person she can rely on is herself. She wanted to lead her own life and take her own decisions.

Other explanations for these problems were that the child or young person had 'got in with the wrong sort':

> She got mixed up with the wrong crowd, a lot older than herself. She stayed out all night drinking and taking drugs.

> He could not cope with moving from a small primary school to a large comprehensive...this made him far more aggressive.

These difficulties resulted in problems inside the home and in worries about what might happen outside it:

> Involved himself with two lads. He was stealing from me for them and for himself. (Foster carer describing a situation apparently involving drugs)

> Foster carers did not approve of boyfriend who had been a drug-taker. (Social worker)

There was a question of how far it was appropriate to persist with placements in difficulty:

> At the point where child's behaviour began to challenge the carer's confidence and ability at around 15 months it could be said the placement became non-beneficial to both carer and child. (Family placement social worker)

Just as a positive response to a carer provoked a benign circle, so a negative one could provoke disappointment, criticism of the young person, and even rejection.

The carers

One family placement social worker responded to our request for an explanation for the placement's success or lack of it:

> These carers fostered teenagers from the time that their first child was an infant. This worked well as the carer's children were so much younger than the foster children that there was no 'competition' between them for attention and needs were very different. Additionally the male carer had been a child in care and was very motivated to give to other children. The female carer has [foreign] parents and culturally has a view of children and family life which values children very highly. Who knows really why placements work? These people do not care about the under-financing of foster care –

they love young people and are committed to them in a mature, practical and consistent way. I feel privileged to work with them.

Despite her agnosticism about the reasons for placement success, this worker identified a number of reasons which were also given by others. There seemed to be widespread agreement that the carers were key to the success of the placement, about the kind of environments they provided, and the qualities required to do this.

The key role of carers was emphasised by numerous comments suggesting that some were better than others – either absolutely or in relation to particular kinds of children:

> I believe she has received the appropriate placement and I wish there were more carers like these. They are exceptional. (Social worker)

> After fostering for 27 years we are pretty good at our job. We have now moved on to private fostering. (Foster carer)

> I believe that some people are recruited who may have financial reasons for fostering rather than the care needs of children to the fore (personal and subjective comment but felt by the majority of social workers here). (Social worker)

In practice, as illustrated later, any negative comments about carers were generally phrased in terms of the carers' unsuitability for particular types of case, or for cases of this kind at this particular stage in their fostering career.

Carers and social workers seemed broadly agreed on the environment a foster home should provide. It should be stable, safe and caring, and it should allow the child to develop in a normal family where he or she is encouraged, offered opportunities and made subject to reasonable expectations. To provide such environments, carers needed to be committed, persistent, caring, willing to spend time with the child and to listen and encourage, and to set limits where necessary.

Stability, commitment, care and love

Stability was a word which recurred frequently. However, it was coupled with others of varying meaning. Some emphasised the importance of continuity and the damage produced by breakdowns:

> I put every effort into caring for my children. I will not put them into respite. I feel losing birth parents is a big loss on its own.

Unplanned moves are disruptive, traumatic and cause great psychological distress…and feelings of guilt and anger.

The positive side of this coin was the value of 'being there' for the child, if necessary, beyond the statutory limits of the care system:

> She had the chance to experience what all children whoever or wherever they live should have: love, patience and a safe environment to allow them to grow into happy individuals. (Foster carer)

> He is now going through the stage of 'I am nearly 18, where do I go from here?'. He still needs to know we are always going to be there for him. (Foster carer)

On a day-to-day basis, carers stressed the need to spend time with the child, and for listening, joint activities which the child liked, encouraging the child to go to sports or clubs, and encouraging them in their successes:

> We try to talk through problems whatever they are and we encourage them to try different outlets, swimming, clubs etc. We do things together as a family, i.e. pictures, McDonald's etc. (Foster carer)

'Being there', however, was not something that was always easily endured. For one carer it involved:

> Constantly reassuring her she isn't going to move any more. Not backing down when her behaviour has been sometimes intolerable. Treating her as one of my own family, and not making her feel different although she constantly throws that statement back at me. Telling her we love her! (Foster carer)

These themes of commitment, persistence, equal treatment and love recurred throughout the carers' accounts.

Commitment was seen as a prerequisite for stability. It carried with it implications of 'stickability', persistence, 'hard work' (a common phrase), an ability not to be thrown off course by difficult behaviour (something which might be encouraged by an understanding of the reasons for the behaviour):

> It's been a success because I work as hard as I can at it. It is hard but I never give up. (Foster carer)

In this respect commitment shaded into patience, an ability to wait as a child's frozen capacity for feeling thawed, or a child with learning disabilities acquired small skills:

> He came a very disturbed 18 month old and it took about five years to get him to trust and relax.

> A lot of time and patience was needed to get her eating and mobile.

For others commitment implied something more assertive – a willingness to fight for the child, against the social services if necessary, to require 'statementing' from reluctant education authorities, or to offer a home and 'mean it'. Children, it was argued, who saw their carers go out on a limb for them became committed to the carers in their turn:

> We have worked long and hard with him, giving him four years of stability and a loving home. There were times when we felt we couldn't go on with him due to no support at all from the social services team…but we know they would just dump him in rooms somewhere out of the area with no back-up. That is what has made us hang on to Kevin. (Foster carer)

> We fought so hard for him against the powers that be that he could not doubt our love for him. (Foster carer)

Care was also a word which was frequently used, but with varying implications. At the minimum it implied good physical care, good food, taking the child to the doctor when necessary. For many carers it was associated with 'love', a word they used without embarrassment:

> She was failing to thrive but with love and regular meals and routines… (Foster carer)

With older children, however, the word was often 'like'. At its best this did not appear to us a weak emotion – a watered-down version of love – but rather a positive response to the child's individuality. It required an accurate perception of what the child was like and an 'acceptance' (another key word) of it:

> We looked beyond her anger and saw the real Virginia. (Foster carer)

The essence of this process seemed to be that the carers saw what the child was like and liked what they saw. The result could be expressed in trust – for example, by leaving the child on their own in the house – or even in battles which resulted in each side having a doughty respect for the other:

We are very fond of Trevor so we would strive to solve whatever the problem is. The key to managing a difficult child is to like them. (Foster carer)

As personalities, we are very different, and, it must be said, not very compatible. We did very well with each other all things considered, and still see each other regularly. In fact for your information she has just come back to stay for the weeks leading up to her A level exams to help her revise and get through them. (Foster carer)

Social training

Foster care seemed to involve discipline or 'setting limits' as well as love. Whereas no one seemed to deny the need for some limits, attitudes towards them seemed to vary from the somewhat draconian, through the highly structured, to the nearly *laissez-faire*.

Some, it seemed, looked to love and time to enable a transformation:

She was able to grow and develop in a safe environment. (Foster carer)

Others relied on the normality and consistency of everyday life, which they contrasted with the children's allegedly chaotic home environments. So they emphasised the need to provide structure, rules and routine:

She herself wanted a more ordered life and we could offer this to her. (Foster carer)

Others viewed matters more proactively and valued the teaching of skills and the enforcement of reasonable behaviour. Some techniques were forceful:

Being persistent with punishments and letting him know who was in control. (Foster carer)

I am a very strong personality and have not allowed her behaviour to win. The child found safety in this and so feels very safe because she cannot go out of control because I have never let her. (Foster carer)

Other approaches involved reasoning, for example by appealing to the child's self-interest, or to generally accepted standards, and negotiation:

Helping her to understand about her culture, to love herself and her body, and how to improve her behaviour, and how people have changed since her behaviour has improved. (Foster carer)

> Being a young adult she is very sensible but sometimes can forget about time
> limits i.e. coming in late, but we can always come up with solutions to give
> her space i.e. as long as we know who she is with. (Foster carer)

Undoubtedly these matters went more easily in the context of a good relationship:

> I like all children very much and like to see them laugh. I taught Dawn not to
> keep losing her temper and not to bear grudges. (Foster carer)

> Constant guidelines and boundaries, being fair with him, showing we love
> him unconditionally. (Foster carer)

In some cases, however, the relationship was fraught and the carers had to rely
on persistence and consistency:

> Despite a police investigation into ourselves, following false allegations by
> this child, and a further even worse disruption, she is still here and making
> small steps in the right direction. She is responding better to our demands
> that there are rules which must be followed and that society expects this too.
> (Foster carer)

Matching and interaction between carers and children

Social workers were clear that similar children might elicit different reactions
from different carers. As seen earlier they tried to allow for this by matching
child and foster family. We have already given examples of the kinds of criteria
used in matching. The three that were most stressed in their concluding
comments seemed to be capacity (sometimes equated with experience), length
of stay and what might be called 'emotional fit'.

In general it was felt that difficult children should go to highly competent
and experienced carers:

> The child was well placed with his foster carers who were extremely profes-
> sional and caring. It could have been a disaster if he was placed in another
> emergency placement with a family that were not experienced. (Social
> worker)

> I was not trained or been fostering long enough to know how to handle this
> child's needs. (Foster carer)

A second criterion was that the length of placement should be matched to
carers' expectations. Some carers were seen as good at managing difficult

behaviour in the short-term, but unwilling to put up with it in the longer-term (although it was acknowledged that some temporary placements had nevertheless worked out well):

> The lesson we always learn is that if placements lasted for the predicted length of time then we would have many more successes. We know carers can cope for a defined length of time with even very difficult behaviour but it's when placements drag on and the child cannot be moved on, then either the carer reaches the end of their tether with the child or the child whose needs are not being met will engineer a breakdown. Thus carer and child experience the stigma of an unnecessary breakdown because of lack of resources. (Family placement social worker)

Failure to match carer and child adequately was perceived in some cases as leading to the 'guilt and distress of breakdown' or even in one case to deregistration:

> Sadly this carer was deregistered due to an unexplained injury to an older child. The child was extremely difficult and we were desperate to place him. I was reluctant to go placing him with this carer as her strengths are with non-organic failure to thrive babies. (Family placement social worker)

Some children were seen as either too difficult for almost any carer or alternatively as presenting a combination of needs which were peculiarly difficult to meet:

> It was my feeling in the past, as social worker for the child, that we as an authority were asking the foster carers to take on more than anyone should be expected to cope with. (Social worker)

Other problems arose because of particular features of the carer and the child, what we called above 'emotional fit'. The most common of these seemed to relate to *attachment, behaviour* and *'family fit'*.

Matching and attachment

Attachment difficulties arose when the child wanted a closer or less close relationship than the carer wanted to provide. Conversely, attachment needs were well met when each side wanted the degree of closeness that the other wanted to offer:

> Carers sometimes cannot reach all of a child's needs. Whilst carers could deal with difficult behaviour they cannot always meet some of this child's other

needs – i.e. to be nurtured, cuddled. Difficult situation because some of the more nurturing carers could not tolerate the aggressive/abusive behaviour shown by this young person. (Family placement social worker)

In contrast to this situation, carers frequently referred to the 'bond' which existed between them and the foster child. Other words which seemed to cover a similar phenomenon included 'chemistry', 'emotional tie' and 'attachment':

> I love Jimmy. He is loved by all our family very much and he loves us. (Foster carer)

This tie was a reciprocal matter – an issue of chemistry – and difficult to predict:

> Placements that do not have the matching potential criteria can sometimes have the best outcome because of attachments, commitments and personality. In short just 'clicking'. (Family placement social worker)

This sometimes seemed to arise because the child's love or need for love evoked a response in the carer:

> This one was different. She needed us so much. (Foster carer)

Carers also varied in their need for love or for a response. Some carers were pleased when their foster child called them 'mum' or 'dad' or expressed love:

> [I think it is a success because] she said she loved me and has never said that to other foster parents. (Foster carer)

However, one carer found the closeness expected by the child difficult – albeit apparently going along with what the child wanted:

> She has always called us mum and dad, even changed her name to ours, and I personally have always found the role hard as I cannot accept her as my own. I never felt that was supposed to be my role. (Foster carer)

But in this preference the carer contrasted with others who fought to adopt their foster children, sometimes despite opposition from their local authorities, who mourned the departure of foster children on adoption or who seemed to expect more closeness than the child wished to give:

> The foster carers seemed to expect gratitude and emotional involvement which a child such as Zak was unable to give. (Social worker)

Matching and behaviour

There were similar variations in relation to handling behaviour. In general, *difficult behaviour* made a poor outcome more likely. It did not, however, make it inevitable. Much depended on the way the carers interpreted and reacted to the behaviour, and on the existence of perceived compensations. Some behaviour was seen as ungrateful and intolerable:

> Started going out with her friends and took little notice of me, thought she could come and go as she pleased. (Foster carer)

Other carers might describe similar behaviour but be more prepared to tolerate it, seeing it, for example, as the sort of thing to be expected of teenagers in a family:

> She's become a typical teenager. Knows everything, treats us like a B and B, and bites our heads off when questioned about the simplest of things. She thinks life is all about clubbing and boys. [Yet] she has always called us mum and dad. (Foster carer)

The way behaviour was then interpreted seemed to have global repercussions on the way the young person was (and presumably was treated), and the outcome of the placement:

> Less successful was the relationship between myself and young person who tended to view everything as her god given right. (Foster carer)

> Child was aggressive, ill-mannered, arrogant and abusive – impossible to live with. (Foster carer)

Others, by contrast, rode such difficulties and the outcome was not separation:

> Because of my experience I did not take notice of his 'bad behaviour'. (Foster carer)

> These carers have bags of patience and tenacity. They were able to interpret child's behaviour as communication. (Social worker)

Matching and family fit

Irrespective of whether the foster child 'bonded' with a member of a foster family it was important that they 'fitted in'. This meant that they were able to adapt to the family's way of life, got on with their siblings or other members of the family if they were there, and got on with the carer's own children and her partner if present. On occasion extended families were also important, and these could include the carer's own children and sometimes former foster children.

Although comments on 'fit' were extremely common they were generally unelaborated:

> Acceptance of child within wider family network. Child felt a sense of belonging. (Social worker)

> Things worked well for our family and Graham because he was a pleasant child and fitted in so well.

Some comments referred to clashes within the family:

> Extreme adolescent behaviour was seriously affecting other foster family members, also neighbours and extended foster family members were becoming unsupportive. (Foster carer)

> He wanted all the attention for himself. Our children suffered and life got very difficult. (Foster carer)

Factors which made a difference to whether a child fitted in or not seemed to include:

- the child's personality – 'pleasant' children fitted in, less 'pleasant' ones were more difficult to accommodate
- the length of time the child had been in the placement – children who had been placed young and spent a long time in the placement might become *de facto* members of the family
- the approach of the foster carers, who themselves seemed to stress the importance of treating all children equally
- the degree to which the child was seen as a threat or a rival to other members of the family.

The carers and the wider environment

Social workers, while apparently agreeing with carers on the main virtues listed above, added others of their own. Many of their requirements could be summarised under the heading of professionalism. Carers, it seemed, should *not want to work on their own*, but should:

- be able to work with professionals and family
- take on board guidance and advice and
- advocate for their own needs.

Social workers could also acknowledge that some maverick carers could perform well in certain respects without these virtues:

> Socially behaviourally emotionally the match has been OK. The carers' commitment has been 100% despite their antagonism to the department.

However, commitment might conflict with a capacity to let the child go, an attribute which was valued:

> Foster carer was excellent – nurtured child but was also able to move child on. (Social worker)

In order to be able to respond to the child's needs, the carer also had to have enough of her own met:

> With my health deteriorating I couldn't cope with these increasing verbal and physical attacks. (Foster carer)

> The foster father died suddenly and unexpectedly causing enormous distress to his wife and the children placed with them. This could not be foreseen. The foster carer was committed to care for the children but has frequently not felt strong enough to focus on their needs. (Social worker)

Ideally, the carers were also able to see the birth family as part of the placement team. This lessened the likelihood that the child would experience conflicts of loyalty whether in the foster home or later in their own:

> We as carers get on well with James' birth family for the better which James understands. As we have said we understand James' needs to be with his birth family as we have a family of our own and understand how important it is to be together. We have a good understanding with James and his family. I keep in contact with them and see needs on both sides and it all works out well. (Foster carer)

> I think the contact between him and his birth family is very important and we've always encouraged this and I'm sure this has helped him to be more settled in our home. (Foster carer)

> He wanted nothing more than for his dad to want him which he did when he was 18. So this made him happy. He was apprehensive at first not wanting to hurt me, but when I OK'd it he was happy to move on. (Foster carer)

In other cases the carer seemed to be involved in direct work with the birth family:

Working with the parents, teaching them parenting skills etc. and being very truthful with them and honest, if anything was not correct in what they did with the child we would tell them so.

Mother was giving him loads of sweets and junk food in the nursery as she wasn't allowed contact in the foster home, then he wouldn't eat proper food in the foster home and was even more hyperactive. I had a chance to put some of the junk food away when mum came to visit the child in my home. I'd say do you mind if he has them after his dinner/tea.

This work with parents could involve building them up and offering friendly support as well as pointing to errors in their ways:

The relationship between foster carer and parent is very important. This foster carer works very well in partnership with parent. She has built parent self-esteem and made her feel that she is very important in her child's life. Parent was ready to relinquish responsibility feeling it was best if she handed him over to carer to become carer's responsibility. Foster carer worked hard to make mum understand that she can never replace her in child's eye – he needs her around.

The other side of the coin was that carers had to work with the child about the way their parents behaved and the likelihood of return. Anxieties about returning or (or not returning) affected the child and were something with which some carers tried to wrestle:

There have been problems with the mother wanting her back and then changing her mind and because she has a new partner and is known to be violent.

He has a clear view of his family as far as he can. Some things are hard to understand.

Conclusion

The qualitative material in this chapter suggests a linked set of hypotheses or model. In broad outline, it seems likely that outcomes depend heavily on the characteristics of *the child, the foster family* and the *interaction between the two*. This interaction, however, takes place within a context in which both the social worker and the child's family play important parts. Foster carers have to be able to deal with this external environment as well as with the child. This schema can be filled in with more detail on each of these broad areas.

Children seemed likely to succeed in a placement because they were *attractive* (either because of their needs or their personalities), they *wanted the placement to succeed* and put something into it, and they did not present marked *difficulties*. Difficulties included sexually disturbed behaviour, problems related to attachment (e.g. wanting all the attention and love, or alternatively an inability to commit to any relationship), violent or dishonest behaviour within the home, a cluster of 'deviant' activities (truancy, drug-taking, heavy drinking and delinquency), and 'adolescent behaviour' (i.e. staying out late without notice, treating the home as a 'hotel' and a generally 'negative attitude'). In a small minority of cases the children were severely disabled and this raised issues related to risk and to the increased amount of help and services that were needed.

In order to cope with such children, *foster carers* needed to offer *stability* (something which required commitment and hard work, and which was made easier by the ability to re-frame difficult behaviour as something other than a personal attack). They needed to *like and respond to children as individuals*. They needed to *provide social training*, providing appropriate limits, direction and encouragement.

Such committed and skilled concern was more likely to take place in a context where the *child fitted into the family*. This 'fit' depended on the carers' treating the child on the same footing as others in the family, and was more likely if the child had spent a long time in the family and become a *de facto* member of it. It was discouraged if the child's age or personality made her or him a potential rival to other children in the house. Fundamentally, however, the fit depended on the *chemistry* between the main carer and the child – a match in terms of needs for closeness, the capacity of the carer to deal with the child's behaviour, and the consequent liking of each for the other.

From the point of view of the social workers, the skills needed to be complemented by a *professional approach*. This seemed to mean an ability to accept advice and direction, to work well with other professionals within an agreed framework. It was particularly important that the carers should deal well with the child's birth family and in a way which did not expose the child to divided loyalties. All this depended on, and required an ability, both to commit to the child and to be prepared to give her or him up without being swayed by their own feelings. Such dispassionate love was easier if carers were experienced and were not being overwhelmed by troubles of their own.

These hypotheses do not seem unreasonable. They are in keeping with common sense – it would be surprising, indeed, if placements were more likely to work where the carer disliked the child and failed to encourage their achievements. In general, they are also in keeping with the findings of research as summarised, for example, by Beek and Schofield (2004), Berridge (1997), Sellick and Thoburn (1996) and Triseliotis (1989) or with the approach advocated by Beek and Schofield (2004). There are, it is true, some differences of emphasis. The foster carers seemed to give more emphasis to the positive aspects of the child's personality rather than their difficulties (although positive aspects were considered by Rowe and her colleagues (1989)). The foster carers also emphasised the positive contribution of other children in the household and not simply the potential for rivalry, which has been the main concern of previous work. And whereas some carers emphasised the professional virtues of experience, skill and team-working, others gave equal or greater prominence to love and a fierce commitment to the child.

Chapter Seven

The Case Studies

Introduction

The qualitative material from the questionnaires just described has consider-able value. It draws on the experience of very large numbers of carers and social workers. The questions allowed them to respond in a wide variety of different ways, encapsulating in a few words the criteria against which they were evaluating the placement and why they thought a given outcome had occurred. However, the material also has disadvantages:

- It lacks detail – we do not know what exactly the parties did in achieving this result.

- It lacks a history and context – we know little of the circumstances within which outcomes did or did not occur and generally (not always) lack information on how the case evolved over time.

- It lacks systematic testing – the explanations given by carers are plausible but specific to the particular case, so that we were unable to test them by applying them systematically to all cases.

The case studies which we now consider make up for a number of these disad-vantages. They are more detailed, providing concrete examples of what exactly children and carers did. They can be grounded in the history and context of the placement so that it becomes possible to see connections between changes in aspect of the placement and changes in others. They are fuller so that it is possible to see how far the model initially developed from the questionnaires could be used to explain *all* the case studies or needed further modification. They can themselves be used to develop theory, so that explanations that appear to apply to one case can be tested and modified against subsequent cases (cf. Glaser and Strauss 1967).

The aim of the next two chapters[1] is to test our emerging ideas against the more detailed case studies. We do this by analysing four cases in some detail, and then drawing on a number of others to highlight aspects of the model.

The model we develop contains two main components:

- *Responsive parenting* – the way in which the carer deals with the child.

- *Conditions* – the prior conditions which make this kind of interaction more or less likely. In what follows we have distinguished two types of conditions:

    ○ central conditions to do with the child, the foster carer and the compatibility between them

    ○ those to do with the wider context.

Responsive parenting is a necessary characteristic of a successful placement. The various *conditions* are not necessary or sufficient for success but they do make it more or less likely. An analogy may be provided by a tennis match. For a tennis player to win he or she must deal skilfully with the balls they have to play. If they hit them continually into the net, they will almost certainly lose the game. The likelihood of their playing the balls skilfully is however related to prior conditions – their own level of skill, the degree to which their style of play is adapted to that of their opponent, the nature of the surface and so on. This distinction between skilled performance in a particular situation and the conditions which make this likely is the one we are trying to make.

In the case of foster care, the prior conditions relate to the characteristics of the foster child, particular attributes of the foster carer, for example her/his general skill and the presence/absence of a sense of strain, and the compatibility between the carer and the child in question. Other conditions reflect the wider context, including the care plans for the child, and the involvement of the birth family members and members of the foster carer's own family. The effect of these conditions is not independent of the child or carer. For example, the impact of the child's family on the placement depends partly on the way the carer responds to the birth parents.

As throughout this book names and details have been changed to preserve confidentiality.

The cases

The cases included in this part of the research were selected because they had been judged to be 'successful' or 'less successful' according to the research study criteria. These were based on the foster carers' responses to the second questionnaire (see Appendix 2). The sample was matched as far as possible on age, gender and length of time in placement, although, in the event, 13 'successful' and 11 'less successful' placements were sampled. Definitions of 'success' were not always shared by the foster carers and/or the social workers: by the time the interviews were completed, one 'successful' placement was on the point of breakdown and others were less clearly regarded as successful by either the foster carer or the social worker, while in other cases, the foster carers were more positive than hitherto.

A number of children and young people, who ranged in age from 18 months to 20 years (and hence strictly speaking not a foster child at all), were described as having special needs ranging from severe to mild learning difficulties, speech and hearing impairments. Most were described as having additional social or behavioural problems either in the home environment or school or both. A majority had been neglected or abused, some very seriously. The sample was made up of 14 boys and 10 girls; all children were of white British ethnicity and culture apart from three children, one of Asian, one of Iranian/white British and one of African-Caribbean family background. Most children had had or went on to experience more than one placement.

Face-to-face interviews were conducted with 25 foster carers, who included 22 females, one male and one couple interviewed together. Eight lived in single adult households or with other adults in a non-marital relationship. Twenty-one foster carers were of white British ethnicity and culture, one was of African-Asian and two of African-Caribbean ethnicity. Telephone interviews were conducted with 23 social workers, of whom one was a family placement worker and the remainder were the social worker for the child.

James: 'love unillusioned is not love disenchanted'

Our first case was seen by all concerned as successful. James is nine years old and has a learning difficulty. He came into care when he was five years old, following his brother's disclosure of physical abuse at the hands of his father, and was placed with his paternal grandmother. She cared for him until she became unable to cope with his increasingly unruly, violent behaviour, which included physical attacks, and setting fire to his bedroom, and other small fires in the kitchen and living room. He was placed with his present foster family initially for an eight week assessment, and had been there at the time of the interview for two and a half years. Some time after the placement had been confirmed as permanent, James disclosed to his foster mother that his father had sexually abused him, but although a medical examination substantiated that his anus was torn, the police decided that there was insufficient evidence to press charges.

His foster family consists of a married couple, and five birth and foster children, all older than James and including a 16-year-old foster child whom they are in the process of adopting. Mrs Stanton is an experienced foster carer, who worked in residential child care before fostering, and now chiefly undertakes time-limited assessments of 'looked after' children for the local authority. She comes across as a warm, articulate individual, very confident about what she and her family can offer the children they look after. She says that she 'loves James to bits', that he is part of the family, and sees the family as providing a permanent home for him.

Asked about the beginning of the placement, Mrs Stanton described an immediate mutual attraction between her and James:

> I think chemistry has got a lot to do with it...in all honesty, there's some you bond with and some you don't – James I instantly bonded with...he just gave me a look, and I thought – ooh – I've got my hands full here. But I thought I'd jump at the challenge, because I love a challenge.

During the first eight weeks, James's behaviour was extremely difficult:

> He was verbally abusive to the children in the household, he used to hurt them. He was very frightened. Unsure what was happening to him. He soiled and smeared. He ripped furniture and bedding. Oh he just weed everywhere, swung from the light fittings. We took him away to our caravan and he set it on fire. He threw food – he wouldn't eat it. He got a knife to me at one point.

After weathering these serious difficulties and seeing him beginning to settle and become trustful, neither she nor her family felt they could let him go to another family:

> I mean, the kids were coming up to me and saying, we can't let him go, after all we've gone through with him. And as a family we're about – well being a family; but also as my kids put it – it's a bit hypocritical, Mum, if we're here to look after children, and then they're learning to love us and we love them and then we're sending them away.

The social services department agreed with some evident relief to their request that he should remain with them on a permanent basis.

Over time, James settled increasingly well into the placement, and his extremely difficult behaviour diminished to the point where after two years he was showing only occasional outbursts of temper – his soiling and enuresis had ceased, he got on well with the other children at home, and helped to look after a newer, younger foster child. He began to enjoy his food and was willing to try out more exotic meals, and his behaviour at school became calmer and more manageable. His problems were sufficiently severe to prompt Mrs Stanton to press for a diagnosis of ADHD (attention deficit hyperactivity disorder) and a prescription for Ritalin, and this, as Mrs Stanton described it, calmed him sufficiently to enable her to help him with certain moods. Although she recognises that he will continue to have problems – 'with James it's never ever going to be easy' – James' story is, in the words of his social worker:

> ...so far, more of a success than we could ever have dreamed of for him.

The central conditions

We turn now to our model. As we have seen, many of the central conditions for the placement seem to have been favourable. Mrs Stanton is a skilful and experienced foster carer, whose qualities include general skill and motivation to foster, a realistic and clear-sighted commitment to the children she fosters, a sense of professionalism, and a relative absence of strain.

Her level of skill is evident from her ability to assess and work with a variety of children, and from the professionalism with which she approached this particular placement. Her response to James was to see him as a challenge, which she would enjoy ('I love a challenge') rather than to be dismayed by him. Although entirely committed to James, she was also realistic in her expectations and plans for him, acknowledging that she will always need a back-up because 'with James it is never going to be easy', or when she reflected on the possible future with him. Her behaviour is also characterised by an absence of strain, and the capacity to judge how much she can take on by herself, and what she needs in addition (for example, time off, or advice from the psychologist) in order to enable her to do her job properly. She has the ability to identify the help which she considered she needed to work with James, and accessed and used this appropriately. Such help included members of her own family, social workers, psychologists, James' school, and additional domestic help, as well as a referral to a paediatrician when she was concerned to explore a possible alternative explanation for some of his disturbed behaviour.

It is somewhat more doubtful whether James, with his 'horrendous' behaviour, his learning difficulties and poor speech, his aggression, soiling, smearing and habit of setting small fires around the house, would be seen in conventional terms as a favourable factor. However, Mrs Stanton's account clearly shows James himself, his personality and responsiveness, as contributing to making the placement work. She sees James, despite his problematic behaviour, as an endearing and rewarding child, in that he is loving and giving in his behaviour in the family:

> James would always give you something back which made you feel good about the relationship you'd got [when John had broken his leg]...he'd come each day and stroke John's leg, and say, are you all right, John?

His responsiveness was a factor in the wish expressed by other members of the family that he should be allowed to stay permanently. Mrs Stanton's sense of attraction to him:

> in all honesty there's some you bond with and some you don't – James I instantly bonded

suggests that the special feeling she immediately had towards him was important in getting their relationship going.

Although, then, it would be difficult – indeed perverse – to describe James' behaviour initially as showing a commitment to being in the placement, there seems to have been enough from the beginning to make him rewarding to the carers. As time went on, he became more settled and more committed to staying:

> Slowly he was giving more and more, and he was starting to trust. And he started calling me Mum. And I just couldn't let him go.

The conditions of the wider context also worked in favour of the placement. As we have seen, Mrs Stanton's family were 'on side' in wanting him to stay, and she used other family members to support her care of James, being very clear about the different roles they were to play:

> James adores John [her husband], and John does him. And what we did was, I decided that if John was – if James played up in front of John, John would deal with it there and then, with issues of normal behaviour problems.

Q: Like table manners and things like that?

Yes, everyday issues. All the other work that was – you know – tackling his behaviour, the soiling – everything else, I dealt with. And we felt it was important that James had a safe person, just there for cuddles now and again, and to play with or get computer games. And he had that with the other children, but because James had had a violent father, we felt he needed the complete contrast within this home, and so John has...to encourage him to turn to John and get a positive feeling, you know, of a father figure. And so as I say, we maintained that, and John would be the one that he would go to afterwards, and he would be there for him.

Another aspect of the wider context which can work either to support or unbalance the placement is that of the child's birth family. In this case, Mrs Stanton has helped by being flexible and indeed encouraging of his relationship with his grandmother, and tolerant of his relationship with his birth mother, so that James has not experienced tensions around having to choose between his foster family and his other relationships or conflict between carers and birth family. James' grandmother visits about once a fortnight and he sees his brother every now and again. There is no contact with James' father, and his mother, whom Mrs Stanton knew when she was young, can visit him three times a year:

> Personally, I don't think the contact with his mother has any significance whatsoever. I think in everybody's interest it would just be better if she would take a back seat, because she can antagonise the situation through his Nana. But I'll wait until it's James' choice. And I'm just waiting for James to sort of think, is it worthwhile? And the more he's becoming involved in our family, I do feel the more he will sort of switch off. As he gets older, and he identifies that there's nothing out of it, either materially or emotionally, for him. I think he'll learn. And it'll be his choice. Whereas with his Nana, oh, he loves her to bits. And he's very concerned, with us moving, because he doesn't want to lose his Nan. So we'll have a spare room on the ground floor, and what we've said is, she can come for a few days and she can stop with us. Her love for him is so genuine and so positive. She was his lifeline, so you can't take that away from him. And it's as strong now as it was when he was living there.

In order to create the conditions for success, relationships between foster carers and other agencies and professionals, most importantly social workers, need to be at least minimally supportive, and there must be a shared view of the child's needs and the purpose of the placement. In Mrs Stanton's case, she acknowledges in general the need for social work support, commenting on the inappropriateness of adoption for many of the children she has fostered:

> I have an awful lot of experience, through friends, through children I've had placed with me, to know that the children I foster have immense problems. They come to me with immense problems. And I can't tackle those problems on my own. They need support, and I need support.

She considers that with James, for all their love and commitment to him, there are things which the family cannot handle on their own:

> I know that there's no way I would cope without knowing that I've got a back-up system, and that James has got the back-up system more than myself. As he gets on, he's going to need that. And I mean with James it's never, ever going to be easy.

Nor was there any disjuncture between the agency's plans for James in relation, for example, to possible rehabilitation home, or move into residential care or to adoption, and what was occurring inside the placement. In other words, the growing attachment and sense of belonging which James experienced in the foster family was consistent with the plans that the local authority had for him and its expectations of the placement. In this case, Mrs Stanton successfully negotiated an alteration in the agreement, so that from a short-term assessment, the placement was recognised as a long-term one, where it was appropriate for these kinds of relationships to be developed.

Other key agencies, such as the psychological service and the school, also worked effectively together. Mrs Stanton received occasional support and advice from the educational psychologist, and was able to access help when she became concerned that James needed additional medical help. The school worked closely with her and she acknowledged the help they have given:

> The way they've handled James, the support I mean, the head-master himself, he's one in a million. The rapport he builds up with the kids, and the level of understanding that he has of the problems. In fact, they've helped make the placement a success. They've worked alongside me. We've worked together. If James has had a problem, they've pulled him out, they'll fetch him down home, and they'll work together with James. Or they'll send for me, and I'll go up. And so he sees us working side by side. And they're just thrilled to bits with him, how he's come on.

Thus those aspects of the conditions to do with the wider context, i.e. the outside agencies, reflected a common view of how to support James and the foster family, and those involved worked cooperatively for the good of the placement. In relation to the other conditions, the foster family were committed to the placement; although there is more ambiguity about the support from James' birth family, the key relationship here with his grandmother worked well, and the foster carer was skilled and assertive enough to ensure that any disruptions from his birth mother were contained.

Responsive parenting

In our view, the way in which the foster carer deals with James also shows a high degree of the first component of our model, *responsive parenting*.

Children in foster care are likely to have difficulties in three main areas:

- attachment (they have frequently suffered multiple rejections and losses)
- behaviour (their behaviour is frequently difficult for those who live with them) and
- self-esteem (they typically lack the skills and success on which a sense of worth is built and have suffered numerous assaults on their picture of themselves).

To work successfully with such children, carers need to handle attachment appropriately, to promote self-esteem, and to handle difficult behaviour appropriately. James certainly had reasons to have difficulties in attachment and self-esteem, and certainly behaved in a very difficult way. How did Mrs Stanton respond?

In analysing Mrs Stanton's handling of James, as we are about to do, we simplify the picture. In particular, we ignore the fact that the same behaviour on the part of the carer may serve multiple ends. For example, by speaking of the child as a 'loved child' a carer may simultaneously reduce the child's fear of rejection, increase her/his self-esteem, and reduce the anger and anxiety which may lie behind some difficult behaviour. As we shall see, this ability to handle one area such as behaviour in such a way that other ends (e.g. increasing self-esteem and attachment) are served is highly characteristic of Mrs Stanton.

This simplification acknowledged, Mrs Stanton's parenting of James seems to be characterised by all of the elements identified above. In addition, Mrs Stanton is able to work with the wider environment – her family, the birth family, psychiatrists and so on – in such a way that they support her rather than work against her. Finally, she is able to ride the difficulties that do arise, using them positively rather than reacting to them in a way that exacerbates the situation.

HANDLING ATTACHMENT

As we have seen, Mrs Stanton 'loves James to bits'. This in itself is likely to provide security, in particular because it is constantly communicated.

First, she talks to him and about him *as a loved child*, seeing him, as do members of her own family, as part of the family:

> And I just couldn't let him go. None of us could. I mean, the kids were coming up to me and saying, we can't let him go, after all we've gone through with him. And as a family we're about – well, being a family; but also as my kids put it – it's a bit hypocritical, Mum, if we're here to look after children, and then they're learning to love us and we love them and then we're sending them away. So we ended up that they agreed to let us [keep him].

Second, in communicating this love, Mrs Stanton uses *attachment-sensitive times*, such as moments when he is feeling settled in the evening, or where there has been an upset, to talk to him about himself, and to help him develop self-understanding:

> Say there's been an upset, and he's vulnerable, and he won't identify what the problem is, because he might be frightened. So I say, come on – let's have a quiet half hour – we'll get the photographs out. And going over his past through the albums, and I'll say, oh, look at that James – do you remember that day? And doing that with him, it like opens him up again, and he becomes in touch with his feelings. And he feels safe. And by going through all that, I'm sort of making him aware that he's safe. And then I find out what's wrong with him, and what's worrying him, what's upsetting him.

Third, a key to how Mrs Stanton gets across to James that she loves him almost certainly lies in the way she handles situations where she might be expected not to do so. In general, she provides a *secure base*, by demonstrating sensitivity, availability and consistency. When responding to his difficult behaviour, her voice tone is consistent, she remains near him, providing him both with a constant presence and also an unhurried one, at a time when he will be feeling anxious and stressed, and fear losing control:

> I never altered the way I handled him, so that he got a feeling of knowing what I was going to do. For him to trust me, he had to learn to understand me and how I work. I kept my voice on an even keel all the way through dealing

with him. It worked because it gave him a feeling of – well, not being in control of me as such, but of knowing that I wasn't going to hurt him.

She also shows an ability to promote a secure attachment, by demonstrating *understanding* and *accurate empathy* in exploring the causes of James' behaviour. In reflecting in the interview, for example, on what prompts it, she suggests that it may come from a wish to be naughty, from a wish to hit out in anger, out of fear of having someone trying to control him (by implication because of his earlier experiences of punitive parental care), and from a wish to avoid the experience of failure by not trying to succeed in the first place:

> Because he wanted to be able to have, say, a dry bed. But he knew he'd have problems achieving that, so he'd rather kick off and not try than be a failure.

Elsewhere in the interview, she empathises with his difficulties with his peers:

> I'm not saying that he doesn't have school yard scuffles, because that's the norm for me. But whereas at one point he'd just go and boot somebody for the sake of booting them, and hurt them…[now], there's been a role reversal. Because James has become vulnerable, the kids have bullied James. And James has found that very difficult.

HANDLING BEHAVIOUR

Another characteristic of responsive parenting is the ability to handle difficult behaviour appropriately. In Mrs Stanton's case, she has identified and developed clear behavioural strategies for dealing with the behaviour. These are based on attachment principles (see above) but also involve setting clear, achievable tasks for him to complete, *to the best of his ability*. When he has experienced an upset, which they have talked about together, she repeats the experience in a safe way, soon after, to reinforce what he has learnt:

> So he took that on board, and I put it to the test a couple of days later, because I wasn't here when he came home from school. What I tend to do is if I go through a situation like that with James [she had been out when he came back from trip, and he had thrown a tantrum], I test it fairly afterwards, before he's forgot about it, so that I can acknowledge to him how proud I am if he's coped, and also work with him more if I need to be, around that issue, if it's failed.

> And I'd say, I'm so proud of you, James, because it's been really hard, and you've done really well, and I want to show you how proud I am of you. So

I'd give him a little treat that way. Because I don't like score chart systems. I
don't think that's fair on a child.

She provides *predictable limits*, thus lessening his anxieties and leaving him
more available for personal engagement. The quotation given above bears
repeating as demonstrating the way Mrs Stanton combines the difficult task
of keeping James in order without thereby making him feel more insecure.

As already noted she is able to handle his behaviour in such a way that the
attachment is not shaken:

> The biggest upset for James is if he thinks he's hurt me. If he's physically hurt
> me. He can't abide to think he's physically hurt me. So when he's gone
> off…now, because the bond is so strong, he doesn't want to hurt me. And
> he's flipping, as we call it, and you've got to sort of contain him for his own
> safety. And I get on the floor, and I hold him in my arms, and hold him in.
> And sometimes he'll break free and hit out. But he's not actually hitting out
> at me – he's hitting out at his anger.

> So I had a pattern where at the side of James' bedroom door, which was
> actually next to the bathroom as well, I used to keep a crossword book and a
> pen there, and as soon as James said no, I used to say, 'It's OK James, if you're
> not ready now, it doesn't matter. You've got all the time in the world. I have as
> well.' And I'd sit in a corner, hold my back against the wall and I'd do the
> crossword. I'd be there with him. And then he'd sort of realise that nothing
> was going to alter until he'd done whatever I'd requested him to do. So he
> would end up to the best of his abilities washing out the mess he'd made.

PROMOTING SELF-ESTEEM

A third hallmark of responsive parenting is the way in which foster carers
promote the child's *sense of identity, efficacy* and *self-esteem*. Mrs Stanton talks to
James about his past, helping him to make sense of who he is:

> He'd get his puppets out and he'd talk through them, or he'd come and ask
> me to sort of be a puppet and – that's how we found out about the abuse.
> And you always know if he's dwelling on his past, because he always gets his
> puppets out.

She encourages his intellectual achievements and development while accepting his limitations and also helps him to understand and anticipate his own
moods and behaviours, thereby enhancing his *sense of efficacy*:

And he identifies now times when his tablet is running low. And he can sort of say, well, I'm going up to me room, Mum, because I'm jumpy inside. And I'll go and draw. So he's actually registering himself how to control his own behaviour.

She promotes his self-esteem by seeing him as a loving and giving person:

James would always give you something back which made you feel good about yourself.

She encourages him by identifying his successes and achievements, and praising him for these, rather than dwelling on the negative aspects of his behaviour, and the things that he has done wrong:

And every now and again we have a sit down and a talk about all the positives that's happened to James. And then we sort of don't make a point of being very negative about what's, you know, the bad side of James' behaviour, but what we do is we look at how he could have avoided those situations happening.

She also helps him to see himself as a worthwhile person:

James is enjoying himself now. You know – he's enjoying about finding out about himself, and learning to control what he wants about himself. You know – what he likes about himself. He's enjoying his sense of humour – being able to share jokes, and take a joke without being offended and going off and flipping. Because he thought people were being nasty to him.

We have shown how contact with the child's birth family forms part of the wider conditions in which the placement exists. The way in which this relationship is handled also promotes his sense of identity in that his birth family is an acknowledged part of who he is, with a differentiation made between the relationships he has with the different members. His attachment to his grandmother ('she was his lifeline') and his continuing contact with his birth mother are accepted as a part of his emotional landscape for as long as he needs them:

And we always make sure we take plenty of photographs. And he's got it all in folders. You know – all his events with his Nana. And we make sure we take photographs of his Mum as well. So he's got quite a history in photographs of his time with how he's been with us.

Finally, Mrs Stanton is able to *use objective feelings*, recognising the behaviour as in part the product of their relationship, but not personalising it as an attack on her:

> He's not actually hitting out at me – he's hitting out at his anger. And if he thinks he's hurt me, he's devastated. And that's the big contrast to where he first came, where he'd actually charge at me, and go out to hurt me.

On this point, James' developing trustfulness and the sense that he is becoming more settled and feels himself to be a part of the family is an indication that there is a good 'fit' in terms of what the family can offer, in terms of closeness and what he wants and needs. Mrs Stanton accepted his initial wariness, allowing him to remain more distant but was receptive to and encouraged a developing attachment on his part. The placement therefore offers containment, security, but a permeable boundary, in the sense that outside relationships are accepted without difficulty or a sense of competitiveness or threat.

Although, then, one aspect of the dynamics of the placement was undoubtedly crucial – namely the quality of responsive parenting on the part of Mrs Stanton – the *conditions* worked with this rather than against it, and were important in its success: the child's motivation, personality, and attractiveness to the foster carer, the 'fit' in terms of the level of closeness and intimacy which the placement provided and James needed, and factors in the outer context of the foster family, agency support and planning.

Robert: 'it's as if he's been with us forever'

Our second 'success' story allows us to test the validity of the model, and also to highlight characteristics which may not have been so obvious in the previous case. Robert came into care when he was seven, because his grandparents with whom he was living at the time were found to be neglecting him, and there were concerns about an uncle who was accused of sexually abusing a young girl. Robert made a planned move to his present foster carers (Mr and Mrs Williams) when he was eight, and has been there for nearly four years.

Mr and Mrs Williams are experienced foster carers, with two grown-up children, and consider they were chosen for Robert because they offered a home with firm but loving boundaries, enjoyed outdoor activities and sport, and wanted a long-term placement. They see him very much as one of the family, and treat him as they treated their own children:

All the family – they think that Robert's absolutely wonderful. The people across the road that we met the first day we moved in here 19 years ago – they say it's like Robert's always been a part of the family.

They recognise that he will need academic qualifications to get anywhere, and are prepared to see him through college or university:

He knows that whatever he wants to do, we'll support him.

Along with their commitment to him, and his to them, they accept Robert's attachment to his birth family:

When you foster, you know that you're fostering someone else's child. You don't actually want the child for yourself.

Robert has asked whether the Williams would adopt him, but Mrs Williams feels that his relationship with his birth family is too strong:

For all their faults, they love him. And deep down inside, he loves them. There is that bond there. And I think it's something that should be encouraged. And when Robert's older, it's up to him what he does.

Although Robert's behaviour before he came to the placement was never very problematic, he evidently found it hard early on to accept the carers' standards:

He found it hard to take the discipline, and he thought we were very, very strict…I don't think we are. But Robert had never had real guidance before. He'd more or less been the adult, doing as he pleased.

They were able to set clear limits, which Robert gradually accepted.

In terms of the qualities identified above with Mrs Stanton, Mrs Williams shows a high level of skilled and responsive parenting. She handles attachment issues appropriately, for example by dealing sympathetically with the possible loss of contact with his birth siblings after the latter's adoption, and by offering a sense of security and permanence. We can surmise that her acceptance of Robert's birth family, which is open, tolerant, and shows a predominant concern for what he wants and she feels deep down needs, allows him to feel settled and at ease in the placement. She speaks of him as a loved child and, as we see below, shows appreciation and respect for his qualities. She encourages his successes, treats him with respect and, while having clear goals for him, tries to take account of his own wishes. What has made the placement a success?

Just our lifestyle, basically. The encouragement, and the way we think about children. We don't think of them as people to be ordered about. They are mini adults who deserve respect, and deserve an explanation. We try to guide children, rather than lay down the law. Explain to them why it's no, and explain why we've said yes.

In relation to the *conditions* for the placement, Robert himself seems to have been committed to the placement, very much wanting to be there and motivated to making it work:

He kept on and on, and he was thrilled to bits when I went that Saturday morning and picked him up and brought him here and said, right – you're staying.

He is seen by Mrs Williams (and others, including the social worker) as an attractive child, and does not pose any great challenges in the way he behaves.

Mrs Williams is both committed to the general task of fostering and to Robert and is professional in her approach to being a foster carer. This is evident from the way she describes preparing Robert for the arrival of a younger more difficult child, and ensuring that he continues to feel he can cope with the latter's presence in the household. She is clear about what tasks appropriately belong to the social workers, and accesses help from them when she needs it – for example, when Robert wanted a change in contact arrangements, she asked his social worker to talk the implications of this through with him. Mrs Williams has found the social workers invariably helpful:

A quick phone call, and it's either sorted out over the phone or there's a social worker here to deal with it.

She comes across as neither intrusive or needy – having successfully brought up her own children, she is not looking for a child of her own, and is able to accept and encourage Robert's relationships with his birth family. She is confident, well-supported (both by informal and formal networks) and unstressed.

In terms of the third sub-element of the condition, that of compatibility between carer and child, the fit is a good one – Robert needs a sense of belonging and permanence and the level of emotional closeness which the carers provide. Perhaps more clearly than in the previous placement, we can see that an agreement over behaviour and expectations of achievement and hopes of success has gradually been negotiated:

It's just giving him the opportunities to do what all his school friends do. Giving him the opportunity to be a child, not an adult from the age of five or six. Letting him be a boy, letting him be a teenager, with no responsibilities. And all we ask of him is that he applies himself at school, gets the best grades he can, goes to college, university, art school – he's a brilliant artist. He can just look at a picture and draw it freehand. Most people like him – he's very, very popular.

The *context* of the placement supports what is happening in it. The placement is seen as long-term, where it is appropriate for the child and family to develop close attachments and a sense of belonging. Carers, child and social workers seem to have the same goals for the placement, and those minor upheavals which could have unsettled it (for example, issues over contact with an abusing uncle, loss by Robert of contact with two younger siblings when they were placed for adoption) seem to have been addressed by the social workers in an open and reassuring way. Mrs Williams supports and encourages Robert's contact with his birth family, who pose no threat to the stability of the placement. He fits well into her family, who help her in her handling of him, and are neither threatened by nor in competition with him. The two now grown-up children are available to help in caring for him – for example, the elder son taking him out on a trip when Mrs Williams was preoccupied in handling another difficult placement, or explaining that they were treated just the same:

> And that's where James and Jane both helped with this – 'yes Rob – when she's in the right, she'll nag you until you give in!'

> They both said, yes, she's like that with us. Hard luck – you've got to put up with it now! So he realised it wasn't him I was getting at – it was, you will do it, for your own good, basically.

Giles: 'temper the wind to the shorn lamb'

Those placements which were identified as less successful in the sample tend to support our view that responsive parenting is an essential ingredient in success and also that other conditions in the placement will work towards making it more or less likely to succeed.

In our third case, a boy of ten with moderate learning difficulties who had experienced severe sexual and physical abuse was placed initially as a short-term placement with relatively inexperienced foster carers, where he has remained, despite serious behavioural difficulties, for three years. Giles has a violent temper and has physically attacked his foster mother and his foster brother. He is destructive, kicking through the partition between his bedroom and that of the children of the foster family and breaking furniture if he is taken out. He masturbates at times obsessively, urinates and defecates in his bedroom and in the drawers of the chest of drawers, and exposes himself at the bedroom window. This behaviour shows no sign of diminishing. His foster mother seems overwhelmed by and somewhat fearful of the difficulties he poses, and feels that if he continues as he is, he will become too strong for her to manage. Although there are signs of some attachment to his foster mother he remains troubled and difficult to handle.

Responsive parenting

In analysing the earlier cases, we identified a number of facets of what we described as responsive parenting. In this placement, despite the carer's sincere efforts to care for him, there is not much evidence that Mrs Lowe is able to work with Giles' insecurities over attachment and the need to belong, to help him develop a sure sense of who he is, or that she knows how to handle and help him with his difficult behaviour.

She describes feelings of love for him – 'because we really care about him and I can't imagine being without him' – and her attributions are not entirely negative. Nonetheless, she considers that by and large they see the worst side of his personality:

> He has two characters, a nice side and the nasty side. And we always get the nasty side, as soon as he's displeased.

The carers have shown their commitment to Giles, by keeping him in the placement despite behaviour which has brought it almost to the point of breakdown. However, it is doubtful whether the placement offers him a sufficient degree of security or that he can feel 'at home' with them: Mrs Lowe's sense of the placement as a permanent one is equivocal and she feels unsure as to how long they will be able to manage him:

> We've had to change so much to keep him here... And if he doesn't learn to calm his temper down, then it will eventually break down, because I won't be able to handle him here.

It seems likely that he will get this message of doubt too, and wonder what the future holds in store for him.

She describes the way in which his behaviour deteriorates when they go away on holiday, but, when invited to speculate on the causes of this (e.g. perhaps this is because he feels insecure about being in unfamiliar surroundings), still sees the difficulty largely in terms of the problem of control, and how hard it makes it for the rest of the family rather than working with him to help him feel less anxiety.

When he does show a wish for physical closeness, she finds it difficult now because he is becoming very sexualised. Although at the suggestion of the social worker she had tried to find other ways to allow physical proximity, putting her own feelings to one side and responding to him as a child, she concludes: 'I'm just not comfortable with it'. She finds it difficult to empathise with him when she is feeling upset, and seems unable cognitively or emotionally to allow his feelings or needs to intrude upon her own:

> And he's coming for a cuddle within 10 minutes of exploding. And you're still sort of – you know, angry and sort of thinking to yourself, what on earth does he think he's doing? So it's very difficult to deal with him afterwards.

From her comments on him and on his past relationships it seems unlikely that she is effective in promoting or reinforcing his sense of identity and self-esteem. Although intellectually she understands the effects of his early experiences on current behaviour, this recognition is not apparent in her handling of him and there is no evidence, implicit or explicit, of her helping him to link what he now does to what has happened previously. Although not unsympathetic towards Giles' birth mother, and readily acknowledging his feelings towards her, she does not seem to help him with these and, indeed, seems faintly critical of his tendency to idealise her.

Despite her clearly good intentions, Mrs Lowe speaks about Giles in a predominantly negative fashion, seemingly dwelling on his difficulties, and reverting to speaking about these even when in the interview she has started to try and focus on his good qualities. The level of her negativism suggests she is unlikely to be able to help him manage his own anxieties about his behaviour, and the focus on behaviour control rather than on understanding seems likely to have consequences for his self-esteem.

Mrs Lowe's strategies for managing Giles' behaviour seem to be largely ones of either withdrawal or control. She does try and understand patterns in his behaviour, identifying times in the year, such as birthdays, which may be particularly difficult for him. But rather than working cooperatively with him and attempting to address his difficulties together, she seems to have developed a strategy of withdrawal as a way of handling this:

I've just floated through it. He's done things and I've thought, right, fine –
move on. And it's been awful. Really awful.

She responds in quite an angry and personal way to behaviour which,
although understandably irritating, seems to indicate emotional neediness,
requiring some empathy and discussion with him. For example, she sees it as
'disgusting' when in the middle of the night he had stolen sweets meant for all
the family, and treats behaviour such as smearing as if it was the action of a
naughty child rather than reflecting earlier difficulties. Instead of trying to
explore with him reasons for his difficult behaviour, or helping him find alternative strategies for outbursts of temper, or setting clear and predictable limits,
the strategies adopted seem to be largely mechanical ones, for example, of
putting locks on the doors and alarming his bedroom, or punishment, such as
being sent to his room or into the garden.

And she finds his expressions of remorse difficult to respond to, feeling
apparently that it is manipulative, and that he only says sorry if he wants
something:

He doesn't often say sorry for anything...not for the right things. If he
breaks something. He broke his roller blades at the weekend. We went
through a lot of sorry then.

Conditions: the child, the foster carer and their compatibility

In both the previous cases, we found certain conditions which seemed to have
made it more likely that the placement would be successful. Both children
were appealing to their carers: in one, an emotional dimension, of being
'drawn to' the child, seemed to form a part of their initial relationship, and to
have helped Mrs Stanton through the process of testing out which took place
over the first weeks; in the second, Robert himself was in addition highly
committed to the placement. In contrast, in this case, the account of the initial
encounter seems muted, and Giles is described in terms of being 'quiet, the
easy one to get on with'. The slightly reserved tone of this may not in itself be
significant, but neither is there any acknowledgement, as there was with the
Stantons or the Williams, of Giles himself as an appealing child, who now or
later contributes to making the placement work.

As with the earlier cases (and it is a limitation of our study) we can only
surmise Giles' feelings, and the extent of his motivation to make the placement work, which seemed so evident with, for example, Robert. Initially, it
seems that he was relieved to move from an earlier foster placement, where he

said that he was physically chastised, but this wish to be in the placement is less clear as time has gone on. What is also evident is that what he brings to the placement, in terms of personal attributes and difficult behaviour, makes it harder for the placement to be a success.

Mrs Lowe had had limited experience as a foster carer before having Giles, and this inexperience may have made it more difficult for her to anticipate likely difficulties with Giles, and negotiate better support in terms, say, of respite. There seems to be a mismatch between the kinds of difficult behaviour shown by Giles and Mrs Lowe's general level of competence, resources and strategies for dealing with it. A period of ill-health has left her under considerable strain. She is critical of the social work support she receives, suspecting that she was not given the complete story of Giles' background when he was placed with her:

> He [the social worker] seemed a bit cagey.

She does not consider the relationship between herself and the social workers to be a good one, and finds the help offered inadequate or worse:

> They always seem to be in a rush. They never have enough time for you. And they're not reliable.

She had difficulty in carrying out suggestions for handling Giles.

In terms of the compatibility between Giles and Mrs Lowe there are indications from her account (see above), and from the social worker's comments, that he is looking for a relationship with his carers which is closer, both physically and emotionally, than they are able to offer. One result of this distance/lack of closeness, and his uncertainties about how secure the placement is, may be that he has recently asked to have renewed contact with his birth mother, a request which his foster carer finds perplexing, since in her view the contact was so unsatisfactory and appeared only to make him upset. Whatever the complicated motivation for this, in order to enable him to settle he will need sensitive help in understanding his feelings about his birth family. Although not hostile to the latter, his foster carer seems unlikely to be able to help him, or fully to understand his continuing attachment to his mother. Giles' unresolved feelings about his mother, coupled with what he may pick up about his foster carer's uncertainty about being able to keep him, may make him at least more ambivalent about being in the placement and increase in turn the likelihood that it fails to meet his needs for closeness and belonging.

Conditions: the wider context

The second dimension of the conditions, the wider *context* in which the placement has developed, does not seem at the moment helpful to it. The placement originally was set up as a short-term one, which seems to have drifted into being long-term without any clear decision-making or plan. Our other findings suggest that although this lack of planning may create difficulties in the short-term, changing the plan is not necessarily detrimental, and provided other things are equal, the child and carers can settle down and the placement may become successful. In this placement, the local authority seem to have been uncertain throughout as to whether this was the 'right' placement for Giles, and to have let it continue because of the lack of an alternative, and because, in the words of the social worker, 'better the devil you know'. This sense of defeat, and the now low expectations of the placement, seem likely to have worked against rather than with it. If the foster carers' own uncertainties are reflected in the attitudes of the social workers, both sides are likely to become more pessimistic and the carers less effective.

Other parts of the wider context are also unhelpful. Despite efforts on the foster carer's part, and a not-unhelpful relationship between her and the head-teacher, the school finds Giles difficult to contain and are uncertain whether or not they can keep him:

> He'd been excluded, and he was being disruptive in class, and they generally thought that they weren't managing to teach him anything, or any of the kids either, because of him. So he [the head-teacher] was talking about getting a meeting together, and getting him out then.

Giles' aggression is often directed at the carers' three children, and seems, understandably, to elicit defensive responses from them. They respond to his behaviour by putting up with him, complaining about him, or trying to avoid him:

> Just now the youngest one doesn't [like him] at all. I think the oldest one just accepts that he is what he is. She's been through periods of liking him, disliking him, and I think she's at the stage now where she just accepts that he is – Giles.

Although seemingly tolerating his presence, they do not contribute positively to making the placement work.

Our analysis of our case studies so far suggests that for the placement to meet the needs of the child, the foster carer must be sufficiently skilled to handle the level of difficult behaviour which the child exhibits and responsive in working with attachment. The child needs to offer something to the carers, even if this only evolves over time, either in motivation to be in the placement and to make it work, or because of their attractive personality. The professionalism and absence of strain on the part of the foster carer may also be important in creating the conditions in which the helpful interaction between carer and child may occur. The level of emotional closeness offered by the carers needs to fit with that wanted by the child. It helps if the foster family support and like the foster child, and if the birth family at the least are not disruptive to the placement. And the expectations or context of the placement, especially those derived from the social work agencies, but also educational and health services, which may change or be negotiated, need to be congruent with the kinds of relationships which are developed within it.

Conclusion

So far we have argued that in successful placements, foster carers are able to deal with the attachment needs of the child, handle their behaviour and help them to develop self-esteem. Some children present greater challenges in these respects than others, some carers are more skilled at meeting these needs than others, and some children and carers are better matched than others. In our next chapter we will consider how far this kind of analysis can help in explaining changes in the placement over time. We apply the analysis to a wider range of placements than those we have just discussed, and conclude with a fuller account, derived from the cases, of the components of *responsive parenting*.

Note

1. The chapters are based on material contained in an article that was published in the *British Journal of Social Work* (Wilson, Petrie and Sinclair 2003) and we are grateful to the journal for permission to reproduce it here.

Chapter Eight

Spirals of Interaction

Introduction

It is obvious from the last chapter that once a placement has started it has in a sense a life of its own. A *modus vivendi* may develop between carer and child. Alternatively there may be changes in their interaction or in the outside conditions of the placement which may lead to it either becoming increasingly successful, or increasingly difficult and which may sooner or later lead to disruption.

A full account or model of what explains foster placement success must take these benign or negative spirals into account. Ideally, the variables involved in explaining these dynamics are the same as those involved in the more 'static' accounts of success and failure we gave in the last chapter. They should also account for the range of cases we encountered.

In this chapter we first explore an example of a 'negative' spiral. We then look at a wider range of cases in much less detail. Finally we present our model of what leads to success in foster care placements.

Carole: a residence order which went wrong

In our fourth long example, we trace how a negative spiral developed in a placement which had hitherto been in a relatively satisfactory equilibrium, and the way in which changes in the conditions functioned to produce this. This placement was identified as 'less successful' in our study, and by the time of the interview Carole, after more than seven years in the placement, had left.

She is now 12 years old, and came into care with her brother when she was nearly four, following their severe neglect by their mother, who has mental health problems. She remained in the placement until earlier this year, since when she has moved to a succession of different foster carers. Her brother remains with the foster carer, Mr Roberts, and is described by him as 'like a son'. The placement was initially a short-term one, and drifted into being a long-stay one, without any clear decision-making or planning.

Mr Roberts has two daughters of his own, both now embarking on higher education. He and his wife, who had both cared for the children, divorced about two years ago, and all the children opted to remain with Mr Roberts. He sees the breakdown of the placement as stemming from Carole's unquenchable yearning to return to her mother, and to the lack of social work support at critical moments when these feelings, and Carole's resulting efforts to sabotage the placement so that she could return to live with her mother, emerged most strongly. He bitterly regrets accepting the advice of social services to seek a residence order for Carole (which he considers was motivated in part by pressure from the department to reduce fostering costs). He considers that it did not change Carole's feelings of belonging or security in the placement (the grounds on which he was persuaded), but removed social work support at a critical period. The social workers who are now involved again with Carole accept that there was a lack of proper involvement, partly reflecting restructuring in the authority at the time.

Carole showed some problematic behaviour within a year of coming into the placement (wiping excrement on the walls and masturbating), but these were accepted and understood as classic signs of having been abused and resolved themselves after a short period. She continued to steal and to lie and to be periodically quite confrontational but these seemingly were dealt with in a firm but non-punitive way by Mr Roberts and his ex-wife. However, he seems to have been unequal to the task of helping Carole with her ambivalent attachment towards her mother, perhaps being unable to remain sufficiently open to it and accepting of the latter, of whom he candidly acknowledges his dislike:

I don't like the mother – that is evident. We don't like each other at all.

Carole's feelings, in Mr Roberts' view, were never reciprocated but her fantasies about her mother grew ever stronger, the idealised picture of her mother as described by Mr Roberts showing all the hallmarks of an ambivalent attachment pattern:

And it was really strange – she used to start reminiscing about the past – you know how you chat about the past with the children. And she used to start saying things like, I did this with my Mum. My Mum took me out in a car.

And I'd say, no – your mother can't drive, Carole. And she said, yes, she did, she drove me to Brighton. And I'd say, no, that was Julie (my ex). So she was like replacing the memories she had with Julie in that mother/daughter relationship. And taking Julie's head off and putting her mother's head on.

We may speculate that his capacity for responsive parenting over her attachment difficulties may have diminished at the time of his own marital problems, and that, possibly, the loss of his wife as foster mother also exacerbated Carole's difficulties in a way which Mr Roberts, for understandable reasons, could not acknowledge or help her with effectively.

Carole's wish for contact with her mother was continual, and Mr Roberts finally forbade her to telephone her mother, because her mother was so unreliable and unresponsive, insisting instead that her mother took the initiative (which she rarely, if ever, did). The placement broke down when Carole refused to come home one weekend, and the emergency duty team supported her, instead of insisting that she return. In Mr Roberts' view, this was a crucial moment: from then on, he had lost authority over Carole, and the break had been made. Although Carole now, finding that she still is not with her mother, would like to return, Mr Roberts feels that the relationship has for the moment broken. He is now intending to foster for an independent agency.

In relation to the *conditions*, Carole seems throughout to have seen being in foster care as a poor alternative to life with her mother, feelings which increased as she grew older. Her motivation to be in the placement and to make it work was always fragile, and as she came to feel more of an outsider in the foster family (in contrast to her brother who was well settled, and towards whom she felt no love lost) she became increasingly detached and difficult. This may in turn have led to Mr Roberts feeling less commitment, and offering less encouragement and loving support.

Despite his evident success in working with other children, including Carole's brother, there evolved a certain incompatibility between him and this particular child, reflected in the underlying dynamic of closeness/distance. Carole did not want a close relationship with Mr Roberts, at least at this critical stage of their relationship, and in the face of her increasing disobedience he felt unable to sustain a commitment to her which might have tolerated a longer period of ambivalence. He also at this point seems to have been unable to access the kinds of help from social services which might have relieved the situation, since Carole had begun to blame her foster father for removing her from her mother:

> She thought it was us that came and took her away. And once she said to me that my Mum pays for you to look after me.

The *context* of the placement was also at odds with what was happening within it. A residence order is designed to provide a sense of security and permanence for the child and foster family, and implicitly signals to them that they can be free from local authority scrutiny and supervision. Although this seems to have reflected Mr Roberts' good intentions towards Carole, it certainly did not take account of Carole's ongoing feelings for her mother. Coupled with this, it also meant that social work support was unavailable when needed. The intervention of social services (when Carole was unwilling to return home) undermined the dynamics of the relationship with the carer and child at a crucial moment.

In addition to this, Carole's birth mother was evidently unsupportive of the placement, consistently undermining the foster carers' attempts at discipline, and holding out promises to Carole (about contact and about a future life together) which were or could not be kept. The part which the foster carers' own children played in the placement is unknown. However, the relationship between Carole and her brother was poor, and it seems probable that the breakdown of the foster carers' marriage will have further served to unsettle her.

The process of the placement therefore seems to have formed a *downward spiral*. The foster carers initially were successful, showing responsive parenting in working with Carole's difficult behaviour, and helping her to feel settled in the placement. Their wish to convey commitment and to provide her with a secure base and a sense of permanency was reflected in their willingness to change her care order to a residence order. Nonetheless, however well intentioned, this may not have been sufficiently attuned to Carole's need to resolve her feelings for her mother. As her behaviour in the placement became more difficult, Mr Roberts in turn may have become less able to handle it, possibly because of the stress of his own marriage breakdown. The conditions of the placement – in this case, particularly, Carole's ambivalence about being there, and the failures of the wider context to support sensitively what was happening within the placement – were such that the quality of responsive parenting became more and more tenuous until the placement finally broke down.

The cases in general

The case we have just discussed illustrates the difficulty of isolating particular features of a placement as the key to its outcome. The problems of the last placement probably reflected Carole's attachment to her mother, her mother's unreliability, the loss of Carole's foster mother, Carole's increasingly difficult behaviour, Mr Roberts' dislike of Carole's mother, the way he interpreted Carole's behaviour and his eventual difficulty in handling both that and her wish to be with her mother, the lack of social work support at a critical time, the jealous relationship between Carole and her brother, and the insensitive reaction of the emergency duty team. These variables do not affect outcome by themselves. For example, Carole's attachment to her mother could have been a positive feature if her mother had been more reliable and on better terms with Mr Roberts.

Analytically, however, it is necessary to divide the world in order to describe it. In what follows, we will illustrate the application of our explanations to the wider class of cases, focusing on:

- the handling of attachment and needs for closeness
- the handling of difficult behaviour
- the support that can be offered by outside professionals.

Handling attachment and needs for closeness

Issues in handling the child's need for closeness raised three key issues:

- the 'chemistry' between carer and child
- the relationship between child, carer and birth parent(s) and
- the degree to which the child's need for closeness was compatible with the needs of the carer.

Handling attachment: chemistry

A number of carers described the initial phase of the relationship with their foster child in terms of 'chemistry' as Mrs Stanton described it, or as another foster carer, Mrs Glendon, put it, 'falling in love'. Not all the carers where we felt there to be a good 'fit' could, or probably would, have described the initial phases of the relationship in this way. However, this was common enough for us to feel that it can be significant in helping the placement get established. In the case of the Gs (where the four-year-old was eventually adopted), the placement began with a strong emotional attraction, and continued successfully because the child's need to belong to a family matched the foster carers' willingness to accept him. The fit in terms of need for, and ability to offer, close emotional attachment seemed excellent:

> He wanted to move. It's funny that – he wanted to be here. But I had to need an Oliver. I had to keep telling him – I need an Oliver living with me. Did he ask? Yes. He kept saying – do you need an Oliver? And I kept saying – I do – I'm waiting for an Oliver to move in.

The attachment literature suggests that the attachment relationship is to some extent a reciprocal one. If this is the case, we would expect, as we have demonstrated in the cases above, that an aspect of the fit between carer and child involves the child's engagement with the carer. This engagement certainly occurred:

> He's made this work. How, I don't know, but he has. It's just – brilliant. He's a beautiful child. I mean he had a lot of problems, which it took out of us a lot, but... He's got a lot of love to give.

Or in describing their second meeting, when the then nine-year-old Sally had been behaving 'horrendously' and she had forcefully rebuked her, another carer wept as she remembered how touching Sally had seemed:

> 'Do not say I yelled at you because I didn't.' And Sally burst into tears. And she said, 'I do want you to be my mother.' And we got back to the children's home, and we got to the bedroom, and she put on a tape, and she sang and she danced – this nice little girl. It broke your heart! She was so good [cries].

And another, working with a boy in late adolescence with severe learning difficulties, is clear about what she gets back from him:

> I tried my hardest to work with Donald to see what he's got to offer. Donald was special. Donald was completely unique.

And yet another described the two-year-old's special appeal:

> I think Toby was the one. Probably because he came at such a young age and he stayed for such a long time... He was so good. He was a pleasure to have...everybody loved him. I think at one point he was surgically attached [to the foster carer].

In some cases the attraction developed later, in one case at least in response to a special set of circumstances. In this case the foster carer was initially slightly reserved:

Up until the time she was ill, I was a step away, because I knew she was going to be placed for adoption.

Then a strong attachment became established, because of the special circumstances of the child falling ill:

> She was so desperately ill – I mean, she nearly died. We were put in a side ward waiting for her to die. She was too ill to give anything back. But my commitment to her was, if she lives, let her be mine. And she lived. And so it was a promise really. I wanted her. I loved her. I grew to love her. I let everything go, and there was nothing – nobody was going to take her away.

The local authority accepted this changed relationship, and quite a complex arrangement was negotiated which allowed Helen to remain with Mrs B, while taking into account of the latter's age (she was over 50, making adoption inappropriate, and the intention is that the foster carer's son and his partner would assume Helen's care if need be).

Handling attachment: the child, the carer and the birth parent(s)

We have already seen how Carole's attachment to her mother was a factor in her difficult relationship with Mr Roberts. An analogous situation, this time involving previous adoptive parents, had a rather happier ending.

In this example, the foster child, Susan, did not show very difficult behaviour, although her adoption had broken down after she had acted in what seems to have been a mildly but inappropriately sexualised way towards a younger adoptive sibling. Her needs seem to have been rooted in attachment and identity issues, arising particularly from uncertainties as to whether or not her adoptive parents would ever allow her to return to live with them.

These uncertainties did not prevent the foster carers from continuing to offer tolerant, non-intrusive care, accepting Susan's extreme reluctance for physical closeness, and riding out minor difficulties and a general lack of responsiveness and insensitivity to feelings which included a certain callousness towards others:

> She doesn't seem to realise what hurt is, what feelings are...

while recognising the need underneath the surface:

> She's very close to June, very close... She finds it almost impossible to show affection of any description... But if I'm missing... She wouldn't like me not to be around. I know that. 'Where's June? Where's June?'

Despite this covert attachment to her foster mother, Susan was set on a return to her adoptive parents and so she was not open to a very close relationship, and kept the carers to some extent at arms' length:

> She wants a whole weekend with Mum, and she wants Mum to take her to the cinema, and she wants Mum to love her really. And go on holiday with her. But there's no chance of that. I mean, they're cutting back on visits, cutting back on phone calls, cutting back on everything, really. Trying to withdraw altogether.

The foster carers are skilled and experienced in working with adolescents, providing more of a 'small home' atmosphere. They were able to accept Susan without feeling personally rejected by her wish to be elsewhere and have a clear sense of personal limits, for example, taking time away for themselves. They worked conscientiously and professionally with the adopters, on the instructions of social services, in order to try and help effect Susan's rehabilitation there. The 'fit' between carers and child was a reasonable one, in that what they had to offer her was a supportive but not very close style of relationship which was compatible with her needs at this point.

The context of the placement was, however, initially unhelpful to it, in that Susan's adoptive parents found it difficult to accept her wholeheartedly (they limited her contact with them to an overnight stay once every two weeks, and are highly critical and negative about her), but could not bring themselves finally to admit failure. The continuing uncertainty had a deleterious effect on Susan's behaviour. The 'conditions' have now changed since Susan's therapist insisted that her adoptive parents resolved the uncertainty about her return and they have decided that she should not come back. She seems now more receptive and open to a relationship with her foster mother, especially.

Handling attachment: need for closeness

The happy compatibility between Susan and her carers in handling her needs for closeness was vitiated by the context of the placement. In her case, local authority policies make it unlikely that she can remain in the placement long-term, despite the foster carers' feeling that it would be in her interests to do so:

> Susan will have to move on. They'll be involving the Barnardo's aftercarers at her next review soon, and then when she's 17 next year, they'll start

looking at bedsits and flats with the Barnardo's, and she will have to move on by 18. And that is the system.

Q: Would you keep her if there was more financial support?

Definitely. Yes, definitely. But it's not there. It's just with Susan being a very young person, unless she rapidly matures, then how she'll cope at 18, I dread to think. A disturbed young person with lots of baggage. Because if it was my own daughter – your own children, you don't say, oh, you're nearly 18! One of Brian's sons lived with us until he was about 26, when he was ready to go – you know! You don't say to children, you're nearly 18…I mean, OK, some 18-year-olds are quite mature, but even so, it's a big thing.

So the positive features of the case – which include skill in meeting Susan's needs for closeness without feeling threatened by a lack of response, and the decision to be decisive about her future with her adoptive parents rather than allowing this to drift – are kept in check, rather than spiralling to a more positive outcome, by the negative features of the conditions, which prevent Susan remaining in the placement long-term.

This issue of holding back in the light of an impending departure was highlighted in another placement which was classified as less successful than Susan's and where the placement took a downward spiral until the teenager eventually left. Crucial to the placement's failure was that the carer seemed to lack sufficient skill and the professionalism to recognise her foster daughter's feelings and behaviour, and work with her over these. In contrast to the previous placement, where the foster carers seem to have been able to wait out Susan's ambivalence, and be available when she wanted more, this foster carer is impatient with what she describes as her foster daughter's jealousy at her other relationships, and seemed resentful of the 16-year-old's demands on her. The interview suggested that the foster child was seeking greater emotional closeness, and more of a sense of being cared for, than the carer wanted or felt it appropriate to offer. She seems unable to respond to this helpfully, and her own needs take precedence:

She complained that I wasn't loving enough for her. But you see… I mean, I mean, I was loving towards Christine, but like with all foster kids, you've got to hold a little bit back. Because foster kids can be very selfish, and just think of themselves. And when it comes to anything, they don't think of you, they just move on and they don't give you a second thought or anything like that. And you'll find most foster kids are like that, and things like that, so it's best not to get too involved, so that when they move on, it's not a big wrench.

In another placement, classified as 'unsuccessful', where the eight-year-old boy, Dan, had remained for nearly two years, the foster carer was aware of holding herself back from Dan's expressions of attachment needs, because the placement was short-term (and as a single carer of over 50 she does not feel it is an appropriate long-term one):

> I never wanted him to feel I was the be-all and end-all.

The 'fit' (along with his behaviour) deteriorated as Dan's needs for closeness went unmet: the conditions (what Dan wanted from the placement, and what the local authority planned for it) made it difficult for the foster carer to exercise the kind of responsive parenting which she had initially demonstrated, or to meet the greater challenges of his increasingly demanding behaviour.

On a number of occasions, this lack of congruence, between the feelings engendered in the placement and the context of placement expectations, was difficult to handle. One foster carer (in our pilot study) spoke with great sadness of the special attachment she had formed with a boy fostered as an infant whom she had seen through very difficult times; she had wished to adopt him but had been turned down, and commented: 'they expect you to treat them as your own, but not to get involved'. A similar conflict was expressed by another carer:

> They want you to do it like a job but they also want you to love the children and you can't do both. At least, I can't. Somehow you're supposed to distance yourself from them.

Handling behavioural demands

The cases we have presented have illustrated the role played in placements by the children's behaviour. Clearly, some carers find difficult behaviour less threatening and easier to handle than others. The way they interpreted it and their ability to be firm without being harsh seemed crucial. However, factors external to the child and carer seemed to influence both the likelihood of difficult behaviour and the ease with which it could be managed. The examples given below illustrate the potential influence of other foster children (in this case a sibling), the birth family, and the foster carer's own family on the foster child's behaviour.

Taking on too much

One placement – which had been classified as successful, and seemed to foster carer, social worker and the interviewer to have provided a great deal, in many respects, to the 11-year-old girl, Sally – was, when last contacted, on the point of breakdown. Here the foster carer had matched the foster child's need for emotional closeness with a high level of intimacy and commitment. The cost of this to her own family had been considerable (for example, her son had moved out of the home, because he found Sally's presence so difficult) but what seems to have brought the placement to the point of breakdown was the foster carer's determination to offer a home to Sally's twin sister. The presence of the two girls, both very difficult and vying for attention, had proved too much. The twin had left, and the foster carer's health had been seriously affected. With the very best of intentions, she seems to have failed to evaluate in a sufficiently professional way the likely demands on her, and the inability of the two sisters to share her affection and care. The wider context perhaps also failed to act appropriately in assessing and predicting the probable outcome of placing the additional twin, although one can imagine the temptation to a social worker desperate to place a needy child.

The birth family

The birth family could influence behaviour as well as attachment. In the following placement, for example, the birth mother's pattern of periodically seeking custody is difficult for her child to handle, and the latter's behaviour becomes more and more problematic as her anxiety and uncertainty about the outcome increases:

> Sophie settled down beautifully. We could see a real improvement. We felt we were really getting somewhere. But now over the last three months, we've just seen this awful deterioration again. Her mother's gone to court to try and get her back, and ever since she's found out, her behaviour has deteriorated. She's confused about what she wants. I think she likes the idea of living with her Mum again, but I think deep down she knows it wouldn't work.

In this case, the foster carer's ability to remain tolerant and accepting (although she made it clear how much she wanted Sophie to stay) seems important in enabling the placement to continue. The social worker, commenting that Sophie seems to be accepting the psychologist's recommendation to stay in the foster home, adds:

Barbara (foster carer) has always spoken sympathetically as well about Sophie's Mum. She never said anything sort of condemning or negative. If they had been condemning in any way, I think Sophie would have retaliated against that and been probably more loyal to her mother.

The foster carer's family

The foster carer's family often bear the brunt of a foster child's difficult behaviour. The impact on them (for example, whether they themselves are led astray) and the way they react (for example, whether they want the foster child out of the house) are naturally important to the outcome of the placement.

In one placement, classified as unsuccessful, but where the foster carer's commitment had begun to help the 13-year-old boy to settle, Timothy's birth family encourage him to steal and this pilfering, largely from the foster family, has strained the foster children's relationships with him. Nonetheless, the foster carer continues to support contact with his family. Hers was also one of the placements which seemed consciously to use the foster children to help in handling Timothy's behaviour. The family is a large, busy, friendly one with seven children aged between 7 and 17. They have remained committed to him despite his stealing and (on one occasion, which was handled, to her justified pride, sensitively and non-punitively by the foster carer) a sexual assault on one of them:

> He's picked a lot of things off my kids. But we never, ever, from day one when Timmy came to us, we never decided to show him the ropes as such, like we don't do this and we don't do that. 'Cos we thought, what do kids always do? Teenagers? They hit back at adults who are trying to tell 'em things. So what we did we left it to our kids to do it. Like a morning – 'we don't do that, Timmy'. 'Oh all right.' And he'd do something else. 'Oh, we're not allowed to do that, Tim.' So me and Tony never had to say anything – it was always the kids. And he learnt far quicker off the kids than he would have done off us. And it was good.

The contribution of outside professionals

Intervention by the professionals may be crucial, as we have seen in the case of Susan (where the psychologist insisted that the adopters came to a decision), and in that of Carole (where the psychologist made a recommendation against her returning to live with her mother).

In relation to social work help, the contribution seemed complex and varied, and it was not always easy to unravel the different parts played in the relationship between placement and social worker(s).

In our two first case examples, the foster carers' skills in different ways helped to ensure a successful working partnership. Both saw the social work involvement in the placement as important. In our less successful placements, social work help was viewed negatively, either because it had been needed and was unavailable, or because it was seen as unhelpful. In our other examples, the picture is also varied. On occasion, it seemed from the interview that the social work intervention could be crucial in enabling the foster carer to work more successfully with the foster child. For example, in the following placement, which was seen as viable, but where there were difficulties over contact and the child's behaviour (he continued to soil), the social worker had invested time since she took over the case in making a relationship with the boy and his brother:

> We actually had a session on what a social worker was and what a social worker did. And that – I think that was very useful for them both. And trying to explain – it's very difficult for children – I mean, at that time they were nine and eleven – to understand what the role of a social worker actually is. So we did some work on that. And they were particularly impressed when I explained that to all intents and purposes they were my boys. And they quite like that idea. In terms of, they told me how they felt, and what their problems were, and I tried to help them sort it. And – you know – in meetings or at courses – any other venue. You know, I was there to be an advocate. And I explained things in their sorts of terms. I was a voice for them. And they kind of liked that.

This she felt had enabled them eventually to express their feelings of being 'second best' in the placement, and she was working with the foster carer to help her become more demonstrative towards them, as well as more accepting of the contact with the boys' birth family:

> He was sort of saying that he didn't feel like he could do anything right. And this sort of coincided with Gillian's period of ill-health. And it was felt that he was treated differently to Gillian's natural grandchildren, and was also noticing himself that there were no pictures of himself up in the house, and there were lots of – I'm sure if you've been to the foster placement, you will have seen that there's lots of pictures that relate to her own grandchildren. And the fact that Gillian had sort of said to both boys, 'you're making me ill'. And so all these were issues that I raised with the family placement team.

Together we went and raised them with Gillian. I have to say that both boys seem much more settled. They seem to view themselves as staying there whilst they grow up, really, and things seem to have improved.

In this example, the social worker's intervention seems to be important in creating the conditions in which *responsive parenting* may occur.

On occasion, other professionals may provide the necessary support and direction. For example, in one placement, the secure attachment between carer and five-year-old child, Isobel, was recognised by the child's therapist, who argued successfully that the placement should become a permanent one, rather than that Isobel should be moved on, as originally planned. The therapist in this case also helped the foster carer to adapt her parenting to the child's needs, and to move from a rather intuitive response to a way of handling her which was attuned to the child; and helped her, for example, consciously identify key times in the child's day. Here, then, aspects of the *conditions* promoted the responsive interaction between carer and child.

In other cases, the social work contribution, or that of other professionals, is more difficult to evaluate, so that we do not know whether, for example, in certain cases more active involvement would have turned the placement round. What does seem true is that in the 'successful' placements the foster carers tend to view the social workers positively, even if there have been disagreements along the way, and this is usually reciprocated. The 'less successful' ones, which have remained unchanged or deteriorated, are marked either by a total lack of involvement (as with Mr Roberts), or, more usually, an absence of a sense of planning or skilled activity designed to support the placement.

A curious feature of foster care is the degree to which it is both natural and professional, demanding a degree of what may be described as 'dispassionate love'. We conclude our exploration of the cases with the comment by one foster carer, in reply to the question we asked at the end of all our interviews:

Q: In what way is fostering the same or different to what a good parent would offer?

A: I have to wear two heads. There's the mother in me that actually adores Paul, that doesn't ever want to part with him, and hopes that he's fetching his kids home to me. He's there in our lives permanently. But there again, there's the worker in me, that sees Paul for what he actually is. For the problems he's got.

Conclusion

Each of the components we have identified in the model may be divided into different sub-elements.

Responsive parenting

To show the child responsive parenting, carers must:

- handle attachment appropriately, e.g.
    - deal sensitively with previous attachments and losses
    - offer security with persistence and avoid threats of rejection
    - offer tolerable closeness
    - be sensitive to attachment times and approaches
    - deal sensitively with jealousy and exclusiveness
    - go out of their way to make child feel 'at home'
- reinforce socially acceptable self-esteem/identity, e.g.
    - praise success of whatever kind
    - avoid dwelling on failure
    - set realistic expectations
    - maintain a positive but realistic picture of child
- handle difficult behaviour appropriately, e.g.
    - analyse motives/reasons for behaviour
    - avoid increasing these motives
    - set clear limits
    - negotiate in ways that avoid humiliating child
    - offer alternative ways of meeting needs
    - avoid reinforcing behaviour itself
    - reinforce competing behaviour.

Conditions: the child and the carer

Some of the conditions which make appropriate interaction more or less likely relate to the child, the carer and the compatibility between them. Relevant conditions include:

- the child's
    - attractiveness (to most people and the carer in particular)
    - motivation to make placement work

- propensity to difficult or easy behaviour
- the main carer's
  - general skill and motivation
  - commitment to particular child
  - sense of professional limits
  - degree of strain
- compatibility (or 'fit') between carer and child in relation to
  - attachment/closeness needs
  - definitions of success (e.g. academic)
  - expectations over behaviour.

Conditions: the context of the placement

Other factors may impinge on the placement from its wider context. These include the carer's family, birth family, social services, school etc. Placements are more likely to go easily where:

- the carer's family is committed to the placement
- there are not clashes between child and particular members of family
- members of the birth family are not seeking to disturb placement
- the social services support the carer's preferred view of placement's purpose
- the child's social world (school, friends etc.) supports placement expectations.

Further carer skills

Carers are not simply passive in the face of the conditions that affect their work. They need to be willing and able to elicit help when they need it from their family, the social services, the school, the medical services and so on.

They must also be able to respond appropriately to new difficulties in the placement, riding out difficult behaviour or changes of plan on the part of social services, the birth family and so on. The alternative is to over-react and risk making the situation worse.

We now turn to the chapters reviewing our statistical findings and, following this, link these to the model and comments in the chapters so far.

Chapter Nine

Measuring Success

Introduction

Methodologically our next seven chapters present a sharp contrast to the last six. They are statistical, at times quite heavily so. They are certainly a far cry from the pithy comments of foster children or the individual case histories we have just discussed. That said, we hope that our quantitative and qualitative approaches are complementary. Each considers similar issues. Insofar as they come up with similar messages, we may have more confidence in the two in combination than in either on its own.

In broad outline our statistical model suggests that five groups of factors influence outcomes. These are:

- the characteristics of the child
- the parenting approach of the carers
- the way carer/carer's family and child get on
- the birth parents (in particular contact with birth parents) and
- factors connected with the school.

Each of these groups of factors has featured in our qualitative model. In this way the statistical model can be seen as a test of our qualitative one.

At the same time our two models are not identical. The qualitative model has much to say that cannot easily be picked up by statistical measures – an example is the importance, as we see it, of 'attachment sensitive times'. This model speaks, perhaps, more directly to practitioners. On the other hand our statistics also cover aspects not picked up in our qualitative material. For example, we identify conditions in which contact with parents may be particularly difficult. The qualitative material did show that contact could be very problematic but could not show how common this was, or how damaging it was likely to be in particular circumstances. In this way each of our approaches is a test of the other while also considering a slightly different range of experience.

In order to pursue this complementary statistical approach we needed measures of 'success'. Given such measures we can see how far success can be predicted and whether different interventions increase the chances that it will occur.

Against this background the task of this chapter is twofold. It aims to:

- introduce three measures of success that we will use in the next seven chapters
- relate these measures to the variables introduced in Chapters 2 and 3, that is to:
  - the children's basic characteristics
  - their care careers
  - the way their placements were made
  - the plans made for them
  - their placement at follow-up (e.g. adoption or return home).

Further chapters will then relate our success measures to the key elements of the model which we began to sketch out in the last chapters (e.g. the characteristics of the child).

Measuring success

As explained in Chapter 5, our primary concern is with the success of placements. Judgements of a placement's success have to be made in the context of its purpose. Views about this and its achievement may differ among those involved. So there is a danger that these judgements will be subjective and arbitrary, an unsatisfactory basis for statistical calculation.

In this study we dealt with the problem of subjectivity in two ways. First, we asked for ratings of placement success from three different parties (carers, social workers and family placement social workers) at two points in time. Our assumption was that if all these parties agreed that a case was 'successful' this judgement would be more defensible than if only one did. Second, we looked at 'disruptions' and used avoidance of disruption as a measure of 'success' – for, whatever the purpose of the placement, it is presumably not that relationships between carer and child should deteriorate to the point where the child can no longer remain in it.

In the long run, a key test for these measures lies in the way they are connected with other variables. It is a point in their favour if they relate closely to each other. It is also reassuring if they relate closely to other potential measures of success (e.g. the degree to which a child improves on certain psychological tests or the degree to which the child wants to be in the placement). It is a further point in their favour if they correlate with the predictors of these other potential success measures – for example, if 'skilled parenting' by the foster carers is correlated both with our measures and with beneficial psychological change. Further reassurance would come if this model fitted the qualitative material presented earlier.

Such statistical findings would help to assure us that the model we test through these measures is relevant to some general notion of success. So we would not only be providing evidence that, say, skilled parenting by carers leads to the avoidance of disruption but also that it leads to children who develop well and like their placement. Evidence on these matters is provided in later chapters. For the moment we need to introduce the measures themselves.

Three success ratings

Our first measure (the *first success rating*) was developed from questions put to the foster carer, social worker and family placement worker at the time of the first questionnaire on placements. The question was phrased as follows:

> There are different reasons why children are placed in foster care. Thinking about this placement would you say that from the point of view of the child it has gone very well, as well as can be expected, or not very well.

In general, respondents were optimistic, with 72 per cent of the foster carers and 68 per cent of the family placement social workers and 66 per cent of the children's social workers giving the highest ratings. At the other end of the spectrum, only 5 per cent of the foster carers and even fewer of the social workers gave the lowest rating. The respondents also agreed with each other, if not invariably, at least to a far higher degree than would be expected by chance.

These positive ratings are both encouraging and in keeping with other research that has used social work evaluations. Rowe and her colleagues (1989), for example, found that social workers thought that only 3 per cent of fostering placements had been 'unhelpful' while nearly three-quarters of them were judged by social workers to have met their aims 'fully or in most respects'. Cliffe with Berridge (1991) used similar measures and reported similar results. Cleaver (2000), working from social work records, studied 152 children fostered at some stage in two local authorities in one year whose placements lasted at least three months. Her figures suggest that around eight out of ten of the children adjusted 'adequately' to the foster family.

The small proportion of 'unsuccessful' ratings creates a problem for those wishing to untangle the reasons for greater or lesser success. For this we have adopted a rule of using the most pessimistic rating in order to get a better spread. On this basis just over half the sample (54%) received *only* highly positive ratings, 38 per cent received no negative ratings but at least one of 'as well as can be expected' and 8 per cent were seen by at least one rater as not having gone well. We call this variable the 'first success rating'.

The *second success rating* relied on exactly the same set of questions which we asked again at follow-up. Again the responses were highly positive and we adopted the same rule in putting them together. Overall, 48 per cent were *only* given top ratings, 37 per cent were given at least one rating of 'as well as could be expected' and 15 per cent were seen by at least one of the raters as not going well.

Our third measure (the *third success rating*) was 'disruption' (or, to be precise, the lack of 'disruption'). This measure has traditionally been seen as a relatively hard one (George 1970). In practice, however, as pointed out by Berridge and Cleaver (1987), there is considerable room for interpretation. Planned moves are clearly not disruptions. There are, however, 'grey areas', for example, when a carer demands that a child is removed but agrees to keep her or him until such time as a planned move can take place.

Our informants agreed on the frequency with which the breakdowns took place – social workers noting them in 15 per cent of the cases and family placement workers and carers in 14 per cent.

The informants were not always agreed on whether a particular placement had broken down or not. Adopting our rule of pessimism we counted as a disruption any placement which was said by any informant to have disrupted. On this criterion 21 per cent of the placements were said to 'disrupt'.[1]

Both the first and second success ratings were strongly associated with our measure of disruption:

- Of those placements which did not disrupt, 58 per cent scored the maximum on both the first and second success rating.

- Where placements did disrupt, only 25 per cent gained maximum points on the first success rating and 8 per cent on the second one.

Disrupted cases also received relatively high proportions of the lowest ratings (23% for the first success rating and 48% for the second). There is an argument for using only measures of outcome which were taken at follow-up – for at this point more of the story is available. However, it seemed possible that these second measures were over-influenced by disruptions and paid too little attention to gains which had been made. For this reason we have generally used both the first and second success ratings. We do, however, give more weight to the two measures from the follow-up survey which are more properly seen as 'outcomes'.

Basic characteristics and outcomes

We related the information on age, sex, ethnicity and legal status to our measures of outcome. We found no association between sex and any of our three outcome measures – a finding which replicates those of Berridge and Cleaver (1987), Cleaver (2000), and Farmer and her colleagues (2004) in relation to 'breakdown' and Rowe and her colleagues (1989), who used other measures of success.

Barn (1993) and Berridge and Cleaver (1987) found no relationship between breakdown and ethnicity. Rowe and her colleagues (1989) also found no relationship between ethnicity and their measures of outcome. Thoburn and her colleagues (2000) found that male foster children did 'better' on some of their measures of outcome if they were not in 'same race' placements.

Our findings were in keeping with Thoburn and her colleagues' results. Male foster children from minority ethnic groups were rather less likely to experience a disruption if placed with carers who defined themselves as 'English, Scots or Welsh' than if they were placed with carers who did not define themselves in this way. The converse was true for female foster children. Neither of these differences was significant and the numbers were too small to investigate the finding further. However, the statistics did suggest a 'significant interaction' – that is, the effect of racial matching was different in the two groups ($p=0.039$). Further work on this issue would therefore seem very important.

Table 9.1 Age of child and disruption

| | Years | n | Whether placement disrupted (%) | |
			Yes	No
Age group	0–4	125	7	93
	5–10	136	15	85
	11–15	167	33	67
	16–17	94	24	76
Total	All ages	522	21	79

Source: Foster carer questionnaire at Time 1; disruption measured by all questionnaires at Time 2.

Age was strongly and consistently related to disruption, a finding which again replicates what others have consistently found (Cleaver 2000; George 1970; Parker 1966; Rowe *et al.* 1989; Scottish Office 1991; Trasler 1960).

The group aged between 11 and 15 were most likely to have 'bad' outcomes. This was so whether the measure of outcomes was disruption or the assessments made by foster carers and social workers. At this age, very difficult children may be looked after in residential homes – an option which is rarely available for younger ones. The existence of a residential option for older children may explain why Berridge and Cleaver (1987) did not find adolescents in longer-stay care more at risk of breakdown than children aged 6 to 11. As these researchers point out, many younger children in foster care are also difficult. However, they are not, on our evidence, on average as difficult as the younger teenagers.

There was no evidence that those who were on care orders did any better or worse than the other children in terms of our outcome measures.

Careers, number of placements and outcomes

A key and proper aim of official policy is to keep the number of moves in the care system as low as possible. As we have seen, children also wanted more stability than they got. However, they also, on occasion, wanted to move from placements they were in. So the need for stability has to be balanced against the need to ensure that children are in a placement which suits them. In striking this balance it is important to know how far moves *per se* have a bad effect.

In evaluating the impact of moves, two points need to be borne in mind.

First, the number of moves may be a rather poor indicator of their psychological implications for the children involved. For example, the ending of a placement which stops because all are agreed it is time to move on may have little impact. By contrast the disruption of a placement on which all concerned have placed great hopes may be devastating. What is important is the degree to which the child experiences continuity and a world which is predictable and to some extent in her or his control. The relationship between these fundamentally subjective concepts and measures of number of moves is indirect.

Second, a child's disturbance may be a reason for frequent moves as well as the result of one. Thus the association between measures of instability and measures of outcome may not be as direct as is often supposed.

We used three main measures of instability to explore its relationship with outcome. These were:

- the number of different episodes of care the child had experienced
- the number of different placements in foster care (five or more were treated as five)
- the length of time the child had spent in the placement.

We will deal first with the number of previous moves whether through episodes or repeated placements. We will then consider time in placement.

Number of care episodes and placements

As predicted, we found that the more foster placements a child had had, the worse he or she tended to do on all measures of outcome ($p<0.01$ or less). Children who had had more episodes of 'care' did not do significantly worse on our success ratings but were more likely to experience disruption ($p=0.052$).

As we have also seen, older children had had on average a greater number of previous episodes in care and placements. By taking age into account we were therefore likely to reduce the apparent association between these measures of instability and outcome. In practice, when we took age into account, the relationship between disruption and number of episodes in the care system ceased to be significant. However, children with a greater number of previous placements had worse outcomes on all our three measures even after age had been taken into account.

In order to look further at the relationship between previous breakdowns and outcomes we distinguished between breakdowns which were said to have arisen from the child's behaviour (behavioural breakdowns) and those attributed to other causes. If a greater number of placements is *per se* disturbing, breakdowns or placement movements which did not arise from the child's behaviour should in the future be associated with further disruption. This was a possibility which could be tested.

Our analyses (all of which took account of age) found no relationship between any of our outcome variables and the number of previous placements after breakdowns had been excluded. The apparent implication is that movement which occurs for reasons that do not have to do with the child's behaviour does not affect the child in such a way that he or she becomes more likely to suffer a placement breakdown or less likely to be seen as benefiting from foster care.

By contrast behavioural breakdowns were significantly associated with future disruption ($p < 0.001$) and with poor success ratings on both occasions ($p < 0.001$).

Unsurprisingly, children who had experienced a breakdown which was attributed to their own behaviour or relationship with carers had a higher than average number of placements than those who had not (3.7 as against 2.0). It seemed to be this fact that accounted for the association between the number of placements and outcome. The relationship between future disruption and behavioural breakdown remained significant even when number of placements was taken into account. This may reflect the damaging effect of behavioural breakdowns on the child or characteristics in the child which preceded and led to these breakdowns.

Care needs to be taken over the interpretation of these findings. This result does not suggest that we should cease to aim for stability. Both carers and children wanted placements to be more stable than they were. However, we should be careful about assuming that movement is necessarily damaging and is never required. As we have seen, some children complained because they were not moved when they wanted to be.

Length of time in placement

There was no association between the length of time in placement and our success ratings. Placements were more likely to disrupt if a child had been in placement for less than two years. Twenty-three per cent of those in the placement for less than one year disrupted. The comparable figures for those placed for between 12 and 23 months was 19 per cent. It was 17 per cent for those who had been there for 24 months or more.

Table 9.2 Time in placement and disruption

Time in placement	n	Whether placement disrupted(%)	
		Yes	No
Under 12 months	200	23	77
12 months to 24 months	119	19	81
24 months to 36 months	65	15	85
36 months and over	82	18	82
Total	466	20	80

Sources: All questionnaires at Time 2. Chi square=1.83, df=3, p=NS.

This relatively flat distribution disguises the fact that those in years one and two were much more likely to move for other reasons. Their time at risk for disruption was therefore reduced and the possibility of seeing a move as something other than a disruption increased. Moreover, those who were older (and therefore more likely to disrupt) also tended to have spent a longer period with their current foster carers. If age was taken into account, the expected result was obtained. Among children of similar ages those who had been longer in placement were less likely to suffer disruption. These children were also more likely to have a placement seen as successful at follow-up.[2]

Placement choice and outcome

As we have seen, social workers placed great importance on the 'match' between foster carer and child. The ability to match, as opposed to taking what is on offer, requires a choice of placements, which was often not available. In keeping with these considerations the social worker's assessment that the placement was initially not judged to be completely satisfactory was significantly associated with the first of our success ratings (i.e. the one rated at the time of the first survey). Arguably, this may be a case of being wise after the event. It is, however, what would be expected if the opportunity to match is important.

Further analysis showed stronger relationships between outcome and the initial assessment of placement if account was taken of the time a child had been in placement. Among those who had been in placement for 12 months or more, there was no relationship between reported initial assessments of how satisfactory the placement was and any of our measures of outcome. Among those who had been in placement for less than 12 months this assessment was significantly related to the first success rating but not the others. If age was taken into account in this recently placed group the apparent effect of placement suitability on the avoidance of disruption became almost significant ($p=0.055$).

This analysis suggests that the associations between 'placement matching' and outcome did not simply arise because social workers were wise after the event. They did not yet know of the disruptions and in any case their wisdom should have been as apparent among those who had been long in placement as among those who had been less. A possible explanation is that 'placements shake down'. The risk of initial failure may, perhaps, be reduced by careful matching. If, however, a placement survives despite being apparently mismatched it becomes no more likely to fail than any other. Confirmation of this hypothesis should, however, wait for further research.

Plans, placement at follow-up and success

We related our success measures to the plans made for the children and to their placements at follow-up.

Rowe and her colleagues (1989) found that foster care cases intended to be short-term were on average seen as more successful by social workers than long-term ones. We did not find this in our rather different sample.

Unsurprisingly, children who were expected to stay for a year or more and who were not there at follow-up were very likely to have left through a disruption. They were also judged as having had less successful placements than those who had been expected to stay and did so.

The final placements were also related to success. The highest average success ratings in both surveys went to placements where the child stayed in the placement or moved to adoption. The least successful placements were those where the child moved to residential care or another foster placement. Placements where the child returned home or went to independent living were seen as intermediate.

These ratings partly reflected the part which disruption played in leading to the final placement. Residential care was largely reserved for those who disrupted. Just over two-thirds of the moves to other foster placements were also counted as disruptions. The follow-up placements which attracted intermediate success ratings – rehabilitation and moves into independent living – were less frequently the result of disruption although they seem sometimes seem to have been prompted by one. Disruptions very rarely prompted a move to an adoptive placement and obviously did not occur when the child remained in the placement.

Conclusion

In order to test the hypotheses from our qualitative material we needed measures of success. This chapter has introduced the three we mainly used and explored their relationship to the basic variables describing the children, their previous careers in the care system, the degree to which their placement was seen as 'satisfactory' when first made and their final placement.

In keeping with other research we found that age was an important predictor of outcomes – with those aged 10 to 15 having the 'worst'.

Like other researchers we found that the chance of disruption increased with the number of previous placements. The explanation for this finding seemed more complicated than previously suspected. Those who had had a previous placement which disrupted because of their behaviour or relationship with carers had on average more previous placements and were more likely to disrupt on their current one. Moves which did not result from a behavioural disruption did not predict breakdown.

There was also some evidence that factors which predicted outcomes early in the placement might not necessarily do so later. Children who had placements which were not thought fully satisfactory at the time of placement were after allowing for age rather more likely than others to disrupt in the first year. Thereafter there was no difference. In general, the longer a child was in the placement, the less likely the placement was to disrupt, but this trend only became apparent after we had taken age into account.

In general it is easier to describe these problems than it is to suggest what might be done about them. As we saw in Chapter 2, careful matching (except in the case of long-stay placements) is almost always impossible. This situation is likely to remain. All placements are in short supply and many are made in an emergency. There are a wide variety of criteria against which children may need to be matched with foster carers. An immediate choice of appropriate placements would only be possible if a high proportion of foster carers had vacancies at any given point in time. This increase in carers would require a very large increase in funding both to attract them and to retain them while they are not fostering. In our view, funds are unlikely to allow this.

In practice, as we again saw in Chapter 2, the social workers seemed to manage this problem by making the best short-term placements they could in the circumstances and then taking time to find an appropriate long-term one if this was required. Two problems result. First, some of the short-term placements are considered to be less than fully satisfactory at the time (in 30 per cent of our intended short-term cases this was said to be so, as against only 10 per cent of our long-term ones). Second, short-term placements 'silt up'. Half of the placements which had been intended to be short-term had already lasted for over a year (cf. discussion in Berridge 1997, p.25).

Given that this problem is almost inevitable, thought needs to be given as to how it might be managed. One possible line of approach would be to increase the proportion of carers able and expecting to take a wide variety of children. This would increase the extent of choice in the system without necessarily increasing the number of carers. A second possibility would be to increase the number of children per placement – a step which would have the same effect and whose likely effects we explore later. Irrespective of these steps, it seems inevitable that some children will stay longer than expected, and some may settle so that it becomes undesirable to move them. These possibilities needed to be faced in planning and in preparing foster carers for their role.

Notes

1. This method introduces a possible bias. Other things being equal the greater the number of questionnaires returned, the greater the chance that one of them would judge a placement to be unsuccessful or 'disrupted'. Those on which we had all three of the relevant questionnaires should therefore have a greater chance of 'doing badly'. In practice this effect was not apparent for 'disruption'. There was a significant trend for those with fewer questionnaires to do better on the first success rating ($p=0.004$) and a slight trend for this on the second success rating ($p=0.029$). We found no reason to think that this bias affected our results. As the trend was not apparent for disruption, it certainly should not affect associations with this outcome. In addition disruption is a dichotomous variable. We analysed it using chi square tests and logistic regression. These make fewer assumptions than the tests used for our other outcomes. The fact that the overall picture of what makes for success is similar for disruption as for our other outcome variables is therefore an important confirmation of the analyses of the success ratings.

2. These results hold when time in placement is entered as a 'grouped variable' (i.e. as a variable divided into quartiles or between those less than a year, 12 months to 23 and over). The raw variable was related in the predicted direction but not significantly so. Analysis to be reported in the third book makes it clear that length of time in placement does help to counteract the effect of age on the likelihood of disruption.

Chapter Ten

Foster Children: Characteristics, Personalities and Problems

Introduction

This chapter deals with the children's individual characteristics. We look first at the children's motivation. Did they want to be in this foster placement? We then turn to their histories and personalities. Have they been abused and, if so, in what way? Do they have 'attractive' personalities? What can we say about their degree of disturbance, the ease with which they make relationships and their general development? Our model, common sense, and the general literature on foster care all suggest that these characteristics are likely to have a major effect on outcomes.

In focusing on these variables our aims are:

- to describe – much of this information has not been provided before on a large sample of foster children in England

- to explore the associations between our variables – this may suggest causal chains and also allow simplification as variables which are closely associated can be combined or used as proxies for each other

- to identify variables which are associated with good or poor outcome.

In terms of method we look first at the associations between the variables and outcome. We then examine whether they remain significant if we take account of age. Finally, we try to build a more complex, multi-variate model predicting outcomes on the basis of all the key variables explored in the chapter.

Motivation towards the placement

Our model suggests that the children who want to be in a placement will be much more likely to do well in it.

We had two measures of motivation. The foster carers rated the children in terms of how far they wanted to stay in the placement. Those children who returned the questionnaire also stated how happy they were with the placement being offered. For this purpose they were given a choice of ratings from between 1 (a very smiling face) and 7 (a very miserable face). The two sets of ratings were consistent in the sense that they were strongly associated with each other. Children who, according to the foster carer, were not fully committed to the placement were also three times as likely to indicate they were not fully happy with the placement.

Both sets of answers suggested that on average the children were very contented. Three-quarters of the foster carers stated unequivocally that the child did not want to leave. Eighty-nine per cent of the children gave the highest rating of how happy they were to be in the placement.

The foster carers' assessment of motivation was very strongly associated with all three outcome measures. For example, just under one in five of those whose carers stated they wanted to stay in the placement disrupted. The comparable figures for those for who wanted to leave 'to a certain extent' was 30 per cent. The figure for the very small number who wanted to leave 'a great deal' was 50 per cent. These associations with outcome remained very highly significant after we had taken account of age.

The association between the children's replies and outcome was less highly significant, partly because the numbers were less. However, the children's rating was significantly associated with disruption before we took age into account and was in 'the right direction' even when we had done so. It was significantly associated with the second success ratings even after we had taken age into account.

Overall, our hypotheses on the impact of the children's motivation seemed to be supported.

Abuse

There is evidence that abuse is associated with poor outcomes in foster care (Fratter *et al.* 1991; Thoburn, Wilding and Watson 2000). Sexual abuse in particular may create problems for foster carers, since such children may display sexualised behaviour, even to the extent of abusing others themselves (Farmer and Pollock 1998).

Sadly, the majority of the children came from backgrounds that were perceived, at least by the social workers, as abusive. Table 10.1 sets out the information on those children for whom we have it.

Table 10.1 Types of abuse noted by social workers

Type of abuse	n	No evidence (%)	Some evidence (%)	Strong evidence (%)
Sexual	320	63	24	12
Physical	334	43	28	28
Emotional	369	16	34	50
Neglect	362	23	29	48
Any of above*	411	9	24	67

Source: Social worker questionnaire at Time 1.
* The rating 'strong evidence of abuse' was used if there was strong evidence for any particular kind of abuse.

As can be seen from Table 10.1, the number of social workers responding to these questions rises with the proportion who considered that they had at least some evidence of abuse. This suggests that the social workers in this situation were more likely to answer these questions. For this reason the proportion in the sample where there was, for example, strong evidence of sexual abuse may be overstated and be nearer to 8 per cent than 12 per cent. That said, it remains striking that in only one in nine of the cases did the social workers feel that there was no evidence of abuse of any kind.

The frequency of the reported abuse differed to some extent by sex and ethnicity. Unsurprisingly, females were significantly more likely to have been sexually abused than males (strong evidence was reported for 17% of them as against 8% of the males).

There were differences in the frequency of abuse in the different age groups. Overall there were fewer reports of abuse among the under fives than in the other groups. Analysis by the age at which the children first entered the care system made the picture clearer:

- Children who entered the care system before the age of five were more likely than any other group to be thought to be neglected (there was said to be strong evidence of this for 56% of them).

- Physical and emotional abuse were most commonly found among those entering aged five to ten.

- Sexual abuse was suspected in just over half the cases where the child was aged six to ten or 11 to 14, but in only a quarter of those entering when less than five, and very rarely among the small number of children entering aged 15 or over.

These differences by age group at entry were not so apparent in relation to the age groups of those in the care system. For example, although children did not enter the system because of neglect experienced at 16, many of the 16-year-olds in the system had been neglected at an earlier age.

All our measures of abuse were associated with each other, with the strongest associations being between emotional abuse and the others. Only two of the four measures – emotional abuse and physical abuse – were significantly associated with disruption. The strongest association was with emotional abuse. This remained highly significant even when we took account of age and other forms of abuse. In these analyses, physical abuse was no longer significantly associated with disruption. In comparable analyses, emotional abuse was also significantly associated with the first and second success ratings after taking account of age. So it seems that in this sample what predicts outcome is not so much the fact of abuse but its association with emotional abuse.

Special needs

We asked the social workers if the children had any 'special needs'. As in the case of abuse, our questions on this could with advantage have been more precise. Nevertheless, on the face of it they revealed a surprising amount of difficulty. One hundred and eighteen children (28% of those for whom we had a social worker questionnaire) were said to have learning difficulties. Seven per cent were said to have physical impairments ('special physical needs' was the term used in the questionnaire). Eleven per cent had 'other difficulties' such as autism. Only six out of ten (61%) had none of these problems.

A different estimate of the prevalence of impairments and difficulties was provided by a question to the foster carers. This asked whether the child had faced them with problems related to disability since arrival with them. Just under 17 per cent (one in six) of the sample were said to be disabled on this definition. The concept of 'disability' was treated by the carers as including physical disability but not as restricted to it. Only 3 per cent of those said by the carers not to be disabled were said by the social workers to have special physical needs. The same proportion among those identified by carers as 'disabled' was much higher (38%). Many of the remainder seem to have had 'other problems'. More than seven out of ten of them had, according to their social workers, 'learning difficulties' (these figures can be compared with the 25 per cent of children in foster care estimated by Parker, Loughran and Gordon (1992) to be disabled as defined by the Office for Population, Censuses and Surveys – OPCS).

The frequency of these problems did not vary by sex or ethnicity. Once again, however, there were some interesting differences by age. Those with special physical needs as recorded by the social workers were most likely to enter the care system when they were under five. Sixty-nine per cent of them of were first looked after at this age. Only 10 per cent started being looked after when they were age 11 or more. There was a similar pattern for those with 'other difficulties'. Nearly 58 per cent of them started to be looked after when under five and only 11 per cent when aged 11 or over. By contrast, those with learning difficulties were most likely to start being looked after in their school years, 39 per cent of them starting between the ages of five and ten, and a further 21 per cent when aged 11 to 14.

There were strong relationships between our measure of disability, as defined by the social workers, and outcomes. Those with special physical needs were very unlikely to disrupt. Only 3 per cent did so. After allowing for age, these particular 'special needs' children scored significantly better on the first and second success ratings.

Overall, therefore, this suggests that in dealing with disability in this group, much depends on definition. There is a small group of potentially 'long-stay' children who have special physical needs. These come into the care system at a relatively early age. Another small group with 'other difficulties' also enter the system when relatively young. These difficulties are likely to be emotional or behavioural – the example we gave was 'autism'. We will see later that this group are more likely to show symptoms of disturbance. In addition there is a wider group with 'learning difficulties' who typically enter the care system at a later date.

In terms of outcome, those with physical disabilities do better than others. Those with 'other difficulties' tend to do rather worse, although not significantly so. Those with learning difficulties have outcomes similar to those in the rest of the sample (a result which contrasts with the findings of Cleaver (2000) who found that those with learning difficulties were more likely to disrupt).

Attachment difficulties

We asked eight questions about attachment. These were taken from work by Quinton and his colleagues (1998). Their sample did not include very young children and their questions reflected this. One, for example, asked if 'the child hides any feelings of sadness'. Hiding sadness is quite a sophisticated activity and one would be surprised to find this in babies, although some may be 'wary' or 'frozen'. For this reason we allowed the carers to tick 'not applicable' if the child was thought to be too young for the question to apply. The number of ticks fell from an average of 5.8 among those aged less than one, through 4.8 among one-year-olds to 3.5 among two-year-olds. The number was 2 among three-year-olds, 1.4 among four-year-olds and negligible thereafter. Analysis based on these questions was therefore effectively based on children who were four years old or older.

Table 10.2 Answers to questions on attachment behaviour

	n	Degree of truth		
		Not at all (%)	To some extent (%)	To a large extent (%)
Seeks attention by misbehaving	420	36	38	26
Is more friendly with strangers than I/we would like	434	54	27	19
Seeks a lot of attention	443	27	35	38
Shows affection like a younger child	404	39	34	28
Shows a lot of affection	464	16	38	46
Hides any fear	400	44	45	11
Hides any feelings of sadness	408	43	44	13
Bottles up any emotions	396	28	51	21

Source: Foster carer questionnaire at Time 1.
Note: Questions were not presented in this order.

The questions presented in Table 10.2 were taken from a larger set which we did not have the space to include in the questionnaire. For this reason we needed to know whether all the questions were measuring the same dimension. We therefore carried out a component analysis. This exploits the correlations that exist between a number of variables in order to identify a much smaller number of dimensions or components in terms of which the individuals can be described. For example, it might be expected that individuals with an authoritarian personality would tend to answer certain questions in similar ways. Component analysis would be used to identify a dimension of 'authoritarianism' against which individuals answering the questions could be ranged and which would explain the correlations between their answers.

In the case of the variables in Table 10.2 the analysis identified two main components which together accounted for 58 per cent of the variation.

The first component was heavily loaded on the first four questions (not originally asked in this order) which can be seen, perhaps, in Bowlby's (1971) terms, as a kind of compulsive self-reliance. Individuals who score high on this component show little affection and hide their emotions. We have called the dimension 'aloofness'. We created a score for this dimension by adding the answers (reversing one score for consistency). We only used this score where all four questions had been answered.

The second component was heavily loaded on questions which showed a kind of childishness. Individuals who score high on this component would seek attention and affection if necessary through misbehaviour or indiscriminate friendliness. The component can be seen, perhaps, in Bowlby's terms, as a kind of anxious attachment. Since we cannot show that we have succeeded in measuring anxious attachment, we have called the dimension 'childlike attachment'. We again measured it through a score which we only used where all four questions had been answered.

These different manifestations of attachment difficulties were strongly related to age. Children over the age of 11 scored on average much more highly on 'aloofness' than those who were aged ten or under ($p<0.001$). The pattern was reversed for 'childlike attachment' where the younger children had higher scores than older ones ($p<0.001$). Female children were somewhat less 'aloof' than male ones ($p=0.02$).

In the eyes of social workers, childlike attachment was particularly difficult for foster carers. We asked the workers to rate each of the foster children on a four-point scale: 'From what you know of the child before this placement would you describe her or him as "easy" (e.g. affectionate and lively), "somewhat difficult" (e.g. enuretic or mildly hyperactive), "difficult" (e.g. hyperactive) or "very difficult" (e.g. severely hyperactive)'. This rating correlated 0.39 with our childlike attachment score ($p<0.001$) but was only weakly correlated with the aloofness score ($r=0.14$, $p=0.02$).

The strong correlation between age and our two measures of disturbed attachment behaviour meant that the latter were related to those parts of the child's career in the care system associated with age. For example, those expected to go out into some form of independent living were older and therefore had significantly higher aloofness scores. Similarly, those who scored high on childlike attachment were more likely to have entered the system at a relatively young age. These associations illustrate particular difficulties likely to face those fostering children of different ages – the wear and tear on the nerves of primary school age children eager for attention and willing to misbehave to get it, and the restrained emotional response of some older foster children preparing to make their way in the world on their own.

Our two measures of attachment were associated with our first two measures of success at a very high level of significance. The placements of children who displayed childlike attachment were much less likely to be judged successful at either point. So too were the placements of 'aloof' children. These associations remained when we took account of age. Indeed age ceased to be significantly related to these success outcomes when we took account of our measures of attachment style. From this point of view it may be that how you relate is more important than how old you are.

Aloofness was not significantly related to disruption. Childlike attachment, however, was. Those who were attached in this way were much more likely to disrupt, a finding which remained when we took account of age.

Disturbance and strengths among those aged three and over

Our main measure of disturbance was taken from the Goodman *Strengths and Difficulties Questionnaire* (Goodman and Scott 1997). At a descriptive level, findings derived from this instrument suggested that many of the children were certainly perceived as difficult but that many also had attractive traits. For example, of a third it was said to be certainly true that they were restless, overactive and could not stay still for long. A similar proportion was said with certainty to be argumentative, a similar proportion to be prone to bad temper and an even higher proportion (45%) to have poor concentration. By contrast, half were said with certainty to be kind to younger children, and more than four in ten to be helpful if someone was ill.

The website for this score provides instructions for creating a total score with 'norms' for an ordinary population. These differ somewhat depending on whether the scale is completed by parents or teachers. (Although the scale can be completed by children, no norms are given for this.) A comparison between the scores we obtained and those for an 'ordinary' population of 5–15-year-olds described by their parents suggests that the sample of foster children did indeed have a high degree of mental ill-health. Sixty per cent were 'borderline' or above for mental ill-health whereas the comparable percentage for a normal population would be 20 per cent. Fifty-one per cent were 'abnormal' with scores of 17 or above as opposed to an expected 10 per cent in a normal population.

This score rose with age with the highest average score found among those aged 11 to 15 after which the average decreased. Children rated as difficult to foster by their social workers had significantly higher scores on this measure ($r=0.46$, $p<0.001$) as did children said to have 'other difficulties' and children said to have learning difficulties (both associations significant at less than 0.001 on a one-way analysis of variance). This measure of disturbance also correlated with our measure of aloofness ($r=0.28$, $p<0.001$) and even more strongly with our measure of childlike attachment ($r=0.67$, $p<0.001$). A regression analysis showed that half the variation in this measure (52%) was accounted for by our two measures of disturbed attachment. This suggests that the measures overlap, with both covering behaviour characteristic of disturbed attachment. It also suggests that their origins in temperament or upbringing may well be similar.

In terms of the origins of this 'disturbance', it was interesting that a number of variables were not correlated with the Goodman total score. These included sex, age at which the child entered the care system, and evidence of physical abuse or neglect. Sexual abuse was associated with disturbance but the association was not particularly strong ($p=0.013$). The strong association was with emotional abuse (one-way analysis of variance, $p=0.003$). This association could have arisen because social workers were more likely to notice emotional abuse when the child was disturbed. The most likely interpretation, however, is that the emotional abuse produced the disturbance. This again suggests that within this sample emotional abuse has a greater effect on mental health in the longer term than even sexual or physical abuse.

Behavioural problems

The Goodman scale was constructed for use with ordinary populations and over a wide age range. It does not include some of the more extreme forms of behaviour which may be found in 'care populations', or which may only be displayed by particular age groups. Some of these forms of behaviour are highly problematic for carers and we constructed an *a priori* list to identify them.

The carers were asked: 'Since the child has been living with you he or she may have faced you with problems. Please indicate if this is so and whether the problem seems to be getting better or worse.' Table 10.3 sets out their answers.

Table 10.3 Problems and changes

	n	No problem (%)	Problem getting better (%)	No change (%)	Problem getting worse (%)
Sexual behaviour	452	72	16	6	6
Not going to school	437	86	9	4	1
Bedwetting/soiling	452	74	19	6	2
Alcohol/drugs	442	91	5	3	2
Self-harm/attempted suicide	439	91	7	2	–
Violence/aggression	442	59	27	8	6
Running away	444	86	10	3	1
Continual disobedience	450	54	29	10	7
Stealing	447	74	15	7	4
Lying	451	47	25	18	10
Eating problems	455	64	22	10	4

Source: Foster carer questionnaire at Time 1.

The most common problem – and the only one where the numbers of those said to have improved did not outweigh the number of those said to stay the same or get worse – was lying. This may be an index of the difficulty for foster children of accommodating their previous lives, habits and values to their new environment without alienating their foster carers. Whatever the explanation, the high proportion of those with a problem who are said to improve must be encouraging.

Many of these problems are only likely to be displayed by older children. For example, those under the age of three would not be expected to run away from their foster home. This observation was supported by a component analysis we carried out on the 11 problems in Table 10.3. (We treated the data as a kind of scale whereby no change was 'better' than 'problem getting worse' but not so good as 'problem getting better' which in turn was not so good as 'no problem'.) The main component accounted for 28 per cent of the variation and was particularly heavily loaded on not going to school, drugs and alcohol, and running away. By contrast, it had negative loadings on bedwetting/soiling and eating problems. A factor score from this component correlated significantly with age (r=0.41, $p<0.001$).

We interpreted this component as a measure of deviancy rather than disturbance and named the measure derived from it the 'social behaviour' score. It was positively correlated with a sub-scale measuring 'conduct problems' on the Goodman questionnaire (r=0.46, $p<0.001$) but only weakly correlated with sub-scales measuring emotional problems (r=0.15, $p=0.01$) and hyperactivity (r=0.1, NS). We tried to 'explain' this variable in terms of others. The most efficient combination of variables we could find was: high childlike attachment ($p<0.001$), age ($p<0.001$), unhappy at school ($p=0.009$) and has many friends ($p=0.031$). Taken together these variables account for a quarter of the variation in our social behaviour measure. The pattern suggests (it certainly does not prove) that children who are anxious about their relationships and unhappy at school may as they age 'get in with the wrong crowd' and develop difficult behaviour as a result.

The second component produced by our analysis of these problems related more closely to the kind of disturbed behaviour measured by the Goodman scale with which its factor scores were significantly associated (r=0.52, $p<0.001$). It was most highly loaded on bedwetting/soiling. However, it was also strongly connected with aggression, disobedience, stealing, lying and eating problems. In contrast to the first component it had negative loadings on failure to attend school and on involvement in drink or drugs. Its factor scores were significantly associated with our measure of childlike attachment (r=0.48, $p<0.001$) and with conduct problems (r=0.45, $p<0.001$) and hyperactivity (r=0.45, $p<0.001$). It was uncorrelated with age. (As seen below the association was, in a sense, masked by the negative relationship between age and childlike attachment.)

We tried to predict this score in the same way as our measure for social behaviour. The best combination of variables we found included our childlike attachment score ($p<0.001$), age (the older the child the 'better' the score) ($p<0.001$) and distress over contact with birth family ($p=0.011$). This combination accounted for a quarter of the variation in the score. The score was unrelated to happiness at school or to friends. It may be that it captures the distress of younger children who show their unhappiness within the foster home rather than outside it.

Both measures were strongly associated with our outcomes. The associations remained highly significant after we had taken account of age.

Development measures

We asked the foster carers to assess the development of the foster children in the areas monitored in the looking after children programme (Ward 1998). These covered health, education, special skills and interests, work, self-confidence, emotional ties, existence of close friends, behaviour in social situations, emotional and behavioural development and self-care skills. Obviously, some areas were only relevant for certain children. Ratings related to work and school, for example, could only be made for those in the appropriate age groups.

The results illustrated the differences among foster children. Whereas three-quarters (77%) were said to be in good health, a small number (2%) were said to be frequently ill or failing to thrive. A fifth (21%) were said to be performing at school at a level well below their ability but one in six (16%) were apparently performing better than expected. A quarter of those available for work were out of work and not trying to get any. By contrast, a further quarter were in stable work and committed to it.

We compared these ratings with similar ratings made by the social workers on the same children. The results were reasonably encouraging. The pairs of ratings were all significantly correlated at levels varying from 0.27 ($p<0.001$) to 0.8 ($p<0.001$).

We created two scores, one summarising the foster carer's ratings of the child's development and the other the social worker's. The two scores correlated with each other ($r=0.62$, $p<0.001$). Each was significantly associated with our three outcome measures. Irrespective of who made the rating, the higher the development score, the better the outcomes – a result which was unshaken when we took account of age.

Combining the variables: dimensions for assessment

We carried out one final component analysis. The variables we tried to summarise were: age, sex, the hyperactivity, emotional problems, conduct disorder and peer problems scores on the Goodman Questionnaire, our social behaviour and troubled scores, our measures of childlike attachment and aloofness and the various development scores rated by the social workers and the foster carers (we used whichever score was available, or the average if we had both).

The first three components accounted for half the variance. The first component which accounted for a third of the variation could be described as 'doing well'. It was highly loaded on all the 'positive scores'. High scorers on the second component would be young, high on childlike attachment and would have strong ties with at least one adult. High scorers on the third component would be older, high on our 'deviancy score', high on conduct disorders, but nevertheless doing relatively well at school or work.

So the analysis supported the obvious hypothesis that children who are 'doing well' in one respect tend to be doing well in others. It also suggested that there may be particular types of difficulty – one associated with troubled relationships among younger children, and one associated with a kind of socialised delinquency.

Combining the variables: predicting outcomes

We examined how far these 'personality' variables could be used to predict our outcomes. The variables we used as 'candidates' for predictors were:

- the sub-scales of the Goodman total score (peer problems, emotional problems, conduct problems and hyperactivity)
- the social behaviour score from our problem list
- the 'troubled' score from our problem list
- age
- whether the child was perceived as 'wanting to leave' (motivation)
- the child's development score (as derived from the foster carer ratings)
- our two measures of disturbed attachment.

These variables are associated with each other so that their contributions to prediction 'overlap'. We wanted to pick the best 'set'.[1]

As might be expected the 'best set' differed between the different outcome measures.

- The first success rating was best predicted by a combination of the child's development score, the conduct disorder score and motivation.
- The second success rating was best predicted by motivation and the peer problem score.
- Disruption was best predicted by the childlike attachment score and the social behaviour score.

All these associations were in the expected direction. For example, children who scored 'high' on the conduct problem score had worse outcomes on all three measures as did children who scored high on childlike attachment.

This pattern suggests that outcomes may be influenced by three different but related variables – the child's social behaviour (as measured by the conduct score and the social behaviour score), the child's relationship difficulties as measured by the childlike attachment score, and the child's motivation (whether he or she wanted to be there).

We tested this hypothesis by trying to predict each of the outcome measures using three variables: the social behaviour score, the motivation measure and the childlike attachment score. The results were broadly but not completely in keeping with our predictions. When all three variables were used at once:

- Social behaviour was related to all three outcomes.
- Childlike attachment was negatively associated with the first success rating ($p<0.001$), almost significantly associated with the second success rating ($p=0.062$) and disruption ($p=0.058$).
- Motivation was associated with the first success rating ($p<0.001$), but not significantly associated with the other two outcomes measures although the association was as predicted ($p=0.142$ and $p=0.102$).

Conclusion

The foster children in the sample often showed admirable traits – for example, kindness to others. Many of them were also seen as difficult and the problems they presented took different forms – disability, disturbed behaviour within the home, aloofness, and anti-social behaviour outside the home.

In general, disability did not predict outcome. Physical impairment was, if anything, associated with good outcomes. The other difficulties we have discussed were almost all associated with poor ones. Children who had them 'did worse' than children who did not. Similarly, children who were said to have many 'good' traits did better than others.

Some of the problems seemed to have their origins in the children's histories. The great majority of them were thought to have been abused. Those who were said to have been emotionally abused fared particularly badly. Such emotional abuse seemed to be more important in predicting outcomes than the existence of other more concrete forms of abuse. In keeping with this finding, attachment difficulties predicted poor outcomes and were strongly associated with measures of disturbed behaviour. Such correlations suggest but do not prove causation.

Overall, the results support the relevant hypotheses in our model. Poor outcomes are more likely when the child is seen as difficult, does not want to stay in the placement and is not perceived as having redeeming features. The results suggest, but do not prove, that the difficulties often have their origins in the child's early relationships. These can be reflected in their behaviour within the foster home. They may also be played out in social situations.

Note

1. We used stepwise regression for the two success ratings and forward conditional logistic regression for disruption.

Chapter Eleven

Birth Families: Characteristics and Patterns of Contact

Introduction

This chapter is about birth families and their contacts with the foster child.[1] No one doubts the importance of this issue. Qualitative studies have shown how children and their families struggle to make sense of the child's entry to the care system (e.g. Bullock *et al*. 1993; Fisher *et al*. 1986; Kahan 1979; Loveday 1985; Stein and Carey 1986; Triseliotis *et al*. 1995; Whitaker 1985). In doing so they variously blame themselves, each other and the social workers, strive or fail to strive to get back together and variously find as time passes that absence makes the heart fonder, that family loyalties prohibit new attachments, that past relationships become as ghosts or that memories and their links to identity grow idealised or faint.

In keeping with some of these observations, official and professional advice is that children and their families should be kept together where possible and kept in touch if not (Department of Health 1989; Thoburn 1994). The reasons advanced are diverse. Some relate to the economic and other advantages of preventive work. Many relate to the inability of the state to act as a good parent. It is seen as incapable of providing permanent security or even a reasonable education. Placements do not always work out and a fall-back is needed. Children who lose their parents often lose touch with their siblings and thus potential nephews and nieces, not to mention their own grandparents, aunts and uncles. And even without these arguments, children usually want their own families, and their parents want them. It is neither legally possible nor ethically desirable to separate them.

So the rationale for contacts is that they are needed to keep family relationships in repair, to prevent unhelpful idealisation, to provide a sense of roots and identity, and, above all perhaps, to increase the chance of return home.

Other policies promote similar ends. Thus the official view is that where children are looked after in the care system, siblings should, if possible, be placed together. In addition thought should be given to placing children with relatives – a step which research suggests may be associated with greater stability (Hunt 2001). Wider but related trends include the growing popularity of open adoption, the increased availability of information on birth families for adult adoptees and, at the other end of the spectrum, experiments with family group conferences.

Such developments reflect ideology as well professional views of good practice, for there is an injustice in punishing the victims of poverty by removing their children, and a desire to ameliorate this process for families when possible.

Not surprisingly, research which has taken place within this context has generally assumed that lack of contact with parents is in itself bad for the child and does not simply reflect a bad situation (e.g. Millham *et al.* 1986). There are powerful accounts of the feelings of loss, uncertain identity, and yearning experienced by some who have been adopted or long-term in the care system (e.g. Fever 1994; Kahan 1979; Triseliotis 1973). There are assertions stemming from research by Weinstein (1960) that more frequent contact is associated with a better self-concept or well-being and also that contacts facilitate return home. There is English and American research support for the idea that relative placements have considerable advantages (Berridge and Cleaver 1987; Hunt 2001; Lahti 1982; Maluccio *et al.* 1986; Rowe *et al.* 1984; Rowe *et al.* 1989) and that siblings should be kept together (Fratter *et al.* 1991; Wedge and Mantle 1991). By contrast, there is a widespread belief that care progressively disrupts contacts with birth families and does not simply keep for longer those whose contacts are less (Millham *et al.* 1986).

Unfortunately this evidence is not conclusive. Qualitative material does not always suggest that children want to return home or even to have contact with their parents. They may want to have nothing to do with their parents, to identify with their foster carers, or to have contact without return, or to live independently with regular contact with their families (see e.g. Arden 1977; Rowe *et al.* 1984; Sinclair and Gibbs 1998). Research has failed to find consistent evidence that contact promotes well-being or suggested both positive and negative effects (Rowe *et al.* 1984; Thorpe 1974; Wolkind 1977). Contacts between parents and children in the care system are certainly associated with return (Aldgate 1980; Bullock *et al.* 1993; Quinton and Rutter 1988). It is not certain they produce it (Quinton *et al.* 1997). Nor is there clear evidence that contacts are eroded by the care system.

Against this background, our qualitative material has suggested that birth families and contacts with them are a major issue in foster care. It has not suggested that this issue can be resolved by simple rules of thumb – for example, to the effect that 'contact is always good'. This chapter will provide statistical evidence relevant to this debate. In more detail we will examine:

- evidence on the birth families from which the children come
- whether children placed with relatives do better
- whether children placed with siblings do better
- the frequency, character and purpose of contacts with birth families
- the determinants of contact frequency
- the relationship between contact frequency and outcome
- prohibitions on contact and outcome.

Family composition

We asked the social workers to give us information on the child's family, which we defined as the family unit which they would be most likely to contact or return to on leaving. Table 11.1 sets out their replies.

Table 11.1 Composition of foster children's birth families

	n	%
Birth mother only	92	32
Birth father only	18	6
Birth mother and birth father	38	13
Birth mother and step-father/cohab	48	18
Birth father and step-mother/cohab	9	4
Adoptive parents	30	10
Other relations	24	9
No family	11	4
Other	15	5

Source: Social worker questionnaire at Time 1.

As can be seen, 'traditional' families involving the child's birth father and mother were rare. Fewer than one in seven conformed to this pattern. The most common form was a lone parent family, generally but not always involving the child's own mother. Around four in ten of the children had this kind of family. The next most common form was a step-family which accounted for around one in five.

At first sight the most striking feature of Table 11.1 is the frequency of 'other relations' and – particularly – of adoptive parents. The number of adoptive families in the population is clearly nothing approaching 10 per cent. Some of those identified in this way were older children who had experienced an adoption breakdown. Seven out of ten, however, had plans for adoption and the same proportion were adopted when followed up three years later. Our question asked the social workers to 'identify the family unit which the child would be most likely to contact or return to on leaving'. Where the plans were for adoption, they probably identified this as an adoptive family rather than the original birth family.

The distribution set out in Table 11.1 did not differ by ethnicity or sex. There were, however, quite large differences by age, with adoptive parents being involved with younger children and lone fathers or fathers and step-mothers being involved with older ones. Children with different kinds of family did not differ significantly in terms of our success ratings or the likelihood of disruption.

Overall, the children's backgrounds seem to be marked by confusion and loss. Almost all of them had, in a sense, more than one birth family with the potential for confused and conflicting emotions that this implies. Inevitably, they had experienced at least one loss when they came into the care system. Most, however, had experienced a series of losses as first one parent and then another stopped living with them. Some of them had suffered additional losses when arrangements set up with relatives or adoptive parents failed to work out.

Relative placements

Placements with relatives were almost certainly under-represented in our sample. Our original survey found 71 relatives among 944 foster carers, a rate of just under 8 per cent. By contrast, we had only 25 children known to be placed with relative foster carers, a rate of just over 4 per cent.

Research on relative fostering is now growing and the results have generally been favourable to it (Broad 1999; Rowe et al. 1984). We had expected the small number of placements with relatives to have a below average rate of breakdown. In fact the rate was very little different. When we took account of background factors in the children those fostered with relatives were, if anything, slightly more likely to experience a disruption although the difference was not significant ($p=0.15$).

Why did we fail to find that relatives did better? One explanation may be bias in our sample. Relative carers who were having successful placements may have seen themselves as relatives rather than foster carers and experienced our questionnaire as intrusive or irrelevant. It is also possible that many relative carers would not be eligible for the survey. Cost-conscious social services departments may fear the financial implications of treating children happily placed with relatives under fostering regulations – preferring to go for 'cheaper' options such as residence orders or support under the preventive sections of the Children Act. Fostering may only be used when there are grounds for thinking that the carers need particular support. Or the relationship between relative fostering and breakdown may have changed as the Children Act regulations encourage social workers to take greater risks in relative fostering.

However that may be, qualitative material suggested that, as might be expected, placement with relatives had both advantages and disadvantages. Things could go well:

> The main carer [is] her maternal grandmother. Placement suits her needs perfectly. She has daily contact with her mother who cannot care for her due to illness and also lives with her elder sister. (Social worker)

> They are our own grandchildren and we have brought them up as our own and have limited contact with their mother, so they are quite happy with the situation, and so is their mother and we as foster parents feel everything is going just fine. (Foster carer)

Such placements were not, however, necessarily without problems. Some argued that the placements were made uncritically and with too little support:

> Main placement was with extended family…I do not feel the family's assessment fully explored their ability to deal with children with emotional difficulties… Their difficulties in dealing with those problems have, I believe, led to a degree of further emotional abuse having been experienced by Sharon. (Social worker)

> I believe we've been treated second class due to fostering a [-shire] child in a different county and she is family. I equally believe fostering within family is

sometimes harder for carers though more stable and long-term for child. (Foster carer)

In some cases the difficulties could be exacerbated by family conflicts or by a feeling on the part of the birth parent that placement with other relatives put additional barriers to the child's return to them:

> Social workers need to take account of extended family problems in such placements. Family dynamics are inevitably much more powerful/subversive in kinship care. (Social worker)

It could be harder for carers to deal with some problems in a context where they were subject to family scrutiny and advice:

> Carers have had some difficulties in dealing with natural mum's mental health difficulties and pressures put on them because they are family. (Social worker)

Sometimes placements exacerbated family relationships:

> A fall out between the carer and her sister (Naomi's mother) caused them to request serious changes to contact routine...(i.e. previously the carers had supervised, used their house as a venue etc.). This angered the mother and caused failure to attend contact, a contested court hearing and a S34 order and problems for Naomi and her siblings. (Social worker)

> Because I was a relative carer when the placement broke down the rest of my family were affected. As a result communications between myself and my family were a little strained. (Foster carer)

So relative placements offer a mix of advantages and disadvantages. On the positive side there is continuity, the commitment of relatives, and the fact that they should have a good sense of what they are taking on. On the negative side, the placement may get caught up in existing family quarrels and myths. It may also be the case that the local authority finds it difficult to think through its attitude to fostering, failing to provide the supports (money, training, social work visits) which are available to other carers and seeing no reason to subject the carers to an equally rigorous assessment:

> Placing a child with family members can have positive outcome and be in the child's best interests. However if there is a degree of animosity between family members this can be difficult to resolve as family tend to do what they feel is best. (Social worker)

Siblings

There is a general presumption that children should be placed with siblings where possible. This raises questions about what is meant by siblings – children may have brothers and sisters they have never seen, but be brought up with children to whom they are genetically unrelated. However, these subtleties apart, it is argued that children have a right to be placed with their siblings and their placements are more likely to succeed if they do (Department of Health 1989; Maclean 1999; Quinton *et al.* 1998).

Frequency of placement with siblings

Most of these children (92%) were said to have birth or step-brothers or sisters, a figure higher than, although comparable with, that found in other research, which suggests a percentage in the mid eighties (Bilson and Barker 1992; Wedge and Phelan 1986). It was, however, uncommon for them to be in the same foster home. Only a quarter of the children with siblings had one living with them. This figure is very similar to the proportion of adoptive placements said to involve a sibling (British Agencies for Adoption and Fostering 1997). It is lower than the 37 per cent reported for Bradford by Maclean (1999) but this study included respite fostering and excluded 'traditional long-term and relative fostering' and thus covered a very different sample.

The likelihood of being placed with a sibling dropped steadily with the age of the foster child. Thirty-nine per cent of those aged four or less lived with one of their siblings as did 31 per cent of those aged five to ten. The same was true of only 18 per cent of those aged 11 to 15 and 11 per cent of those aged 16 or more.

This trend is not simply the result of elder children having fewer brothers or sisters. They had on average rather more – an unsurprising fact since they had had more time to acquire them. Some of these, however, were too old to be in the care system. No doubt partly for this reason, among those who had siblings the proportion with siblings who were looked after dropped from 76 per cent among the under fives to 53 per cent among those aged 16 or over.

The fact that older children had fewer siblings in the care system does not fully account for the fact that they were less likely to live with one. Overall, around six out of ten (66%) of those with siblings had at least one sibling or step-sibling within the care system. Around four out of ten of those in this position had a sibling with them. The likelihood of their doing so again dropped steadily with age from 60 per cent among the under fives to 19 per cent among those aged 16 or over.

The reasons for this drop are probably varied. Younger children may be more likely to enter the care system because of problems affecting the whole family; older ones may have more individual reasons such as difficult behaviour. Older children need a room of their own; younger ones may at a pinch be put in a room together. There may be good practice reasons for not placing extremely rivalrous children together. And over the course of a long care career, a great variety of reasons may lead to children who were initially placed together finding themselves placed apart. Whatever the reasons, loss of close contact with siblings is a further loss which foster children commonly have to face.

Outcomes and living with siblings

The effects of placement with siblings have been a matter of some doubt. Early work (George 1970; Parker 1966) found that children placed with siblings were more likely to have placements which broke down (although in Parker's case the association was not significant). Rowe and her colleagues reported in 1984 that children in long-stay foster care seemed untroubled by separation from siblings – possibly because they were separated before they got to know one another. By contrast, Berridge and Cleaver (1987) reported higher rates of breakdown when children were separated from all their siblings. More recent research (Fratter *et al.* 1991; Wedge and Mantle 1991) suggests that children placed with siblings have better outcomes.

More recently, Quinton and his colleagues (1998) reported a strong and significant association between placement with siblings and good outcomes. It seems likely, however, that this effect depends on the existence of emotional abuse. Children who have been particularly rejected seem to do better if placed with siblings and worse if placed apart from them (Rushton *et al.* 2001).

In this study, children who had siblings and were placed with them were less likely to disrupt than when placed apart from them. The difference was marginal when the contrast was between living with one sibling or living with no other sibling – 21 per cent of the former placements disrupted as against 25 per cent of the latter. However, none of the small number living with two or more siblings disrupted and the overall difference was significant. It should be remembered that younger children were more likely to be living with siblings than older ones. Younger children were also less likely to experience a disruption. The apparent association between disruption and living with siblings was not significant (although still in the same direction, $p=0.28$) if we took account of the age.

An unexpected finding was that children who had siblings living with their birth parents were significantly more likely to disrupt and scored significantly worse on judgements of placement success. Where the child had no siblings at home only 12 per cent of the placements disrupted. This rose to 28 per cent where the child had one sibling at home and 42 per cent when there was more than one at home (a highly significant trend, $p<0.001$). Children who had siblings at home were on average older. The association with outcome remained, however, when age was taken into account.

In keeping with the findings of Rushton and his colleagues (2001) emotional abuse was significantly associated with disruption when the child had no siblings in the foster home and also when the child had siblings looked after elsewhere. In other conditions the association between emotional abuse and disruption was not significant although it was in the same direction.

So what do these findings suggest about the relationship between placement with siblings and outcome? First, there is no evidence that it is in general harmful. So if children want to be placed together, there must be a presumption that this should happen unless there are good reasons against it. Second, there may be some cases where a number of young children are removed together for family reasons, see themselves as a family unit and support each other. Separation in such cases could well be harmful. Third, some studies may have overestimated the associations between having siblings in the same placement and good outcomes, by being unable to take account of age or the association with having siblings at home. Fourth, those with siblings at home may well be more difficult than others (they scored higher on our social difficulty and disturbance measures). They may move into care for 'individual' reasons, for example, because they have unusually difficult temperaments, or they have, for some other reason, suffered from being 'scapegoated' at home (Quinton *et al.* 1998). Additionally, they may feel jealous towards those who are left behind, and this may be a factor in their poorer outcomes.

Contact

In this section we give some descriptive data on contacts with birth families. We then tackle the vexed question of the impact of contacts on outcomes.

Purposes of contact

Cleaver (2000) found that social workers saw contact as mainly serving one of four purposes – preparing for return, keeping parent and child in touch, improving relationships and providing reassurance. Our own study explored similar issues. Where there was some contact between family and child, we asked the social workers what they themselves saw as its purpose. We provided a fixed list of possible reasons, together with an 'other' category which, it turned out, was rarely used. The workers were also invited to tick more than one purpose if they thought this appropriate. The percentages we give below are based on all those who received at least one visit.

The most striking result of this exercise was the rarity with which the social workers ticked 'prepare for return home'. In only 11 per cent of cases did they do so. The most common reason given was to 'maintain relationships' (81% of cases), followed by 'to meet children's wishes' (47%) and 'to meet parents' wishes' (34%). Other reasons – 'to allow for assessment' (10%), 'to meet the requirements of the court' (18%) and 'other' (10%) – were given less frequently.

These different purposes fell into two main clusters. Visits that were intended to provide assessment, meet court requirements or prepare for return home overlapped. If the social workers ticked one of these purposes they were very much more likely to tick one of the others. They were also more likely to tick 'to meet parents' wishes', although the level of significance was lower (albeit still less than 0.005). Interestingly they were significantly less likely to see the visit as intended to meet the wishes of the child. It is hoped that children's wishes were taken into account by the court and the social workers at an earlier stage. At the time, however, they were clearly not the main thing in the social workers' minds.

The second group of purposes was focused on maintaining relationships, meeting the wishes of the parents and meeting the wishes of the child. Social workers who ticked one of these purposes were significantly more likely to tick one of the others.

These results emphasise the moral or ethical imperative behind visits. If parents or children want them they should not be lightly denied. They may also emphasise the need for visits to provide an anchor for identity and a backstop for future emergencies (reasons perhaps for maintaining relationships). They do not suggest that with this group the key role of visits is to promote return home.

Role of foster carers in visits

We asked the foster carers whether the social services expected them to play a role in these contacts. Commonly (in around seven out of ten cases) they did.

Again we provided a fixed list of possible roles together with an 'other' category. The most common role (ticked in 35% of cases where there was contact) was 'keeping an eye on things'. This was followed by 'providing support for the children', 'providing transport', and 'assessing what goes on', which were all ticked in about a quarter of cases. In 15 per cent of cases, carers said they were expected to support birth parents.

Frequency of contacts

We asked the foster carers how often the children saw a variety of relatives. The question covered fathers, mothers, grandparents, aunts and uncles, and step-parents.

Nearly half the sample (44%) saw at least one of these relatives weekly or more often. Nearly seven out of ten (69%) saw a relative monthly or more often. Around three in ten seemed somewhat isolated from their relatives, seeing none of them as often as monthly. One in nine (11%) were said to see no relatives at all.

The frequency and likelihood of contact varied with the type of relative involved. Nearly half saw their mother at least monthly. The comparable figure for fathers was 26 per cent, and for brothers and sisters (taking the most frequent visitor) 45 per cent. Only 19 per cent saw a maternal grandparent this often and only 11 per cent a paternal grandparent. Aunts/uncles were seen as often as this by around 15 per cent and step-parents by around 11 per cent.

Time, distance and other barriers to contact

The most influential study of contact was carried out by Millham and his colleagues (1986). They felt that the care system operated in such a way as to reduce contact with families over time. They also distinguished between formal barriers to contact (i.e. prohibition on contact for one or more family members) and informal barriers. The latter included distance from home, discouragement of contact by the carers, and the unnatural and awkward circumstances in which family and child had to deal with each other.

In keeping with Millham and his colleagues' conclusions, weekly contacts with at least one family member were significantly less common among those who had been longer in placement. There was, however, no way of knowing whether this reflected selection – those who were visited frequently returned home – or discouragement – parents 'gave up' on children who did not return home and visited them less frequently.

Partly, perhaps, in response to the earlier research findings the frequency with which contact is forbidden appears to have dropped. According to the foster carers 27 per cent of the sample had at least one potential visitor who had been forbidden contact. The figure for those who had been in the care system for at least six months was slightly higher (29%) but in any case considerably lower than the 49 per cent reported by Millham et al. (1986) for those staying over six months in the early 1980s. Where someone had been forbidden contact, the likelihood that any relative was in weekly contact was less (37% v. 47%, $p=0.05$) – a finding in keeping with Millham and his colleagues' analysis.

As these researchers would also have predicted frequency of contact was related to the carer's attitude to it. Satisfaction with the arrangements was higher when the child was visited weekly or more often ($p=0.0001$). It also rose with the foster carer's rating of the reliability of the visits ($p<0.001$). These associations leave questions of cause unclear. Are carers satisfied because families visit regularly? Or do families visit regularly because carers are pleased to see them? Or is there some other factor that explains the association? Other qualitative research strongly suggests that some of the association arises because of the reluctance of families to visit foster families whom they perceive as disapproving of them or as rivals (e.g. Aldgate 1980).

As Cleaver (2000) found, distance from birth family was strongly related to frequency of contact. The proportions of children with weekly contact dropped from 60 per cent among those fostered within one or two miles from their families, through 53 per cent (three to five miles), 45 per cent (six to ten miles) to 29 per cent (11 miles or more).

We also expected that distance would be related to plans for restoration. Contrary to what we expected, current plans were not related to distance. According to the social workers, 24 per cent of those for whom rehabilitation was planned lived more than ten miles away from their nearest family member, as did exactly the same proportion of those for whom rehabilitation was not planned. So social workers were no more likely to be planning returns for those who were close to their families than they were if the family was far away.

Social work plans were, however, strongly related to whether a child returned. Sixty-five per cent of those for whom social workers planned a return home had done so on follow-up. The same was true of only 5 per cent of those for whom the social workers had not planned return home. By contrast there was no association between distance and the likelihood of return.

Foster carers' views of contacts

We asked the foster carers how satisfied they were with the arrangements for contact between the child and her or his family. In one in eight cases (12%), the question could not be answered since the child had effectively no contact. However, in four in ten of the cases they were satisfied or very satisfied with the arrangements, and in around a third of the cases they had mixed views. In around a sixth (16%) they were either dissatisfied or very dissatisfied with them.

A rather similar distribution was found when we asked them whether they themselves found the visits stressful or enjoyable. In cases where the child was visited, one in six found the visits stressful or very stressful. One in five found them enjoyable (hardly anyone found them very enjoyable). The majority opted for a middle rating and said their experience was 'mixed'.

Their open-ended comments revealed a wide range of experience. Some of this diversity related to who visited and how important their visits seemed to be. Grandparents and siblings could play a key role, as well as birth parents:

> Anna's maternal grandad and his partner who do not live locally ring about once per week and send letters. They try to see her every month and take her out. Her mother has given up and does not want much contact. Anna is upset about her mother… She loves visits from her grandfather.

> Mixed feelings when mum does not turn up but loves going to see his brother and sister.

As implied above, the visits also varied in their impact. On the positive side, some children were said to welcome the experience:

> Very pleased for child. Child looks forward to contact.

> From the very beginning we set out to have a good relationship with the birth family. It hasn't been easy but we have learnt to see their (especially mum's) side of things. We have built up a strong relationship to the extent that mum goes on holiday with us occasionally and we socialise with the maternal grandma. Because of how we have reacted to the family the child has responded positively.

Sometimes things were more problematic and mixed:

> The child's maternal grandma is an excellent support both to us and her grandchild. Her positive loving attitude has helped us all. The father has visited the house drunk and uninvited, insisting he sees his children and has never hurt them.

The main problems appeared to relate to the children's behaviour after the visit. Foster carers reported that some children were rude, others regressed to more childish behaviour, others tried to play them off against the birth parents, others had nightmares and others were generally confused and distressed:

> Sometimes she comes back upset and that upsets all the family. She plays me up a lot when she has to leave dad and gets me uncomfortable and doesn't like us much.

> We have to pick up the pieces when John's mother promises him impossible things. He now uses her for material gain.

> The child is often very distressed after contact with mother. His behaviour at school and at home improves significantly when he does not have regular contact with mum and he is much happier and more relaxed.

In the foster carers' eyes, the reasons for upset were varied. Some children wanted more contact with parents than parents were willing to provide. Others felt that the children were being pressured into contact which they did not want. Others were upset by the way the parents treated them – promising the impossible, or saying the foster carers did not love them, or failing to keep appointments, or shouting and increasing the unhelpful excitement, or keeping the children up late and generally accustoming them to a disordered way of life. Some carers said that the birth parents tried to set the foster children against them:

> The contact with the children is going well, but lately one of her sons does not want to go for the contact because the birth mother calls me names and speaks against me to them.

These comments were in keeping with the statistical evidence. Around four in ten of the children (43%) were said to experience no distress. A further fifth (22%) experienced distress but the problem was said to be improving. A quarter (24%) were rated as being distressed with no improvement. In one in nine cases the problem was said to be getting worse. This measure was quite strongly associated with the foster carer's satisfaction with contact from the child's point of view ($r=0.41$, $p<0.001$). It was significantly correlated with a rating of the degree to which the carer herself found the visits stressful.

Barriers to contact and return home

The general assumption is that the likelihood of return home is determined by the frequency of contact. In a sense this is almost certainly true. Social workers who perceive that a parent is unwilling to visit a child are almost certain to be less keen on planning for a return. Conversely plans for return are likely to be accompanied by determined efforts to ensure contact.

An interesting question is whether barriers to contact that do not have their origins in the child or birth family have an impact on return through their impact on contact. In practice none of our three 'barriers' to contact were significantly associated with return. Children were equally likely to return irrespective of how far the birth family lived from the foster home. They were slightly less likely to return if someone had been forbidden contact (14% v. 9%) but the difference was not significant. They were not more likely to return if the foster carer was more or less satisfied with the arrangements. (Where the carer was very satisfied return was more likely and where the carer was very dissatisfied return was less likely (20% v. 4%) but the percentages for satisfied, mixed views, and dissatisfied were almost exactly the same.)

The lack of association between return home and distance between birth family and foster home is interesting. Distance between the two homes is very strongly associated with low contact. It shows no association at all with the likelihood of return home. This does suggest that return is not determined by frequency of contact in any simple way.

Contact and outcomes

The mixed response of carers to visits is in keeping with research. Carers have generally been found to show less enthusiasm for contact and birth families than social workers (see Berridge 1997; Waterhouse 1997). The evidence on the relationship between visiting and breakdowns is similarly unclear, with some studies (Rowe *et al.* 1989) finding no relationship, while others do (Berridge and Cleaver 1987; Fratter *et al.* 1991).

In exploring these issues, we calculated a measure of frequency of contact, adding two if the child had weekly contact with at least one relative outside the house, and one if the child had monthly contact with a relative outside the house. The overall score ran from 0 (no monthly or weekly contact with anyone) to 3 (weekly contact with at least one relative and monthly contact with at least one other).

As others have found, contact was associated with *destinations*. It was more frequent when children returned to their birth families. It was lowest when the children were adopted. It was next lowest when the children remained with the same foster family. However, the measure was *not* significantly associated with any of our evaluative outcome measures (e.g. with the placement being seen as going well or badly). The lack of association remained when we took age and disturbance or adolescent deviance into account.

We examined whether outcomes might depend on the quality of contact. We based our measure of quality on the foster carer's judgements. We counted a child as having unsatisfactory contact if the carer said that contact was unreliable, unsatisfactory from the point of view of the child, or stressful to themselves or the social worker said that contact arrangements were unsatisfactory. Children who were said to be distressed at contact had 'worse scores' on this measure. So too did those who had lower success ratings at the time of the first survey. However, the measure was not related to disruption or the second success rating.

A possible explanation for lack of association between frequency of contact and outcomes was that we were putting together children for whom contact was important with others for whom it was less so. For this reason we predicted that: quality of contact and distress at contact will be more strongly related to outcomes when contact is frequent.

The result was contrary to our prediction. *In cases where no one visited monthly*, our measure of the quality of contact was strongly related to disruption. In this situation only 13 per cent of the children disrupted if there was no adverse comment. Twice the proportion disrupted if there was adverse comment.

We suspected that these results with quality of contact reflected the good outcomes of children who were adopted. These children had little contact with their birth families. They were therefore likely to score well on a measure based on negative comments on contact. However, the association remained significant even when adopted children were omitted.

Taken as a whole, these findings suggest that the relationship between contact and outcome is complex. It seems likely that the impact of contact depends not so much on frequency *per se*, as on the significance of the relatives for the child and the degree to which the child is settled in the placement. Our own initial hypotheses were wrong, because we mistakenly saw the causal process as lying in the effect that the relatives had on the child when they visited. So we assumed that the more frequently they visited, the greater would be the effect. It now seems more likely that the impact depends on the degree of unresolved yearning of the child for its relatives, and the impact of this on the child's desire to be in the placement and ability to attach to the carer.

Outcomes and forbidding contact

As we have seen, policies have changed on forbidding contact. It is now less common than it once was. There is clearly an important question over whether this strategy has a positive or negative effect on outcomes. What evidence did we have on this?

At the simplest level, those for whom contact is forbidden were slightly less likely to have placements which disrupt (18% as against 22%). They were significantly more likely to have a good second success rating ($p=0.026$ on a test for trend). So at first sight it seems unlikely that forbidding contact has a negative effect on outcomes.

All this leaves open the question of whether forbidding contact might have a 'good effect' in some cases and a negative or nil effect in others. In order to test this we examined whether the results were different when there was strong evidence that the children had been subjected to at least one form of abuse.

We first examined the relationship between forbidding contact and 'disruption' when the child had on this definition not been abused. Outcomes were rather better (but not significantly better) if there had been no prohibition. Nineteen per cent disrupted when there had been no restrictions on contact and 29 per cent when there had been. The situation was very different when there was strong evidence the child had been abused. Nearly a third (30%) disrupted when there was no prohibition. By contrast, only 11 per cent disrupted when contact had been restricted – a highly significant difference ($p=0.003$). The difference remained significant when we allowed for age and/or time in the placement (the factors associated both with restriction and with outcome). It was also significant when we allowed for our measures of disturbance and social behaviour (our usual method of testing the association between a factor and outcome).

Similar, but less striking, results were obtained when we looked at our success ratings. When there was strong evidence of abuse, restriction on contact significantly predicted a high second success rating even after allowing for the relevant background variables. It did not predict a high first success rating although the association was in the same direction.

The association between forbidding contact and lack of disruption held true for all categories of abuse. It was very rare for contact not to be forbidden to someone when there was strong evidence of sexual abuse. In this case the association between forbidding contact and avoidance of disruption was not significant. Nevertheless the percentage disrupting was consistently around three times as great where no one was forbidden contact (6% to 27% for sexual abuse ($p=0.17$), 10% to 31% for physical abuse ($p=0.05$), 14% to 35% for emotional abuse ($p<0.01$) and 7% to 25% for neglect ($p<0.01$)).

Table 11.2 sets out the basic pattern for all those for whom we had returns from the social workers in the first survey.

Table 11.2 Evidence of abuse, forbidding contact and disruption

Evidence of abuse	Contact forbidden	n	Disrupted (%)
None/some	Yes	21	29
	No	90	19
Strong	Yes	70	11
	No	153	31

Source: Social worker and foster carer questionnaires at Time 1. Disruption measured through all questionnaires at Time 2.

These results suggest that forbidding contact between the child and particular individuals can have a good effect on outcomes. It is likely that the effect is strongest when the child has been abused. It may even be restricted to such cases.

This, however, leaves open the mechanism that may underlie these effects. Our only evidence on this is negative. Forbidding contact is not associated with lower distress at contact either in the sample as a whole or among those who have been abused. We tested other possible explanations (for example, that the associations with disruption could have arisen because contact was more likely to be forbidden in cases involving adoption). None of our hypotheses were supported.

Conclusion

This chapter has dealt with a number of features of modern fostering and adoption which mark a sharp shift from earlier practice. The adoption of older children is now more common. Fostering by relatives is now encouraged, a practice which has informally always existed, but which is now supported by formal arrangements. Contact between foster children and birth families, once seen as disturbing and undesirable, is now seen as almost a right and its frequency has greatly increased. These all mark a change from the 'either/or' choices of earlier times when a child was either with its own family or, in intention if not in practice (for short-term stays in the workhouse were always common), cut off from family roots by early placement with strangers.

These changes raise a number of issues. First, the problematic nature of some fostering with relatives highlights the need to develop policy and practice in this area. In what circumstances should fostering by relatives be chosen as opposed to fostering by strangers, or support for relatives with a *de facto* foster child through means other than the fostering regulations? How far do these families get the financial and other support they need? (See Broad 1999.)

Second, as far as the social workers are concerned, very few contacts are maintained with the express purpose of preparing for return home. Other rationales must therefore be sought and these are likely to be ethical as well as pragmatic. Contacts should often be maintained, not because they are likely to have a good effect, but because parents or children want them. It is wrong to prevent them unless it can be shown that they are damaging.

Third, in general, placements with siblings and relatives cannot be shown – at least on the evidence of this study – to be damaging. If like is compared with like, neither form of placement is significantly associated with poor outcomes. Certainly both forms of placement have problems. However, foster children commonly yearn for their placements and many value placements with relatives. So the need is for care in making these placements and for additional support for them. The study certainly does not suggest that the frequency of these placements should be reduced.

Fourth, other things being equal, at least three of the parties concerned seemed to want contact. Social workers and foster carers were more satisfied with contacts when these were frequent. In the case of these two groups any chain of cause and effect could run both ways (e.g. foster carers unhappy about contacts could discourage them, thus making them infrequent, or foster carers could be unhappy about contacts because of their infrequency). Children with infrequent contacts who answered our questionnaires were less happy about how often they saw their families. Reverse causation is possible but less likely in this case. In a better world they would have liked more contact with their families. There is a *prima facie* case for enabling them to have it.

Fifth, the case for contacts should not obscure their difficulties:

- Placements with relatives could raise particular difficulties as issues about the child and placement became caught up with other family quarrels. Social workers also suspected that in some cases relative foster carers were too readily recruited and insufficiently supported.

- Most foster children in the sample were seen as being upset by contacts or as having been so in the past. Foster carers commonly had mixed reactions to contacts and in a minority of cases found them highly stressful.

- Where a child had been abused, success on our measures was much more likely when one or more people had been forbidden to have contact with the child.

Sixth, there is as yet no clear theory which might guide social workers through this maze. As far as this research goes, it seems quite likely that everything that has been said about contact is – in some circumstances – true. Other researchers (Farmer *et al.* 2004; Quinton *et al.* 1998) have rated contacts and shown that some seem clearly detrimental – a situation quite compatible with the fact that the same child may also have other more positive contacts with other family members. (In Farmer and her colleagues' study roughly two-thirds of the young people were said to have positive contacts and a similar proportion to have detrimental ones.)

So contacts, like family placements, can help (as the current wisdom is). They can also harm (as previous wisdom would have had it). Decisions about contact, family placement and so on therefore call for a high degree of professional skill – there is a moral presumption in favour of contact, but no rules of thumb that apply in all circumstances. Moreover, the reasons against any decision which is taken – for example, the yearning of a child for abusive parents he or she is forbidden to see – need to be recognised so that the disadvantages can be lessened. And this will only be done if the situation is seen for what it is, if the views of those involved are seen accurately and in their complexity, and if interventions relating to contact are sensitively timed.

Note

1. This chapter reproduces some of the material contained in an article published by *Adoption and Fostering* (Sykes *et al.* 2002) and we are grateful to the journal for allowing us to reproduce this material here.

Chapter Twelve

Foster Families: Characteristics, Reactions to Child and Approach of Main Carer

Introduction

Our model suggests that foster carers have a major influence on outcomes. On this view, some foster carers are more skilled or committed than others. There is also an interaction between child and carer.[1] Some children fit in better with some foster families than they would have done with other families with equal skill and commitment to fostering. Carers themselves acknowledge that 'some you bond with, some you don't'.

These hypotheses are in keeping with common sense and with the emphasis laid by social workers on 'matching'. It is, however, difficult to get evidence for them from the literature. There is some evidence that experienced, 'middle-aged' foster carers who do not have their own children living with them do 'better' (Hill, Lambert and Triseliotis 1989). This evidence, however, is not particularly strong or consistent.

There is very little hard evidence on matching or on the impact of carers' skill. Such evidence as exists suggests that depressed carers (or adoptive parents) and punitive ones may do worse in terms of psychological outcomes (Gibbons, Conroy and Bell 1995). Conversely, carers who are responsive, and able to manage behaviour may do better (Quinton *et al.* 1998). As Quinton and his colleagues point out, responsiveness and sensible control are easier to provide for some children than others. In their study they found that children who had been rejected were more difficult at the beginning of a placement and their difficulties tended to produce a reduction in the parents' skills over time. Farmer and her colleagues' (2004) research on adolescent fostering provides very similar results.

A natural reaction to these findings is to try and train foster carers in appropriate approaches. One American project which trained carers in parenting skills (e.g. in noticing and praising good behaviour and intervening early and effectively with bad behaviour) demonstrated good results with a particular difficult set of young people (Chamberlain 1990; Chamberlain and Reid 1991).

These latter findings are in keeping with what is known of foster children's preferences. They want carers who are warm, encouraging, and do not 'put them down' (Triseliotis and Russell 1984). The findings also fit with the voluminous evidence on the characteristics of parents who have children who 'do well', much of which emphasises the need to provide warmth and security alongside the comparable need to provide firm but non-punitive guidance. Foster care is, however, a special form of parenting, if indeed it should be called parenting at all. How far do our findings suggest that, in foster care, certain characteristics promote good outcomes?

Foster carer characteristics

In this section we look at the relationship between outcome and the more obvious characteristics of the foster carer and their household (for example, age and household composition). We also look at the relationship between previous experience of difficulty in placement (e.g. experience of allegations) and subsequent difficulties such as breakdown. If foster carer characteristics are important we would expect a certain consistency. Thus, after allowing for the difficulty of the child, foster carers who had experienced previous placement disruptions should be more likely to experience future ones.

Age and experience of main carer

Some researchers have found that older, more experienced, carers are less likely to offer placements which disrupt (Hill et al. 1989, for summary). Our findings did not support this view. Instead we found that the older the carer, the more likely the placement was to disrupt. This turned out, however, to be a reflection of the fact that older carers had older children. When age was taken into account the association disappeared. There was no association between the age of carer and ratings of placement success or between the number of years' experience the carer had had and our measures of outcome. Lone carers were somewhat more likely to experience a disruption but not significantly so.

Presence of foster carers' own children

A considerable amount of research has focused on the presence of the foster carers' own children. The balance of evidence suggests that placements are somewhat more likely to disrupt if the carer has her own children in the house, and that this is particularly likely to be so if the foster children and her own children are close in age (Parker 1966; Quinton *et al.* 1998; Wedge and Mantle 1991 – but see Farmer *et al.* 2004 for contradictory evidence).

The comments in our General Questionnaire to foster carers gave a somewhat more equivocal picture of the benefits or otherwise of fostering when there are children in the house. On the negative side, it was obvious that there could be competition for space and the carer's time and attention. The carer's own children could also be led astray, suffer distress at the trouble experiencd by their parent or react negatively if their things were damaged. On the more positive side, carers felt that their own children learnt from the presence of others less fortunate than themselves, and they could be a positive influence and help their parent(s) settle in the foster child and with such tasks as baby-sitting. It is also possible, although the carers only referred to this indirectly, that experience with one's own children can be helpful in dealing with those of others.

More than half the sample (57%) had children living with them at the time they filled in the General Questionnaire. These variables were not related to outcomes in the way we had expected. Those who had at least one child living with them were significantly less likely to experience a disruption (16% v. 27%, $p<0.001$). Moreover the more children there were at home the less likely disruption proved to be. The associations with the success ratings similarly favoured homes where children were present, although this was only significant for the first rating.

Part of the explanation for the surprising association between outcome and the presence of children may have had to do with age. The children placed in families with birth children were on average two years younger (8.8 years as against 11 years). The association between disruption and number of children was no longer significant if we took account of the child's age and the Goodman total difficulties score. Nevertheless the association was still in the same direction. So our evidence did not favour the hypothesis that the presence of the carer's own children had a negative effect on outcome. If anything, it suggested the reverse.

The association that others have found between the presence of children and the disruption of foster placements might be explained on the hypothesis of jealousy or rivalry. In the light of this possibility we asked the carers to rate how far the children liked having the foster child with them. The rating was on a five-point scale from 1 (dislike a lot) to 5 (like a lot). Generally and perhaps optimistically, the foster carers saw their children as approving of the foster children's presence. In only 7 per cent of the cases were they said to dislike the fact that the foster child was there. In a further 20 per cent their reactions were mixed. In 73 per cent of cases the reaction was said to be positive and nearly half the cases the children were said to 'like it a lot'.

Unsurprisingly, this score was strongly associated with both our measures of outcome. It was also associated with the Goodman total score (r=0.50, $p<0.001$), and somewhat less strongly with our measure of social behaviour (r=0.35, $p<0.001$). In short, the children of foster carers seem to prefer foster children who are not disturbed or difficult. Moreover, children whom they prefer are also less likely to experience a disruption and more likely to have placements which are rated successful. The question is how far their dislike leads to the disturbance and to the disruption and how far the causation flows in the opposite direction.

More complicated analysis suggested that the attitude of the children was more important than the Goodman total score in predicting disruption. Indeed the latter did not make a statistically significant contribution to the prediction at all. The social behaviour score did, however, make an independent contribution to this prediction, although this was not as important as the supposed attitude of the children.

Given the importance of the question, we carried out a number of other analyses. We looked at the possibility that negative outcomes were more likely when there was little difference in age, when the foster children were older than the resident children and when there was not a resident child of more than school age. None of these hypotheses was supported, although an incidental finding was that dislike was more common when the age difference was slight.

We are therefore faced with explaining why we did not find an association between the presence of other children and outcome. One possibility is that this is a chance finding or, rather, lack of one. Given the size of the sample and the fact that the association was the reverse of that predicted, we do not think this likely. These facts certainly imply that the predicted association, if it exists, is not strong. Another possibility is that the situation has changed. The dangers of putting children in foster homes where there are other children close to them in age are now more widely understood. As a result, foster carers may be more alert to their children's views when they decide to foster and only do so when their children are in broad agreement. Social workers may also be more careful when placing children in these situations. Interestingly foster children placed in houses where there were birth children were not only younger but also scored significantly better on the social behaviour scores.

The possibility that social workers are now more cautious in placing foster children with birth children seems to us the most likely explanation. If so, the lesson is not that the previous research should be disregarded. Rather, previous research may have been heeded and appropriate conclusions drawn.

Presence of other foster children

Given the previous findings on the apparently negative effects of birth children, it is surprising that the main evidence on the presence of other foster children suggests that this has a positive effect. Berridge and Cleaver (1987) are the most important source of evidence on this point. Their study, however, did not distinguish between children who were placed with siblings and children who were placed with other foster children or between children who had been rejected at home and children who had not – a factor which Rushton and his colleagues (2001) suggest is important in this context. Moreover, the earlier finding is somewhat at odds with the finding by Quinton and his colleagues that foster children do worse when placed with an 'established family' (a concept which seems to have included other foster or adoptive children as well as birth children).

The evidence that the presence of other foster children affected our outcome measures for good or ill was ambiguous. Disruption was significantly more likely where there were other foster children (25% v. 14%, $p=0.003$). So too were poor second success ratings ($p=0.02$). These associations were no longer significant when we took account of the child's Goodman and social behaviour scores.

The foster carer's rating that the child was liked by other foster children was associated with outcome, as in the case of the carer's own children. Again, the analysis suggested that part of the reason was that the more challenging children were less popular. The association between 'popularity' and the avoidance of disruption was no longer significant if we took account of the

Goodman and social behaviour scores. However, the association with the second success rating remained significant ($p<0.001$).

Experience of previous disruptions, allegations and 'other events'

In our first book (Sinclair *et al.* 2004) we developed a list of 'events' which were associated with relatively poor mental health among foster carers. These events were disruptions, allegations of abuse by foster children, family tensions associated with difficult foster children, removal of foster children against their strong advice, and severe difficulties with birth parents. Irrespective of their impact on mental health, there is no doubt that these events could be very distressing to the carers involved.

We argued above that if some carers are less adept than others, they should be more liable to these events. If so, carers who noted more previous 'events' in our first survey should be more likely to have children who disrupted or did not do well in our second survey. We tested this assumption on three variables – previous allegations, previous disruptions, and previous 'events' (the total number of events experienced).

In carrying out these tests we needed to allow for number of years fostering – unsurprisingly, the number of events was strongly related to the number of years in which they could have been accumulated. We also needed to allow for disturbance and adolescent deviance (since some carers took more difficult children) as measured respectively by the Goodman total and social behaviour scores.

For technical reasons we carried out these analyses using a 'multi-level' model. Some carers had more than one child in the survey. Analyses which treated attributes of the carer as attributes of the child (e.g. this child has a carer with experience of allegations) could have led to results which appeared to be more statistically significant than they were. A convenient computer program for handling data of this kind has been developed (Goldstein *et al.* 1998). We used this to produce a regression equation in which the variable to be explained (e.g. the success rating) was related to:

1. variables at carer level (e.g. experience of allegations) and

2. attributes of child (e.g. disturbance score).

The results of this analysis showed that after allowing for adolescent deviancy, disturbance and years of fostering:

- experience of previous disruptions was significantly associated with disruption ($p<0.05$) and a relatively poor second success rating ($p<0.05$)

- experience of allegations was significantly associated with disruption ($p<0.05$) and a relatively poor second success rating ($p<0.05$)

- experience of 'events' was associated with disruption ($p<0.05$) and a relatively low second success rating ($p<0.05$)

- a high distress score was significantly associated with disruption ($p<0.05$) and a relatively poor second success rating ($p<0.05$) and a relatively poor first success rating ($p<0.01$).

As can be seen, only one of the measures was associated with the first success rating. This gives us greater confidence in the results. We were concerned that social workers would be more likely to say that a placement was not working well if previous placements had run into trouble. This effect however, if it occurred, would be more likely to be seen in the first success rating, which was made closer in time to the previous placements. This suggests that associations we found between social workers ratings at Time 1 and outcomes at follow-up were not influenced by social workers' preconceptions based on earlier events.

Effect of foster carer's approach

Our model suggests that some carers are 'better' than others. The analysis just described supports this view, at least to the extent that some carers seem more likely to experience allegations and disruptions than others. In this section we consider how far it is possible to measure the differences between carers and assess their effects.

The areas covered and their measurement

Immediately we will be concerned with three main areas:

- the parental role of the foster carers as assessed by the field social worker and the family placement worker

- the degree to which the carer likes or rejects the foster child as assessed from the carer's replies to questions in the postal questionnaire and

- the degree to which the carer reports that they have been involved in doing things with the child.

Each of these measures was constructed from sets of questions which we put together. This has advantages when analysing the data but can obscure the meaning of the answers given. For example, it is relatively easy to understand the statement that 'in 80 per cent of the cases the foster carers were described by their family placement workers as highly caring'. The statement that 'the average carer support score was 0' carries no obvious meaning and may even be taken as implying that on average carers gave little support.

For this reason it is worth noting that in all three areas the general impression was very positive. Table 12.1 gives the average ratings given by the family placement worker and social workers to the carers of individual children. As can be seen, the averages are close to the maximum of four, a finding which confirms the generally favourable opinion which social workers have of foster carers (see Berridge 1997 for summary). In the case of every rating but one, more than half the cases were given the maximum score. The only exception related to whether the carer was easily upset by the child's failure to respond. Here more than half the social workers and more than half the family placement workers did not give the maximum score. Even in this case, however, no other rating was given as often as the maximum.

Table 12.1 Average carer ratings given by family placement workers and social workers

	Family placement workers	Social workers
Caring	3.8	3.7
Accepting	3.5	3.4
Clear expectations	3.6	3.6
Not easily upset by child's failure to respond	3.1	3.3
Sees things from child's viewpoint	3.5	3.4
Encouraging	3.7	3.7

Sources: Family placement worker and social worker questionnaires at Time 1.

A similar positive impression was given by the answers given to the questions in our *'rejection' score*. These questions were concerned with the degree to which the carer (and partner if any) was fond of the child and/or perceived her or him as 'impossible'. The answers quoted below are for children to whom the question applied (e.g. where the carer had a partner or where the child was old enough for a question about the reasons for misbehaviour to make sense):

- In 4 per cent of cases carers stated that they were not at all fond of the child.

- In 7 per cent they were unsure that they could go on living with/putting up with the child.

- In 11 per cent they acknowledged mixed reactions to having the child (hardly any admitted to disliking the child).

- In 11 per cent they felt that there was no point to telling the child why they did not like her or his misbehaviour.

- In 12 per cent (where question applied) they stated their partner had mixed reactions (again less than 1% admitted there was dislike).

- In 23 per cent of these cases the foster carers were quite sure that there was no 'point in asking the child why he or she misbehaves'.

It is not only that overt rejection is rare. Positive acceptance is common. Eight out of ten carers stated they were very fond of the child.

A rather more mixed picture was given by the questions in the child orientation score. This was made up of a set of 12 questions developed by Marjorie Smith. It is concerned with the degree to which the foster carer does such things as inviting the child's friends to play or takes her or him to McDonald's. Again, carers were given the option to say that the child was too young to take part in activities of this kind.

In this scale the individual answers to questions are harder to interpret. Taking a child to a football match is fine if both child and adult enjoy this. If not, it can be an uninspiring event for both sides. It is therefore not to be expected that in the case of any individual question, high proportions would answer 'yes'. Nevertheless, we did expect that, on average, successful foster placements would involve more joint activities than unsuccessful ones.

We constructed three measures:

- The *carer parenting score* comprised the average of the social worker ratings given in the areas listed in Table 12.1. Where the social worker score was missing, we substituted the family placement worker ratings. In order to ensure that no bias was introduced by the slight tendency for family placement workers to give more generous ratings, we standardised the ratings so that all had an average of 0 and a standard deviation of 1.

- The *rejection score* comprised the mean rating given to the six questions described above, which covered the degree to which the child was seen as incorrigible and the degree to which the carer and her partner was fond of her or him. The scoring of the question was reversed as necessary so that the scoring was consistent. The scores for each question were also standardised with the aim that each question should make the same contribution to the overall total.

- The *child orientation score* comprised the mean rating (never=1, sometimes=2, often=3) given to involvement with the child in the various areas covered.

Internal consistency and other properties of measures

Scores based on the family placement worker ratings had good internal consistency in the sense that the items of which they were made up tended to go together (alpha=0.87), and the internal consistency for the social worker ratings was comparable (alpha=0.89). The consistency between raters was less high than we would have liked, with a correlation between the social worker and family placement worker scores of only 0.38. This was highly significant ($p<0.001$) but nevertheless suggests that we were not measuring our target variable with any great precision.

The rejection (alpha=0.77) and child orientation scores (alpha=0.77) were also internally consistent.

One concern was whether, contrary to our intention, all the scores were effectively measuring the same underlying dimension. This did not seem to be so. The rejection score was negatively correlated with both the carer support score ($r=-0.29$) and the child orientation score ($r=-0.25$). Conversely, the carer support score and child orientation score were positively correlated ($r=0.21$). These correlations are all significant at a level way below one in a thousand, but are nevertheless not so high as to suggest that the variables are measuring the same thing.

A second concern was whether our variables were unduly influenced by the age and difficulty of the child.

The items that make up the measure were clearly likely to be influenced by age – it is, for example, unlikely that a baby will react favourably to being taken to a sporting event or to being told why carers do not like its behaviour. Analyses which use these measures have to exclude children aged less than three.

Similarly, there are items in the rejection score which measure the degree to which the child is seen as impossible. These could reflect the degree to which the child is 'impossible' and thus be a measure of the child's disturbance rather than carer reaction.

For these reasons, we correlated our three main variables with our measures of disturbed attachment, social behaviour and the Goodman total score. All the correlations showed that 'worse' parenting scores went with more disturbed or deviant behaviour and all but one were significant. In most cases, however, the correlations were low, varying from 0.1 to 0.18. The only sizeable correlations involved the rejection score. This correlated 0.18 with the score for social behaviour, 0.27 with the aloofness score, 0.38 with the childlike attachment score and 0.56 with the Goodman total score. To put matters in plainer English, the degree of 'child difficulty' seems to have little impact on the parenting scores but a considerable impact on the rejection score.

There are various possible explanations for these correlations. Disturbance could lead to rejection. Rejection could lead to disturbance. Rejection could lead to a child being seen as disturbed irrespective of whether he or she was. Most likely there is something in all these explanations.

In essence, the proof of these measures must lie in whether they help us to understand outcomes. It is to their relationship with outcome that we turn next.

Relationship between measures and outcomes

With two exceptions all our measures of parenting were related to our measures of outcome at a level of significance of less than one in a thousand. Child orientation was significantly related to disruption and to the first success rating but the significance level were less (0.002 (with disruption) and 0.01 (first success rating)). (See Tables 12.2 to 12.4 for the associations with disruption.)

Table 12.2 Rejection score and disruption

		Whether placement disrupted (%)	
Rejection score	n	Yes	No
Low (below median)	160	13	87
High (above median)	195	33	67
Total	355	24	76

Sources: Foster carer questionnaire at Time 1; disruption measured by all questionaries at Time 2.

Table 12.3 Child orientation score and disruption

Child orientation score	n	Whether placement disrupted (%)	
		Yes	No
Low (below median)	217	28	72
High (above median)	224	16	84
Total	441	22	78

Sources: Foster carer questionnaire at Time 1; disruption measured by all questionnaires at Time 2. Chi square=9.43, df=1, p=0.002.

Table 12.4 Parenting score and disruption

Parenting score	n	Whether placement disrupted (%)	
		Yes	No
Low (below average)	219	32	68
High (above average)	214	13	87
Total	433	22	78

Sources: Family placement worker and social worker questionnaire at Time 1; disruption measured by all questionnaires at Time 2. Chi square=23.3, df=1, p=0.000.

These associations could occur because difficult children produce unsatisfactory parenting rather than vice versa. As a first step to checking this possibility, we related each measure in turn to our two outcome measures in a multi-variate analysis which included the key behavioural correlates of outcome – to wit the Goodman total score and the social behaviour score. As before, we used logistic regression in our attempt to explain disruption and multiple regression in our attempt to explain the rating of placement success. This preliminary analysis suggested that the measures of parenting were associated with outcome even after disturbance was taken into account.

The next step was to include all three measures together with the two individual predictors in the same equations. Basically the pattern remained the same. The child orientation score was not associated with the first outcome measure. With this exception the three parenting measures were all associated with the three outcome measures.[2]

One interesting feature of these analyses concerned the associations between our Goodman total score and the outcome measures. These were significant in the case of the success ratings. However, the score was not associated with disruption once we took account of the rejection score. A plausible explanation is that disturbance only leads to disruption through its association with rejection. In general, disturbed children are more likely to disrupt. However, disturbed children whose carers do not reject them are no more likely to disrupt than other foster children. A rather similar finding is reported by Quinton and his colleagues (1998), who found that although difficult children have less stable placements, the difference is only marked when their new foster or adoptive parents are not 'responsive' to them.

Measures and the carer's experience of previous disruptions, allegations and events

So far our results confirm our hypothesis that some carers do perform better than others. Our model suggests two further refinements. First, the better performing carers should consistently demonstrate better 'parenting'. So they should score higher on our parenting and child orientation scores. Second, there remains an element of 'chemistry'. Relationships within the placement can deteriorate or blossom. Even the most committed carer can therefore be caught in a spiral of interaction which he or she has difficulty in controlling. We tried to measure these spirals with our rejection score which we saw as a measure of the relationship between carer and child rather than a simple attribute of the carer.

We remained concerned that our parenting scores might in effect be acting as an additional measure of disturbance, reducing the association between our intended measures of child difficulty and giving a spurious impression that the carers were contributing to outcome. In order to test this possibility, we examined the relationship between the scores and previous experiences of breakdown.

For this purpose we again used a multi-level model. Our dependent variables in this model were the parenting, child orientation and rejection scores. Our hypotheses were that these scores would be 'worse' when the carer had experienced more allegations, placement disruptions and events than would be expected from the number of years they had fostered and the difficulty of the current child.[3] The results were as follows:

- experience of allegations – this was quite strongly related to the parenting score but not the other measures

- experience of disruptions – this was not related to the rejection score and not quite significantly related to the parenting score but was significantly related to the child orientation score ($p<0.05$)

- experience of events – this was significantly related to the parenting score ($p<0.05$) but not to the child orientation or rejection scores.

As can be seen, none of our event scores predicts rejection. This supports our suggestion that rejection is an attribute of the child or of the interaction between child and carer. It is not a stable attribute of the carer. So carers may take against one child but not against another.

The finding that allegations were not associated with any of the scores could bear different interpretations. As noted above, previous allegations did predict disruptions and poor success with the current placement. This could be a chance finding (the significance level was relatively low). Alternatively, allegations could denote a characteristic not picked up by our foster carer rating (for example, the negative effect of someone in the carer's household other than the carer).

As can be seen, disruptions were associated with child orientation and with the fostering score. This supports the interpretation that some carers are more likely to experience disruptions than others and that this has to do with the way they parent.

The carer scores and outcomes in a multi-level model

As a final test of our model of caring we looked at the relationship between the carer scores and outcomes in a 'multi-level model'. This showed that the rejection, child orientation and parenting scores were associated with the second success rating. The associations remained significant at a level way beyond one in a thousand after we had taken account of the Goodman total score and social behaviour score. After allowing for these variables the multi-level analysis showed that child orientation ($p<0.01$) and the rejection score ($p<0.05$) were both associated with disruption as predicted. However, the association with the parenting score was not significant. By contrast the associations with the first success rating were significant for the parenting and rejection scores but not the child orientation score.

Further analysis suggested that the child orientation score was indeed a measure of some relatively stable characteristic of the foster carers. An estimated 60 per cent of the variation in this score was accounted for by variations between foster carers. This compared with less than 2 per cent of the rejection score and 52 per cent of the parenting score. In keeping with these differences the child orientation score was not related to the social behaviour or Goodman total scores. The parenting score and the rejection scores were related to both.

A final piece in this jigsaw was that high distress scores were significantly related to the rejection and parenting scores even after our two individual variables had been taken into account. If the individual variables were omitted from the analysis the association between the distress score and the rejection score became even stronger (massively so in the case of the rejection score). They were not, however, related to the child orientation scores.

Overall, the results support the hypothesis that some foster carers are consistently less likely to experience breakdowns than others. These carers also seem to have better success. Success and breakdowns are also influenced by the behaviour of the child or young person. One way in which this may occur is through the effect of behaviour on the carer's psychological state. Carers dealing with placements that are not going well may become more distressed. This may both affect the quality of their parenting and their commitment to the child. Over time the chemistry between carer and child can worsen and a disruption may result.

Conclusion

In this study, the basic characteristics (age, family composition) of foster families were not related to outcomes. This does not mean that these aspects of a family are unimportant. For example, it seems likely that the other children in a foster family can help or hinder a placement depending on how they react to the new child. The reactions of the birth children in the family remain crucial, even though we can not say that in general these reactions are likely to be negative.

In general our findings emphasise the crucial importance of the way the carers 'parent' and of relationships within the family. In this respect they seem highly consistent with the work of Quinton and his colleagues (1998) and Farmer and hers (2004). Our results suggest that:

- Some carers are consistently better than others (that is, they are warmer, clearer about what they expect, more empathic with the child, less easily put out by the child's behaviour, and more concerned to do things with the child).

- The child orientation and parenting scores tap dimensions of carer behaviour which distinguish one carer from another and persist over time.

- Carers who score 'well' on these dimensions are more likely to have had successful placements and to be successful in the future.

We also have evidence that outcome depends on features of the particular placement:

- Rejection is heavily a reaction to the difficulty of the child but may also reflect the degree to which a particular carer 'clicks' with a particular child.

- A carer who is accepting (or rejecting) at one time is not necessarily so at another. Hence current rejection does not predict previous disruptions.

- Characteristics of the family situation, other than the carer, may influence outcomes. The reactions of other family members are clearly important.

- Allegations may predict future disruptions but if so they are likely to influence disruption through a mechanism other than the carer characteristics tapped by our parenting and child orientation scores.

- A child's difficulties only lead to disruption if they lead first to rejection within the family. Difficult children placed with families who are committed to them are no more likely than others to disrupt.

In short, the outcomes of a placement reflect the child, the carer and the degree to which the two get on.

Notes

1. Some of the material in this chapter is based on an article in the *British Journal of Social Work* (Sinclair and Wilson 2003) and we are grateful to the journal for permission to reproduce this material here.

2. In the case of the second success rating the association between the rejection score and the second success rating dropped just below significance ($p=0.065$). Given the overall pattern of results it seems reasonable to consider this association a genuine one.

3. Our independent variables were therefore the three event scores, the social behaviour and the Goodman total scores, and number of years fostering (logged for statistical reasons). We considered each event score separately (i.e. without entering the other two into the equation) and estimated nine models overall.

Chapter Thirteen

Social Work Support

Introduction

So far, we have concentrated on factors associated with the child and the foster family, dealing only briefly with the involvement of others in making the placement. We turn next to the factors outside the foster home which may contribute to successful outcomes. Our last book (Sinclair *et al.* 2004) considered the role of the family placement social worker (now commonly known as the supervising social worker). In this chapter we concentrate in particular on the role of the child's social worker.[1]

Social workers did not feature prominently in our 'model' of what leads to successful placements. They were, however, very significant to both carers and children. So it is important to examine what impact they may have on outcomes. In what follows we will concentrate on:

- the nature of the social worker's role
- their performance in this role
- the factors which affect performance
- the relationship between role performance and outcome.

In describing the nature of the role and its performance we are relying on the accounts of foster carers. In looking for the factors which affect performance and its relationship to outcome we use multi-variate analysis.

The nature of the social worker's role

> She gives me advice on managing behaviour problems, she sorts out his extra allowances for holidays on time, she always gets back to me when asked, she

listens to both of us and always forewarns me of decisions made etc. I can't think of any way in which she is unhelpful.

She [social worker] knows J and understands him and his past. This helps him as he has been with her in good and bad times with his mother and father. This is a bond they have and must never be broken.

We asked the carers: 'What does the social worker do that seems particularly helpful or unhelpful?' We analysed 86 of the replies, which were randomly selected. Their overriding tone was favourable. Forty-six were wholly positive, 25 offered both positive and negative comments as requested, ten offered exclusively negative comments, and five were non-committal. The detail of these replies suggested both the general qualities for which carers looked in social workers and the tasks they wanted them to perform – in short, the role they wanted them to play.

In terms of general qualities, carers wanted social workers who were:

- 'there for them' – those who made themselves available were valued; those who were perceived as being continually sick, on leave, or in meetings and who failed to return phone calls or only appeared at a crisis were not

- reliable and prompt – those who came when they said and did what they said within a reasonable time-scale were valued; those who missed appointments, promised the children something they did not perform, or took 'for ever' in sorting out practical matters were not

- respectful of the carer's views – those who listened to what the carer had to say, kept the carer informed on the plans for the children/expectations of the carer and involved them in the planning were valued; those who were seen as looking down on carers, as talking to them in a patronising way, as withholding key information and as making plans without reference to carers were not; particular resentment was felt when carers perceived themselves as having been manipulated into taking an unsuitable child through lack of appropriate information

- considerate – those who took account of the carer's work schedule and childcare commitments were valued; those who arranged meetings when a partner or carer was at work and without reference to their convenience, or who changed arrangements without informing the carer were not

- supportive – understandably, carers valued social workers who were perceived as warm, approving of the carer, and ready to listen.

These excellent qualities were expected to be displayed in all the arenas where the carer perceived the social worker as active. These included:

- sorting out financial and transport arrangements with the department
- arranging the relevant professional networks and services (e.g. health visitors, schools, therapy)
- working with the child's birth family
- working with the child her/himself
- enabling the carer to work better with the child
- supporting the carer.

Comments about work with the department or networks were mainly concerned with the efficiency and diligence of the social worker (or the lack of them). Comments about work with the child and the family were more complicated.

In relation to the child, some of the difficulties related to particular incidents where the social worker was seen as giving poor advice. For example, one child was exposed to racist remarks at school and the social worker basically told the carer that this was to be expected. Some problems related to a feeling on the part of the carer that they were excluded from what went on between carer and social worker ('a little feedback would be good'), or that the latter actually colluded against them – for example, by taking the child to McDonald's after an incident of disruptive behaviour. Some related to major differences of view – for example, over whether it was safe and desirable for the child to return home. Complaints were a particularly sensitive matter with carers likely to feel that the social worker had taken the child's side and not listened to their point of view.

Some of these problems no doubt reflected differences of role. Social workers did not have to live with the child. Moreover, they did not necessarily wish to hear about problems that might lead to a new placement being required:

> Social worker tries to understand the problems that we face but in all honesty does not. He tries to offer advice but at the end of the day he can go home and forget about us and we are left with the problem. He thinks no matter

how bad the problem he can solve it by talking and trying to smooth things over without actually taking any positive action.

By contrast with the above, social workers were valued for their ability to understand a child, to calm her or him down, to give good advice on how to handle problems, and in some cases to act as a friendly mediator or referee between child and carer. Carers appreciated the support which children received from their social workers and the readiness of the social worker to visit the child, take an interest in the child's schooling and so on. They also perceived that in some instances the social worker had 'been through a lot' with the child and was a valued and benign link with a troubled past.

Rather similar issues arose over family contact. What seems to be needed is an appreciation of the foster carer's position and an ability to intervene effectively, by advising the foster carer, dealing directly with the birth parents or mediating between the parties involved:

> In the case of an abusive father…the child's social worker was extremely supportive. Helping us to handle birth parents when difficulties arise.

> Foster child told lies and mum believed him before she had my side of the story. So my link worker called for a meeting with all concerned and got it sorted out. Now mum and myself get on great.

Measuring role performance

Our measures of the social worker's role performance were all taken from the point of view of the carer. They involved a general measure of performance similar to that already introduced for the family placement social worker in our first book. They also included a number of specific questions about the adequacy of the information made available to the carer, the degree of involvement allowed the carer and the degree to which carer and social worker were in dispute over certain issues.

Table 13.1 sets out the distribution of answers to questions about the family placement worker in our General Questionnaire to foster carers. The measure at the bottom of the table (alpha) measures reliability or internal consistency – the degree to which answers to the different questions go together and so may be seen as measuring the 'same thing'. An alpha of 1 reflects perfect reliability, whereas one of 0 suggests that all the items are measuring variables which are independent of each other.

Table 13.1 Foster carers' views of family placement workers

	n	Strongly agree (%)	Agree (%)	Disagree (%)	Strongly disagree (%)
Visits often enough	885	35	52	10	3
Listens carefully	886	49	45	5	1
Does what they say they will do	880	46	45	7	2
Responds promptly when asked	884	47	42	9	2
Appreciates our work	874	56	39	3	1
Offers good advice	877	47	44	8	1
Sorts out practical problems	880	42	48	9	1
Keeps in touch with us enough	887	43	43	12	2

Source: General Questionnaire to foster carers. Alpha=0.93.
Note: the percentages may not add up to 100 across the rows due to rounding.

The items in Table 13.1 go together to a high degree and the scale has an extremely high measure of internal consistency. Overall, carers seem to have a very favourable picture of their link or family social worker.

The picture of the child's social worker was slightly less favourable but still highly positive. In their case we asked a rather longer set of questions reflecting their role with the child as well as the foster carer. Table 13.2 sets out their replies.

Table 13.2 Foster carers' views of child's social worker

	n	Strongly agree (%)	Agree (%)	Disagree (%)	Strongly disagree (%)
Visits often enough	472	23	50	20	7
Listens carefully	477	28	54	15	4
Does what s/he promises to do	472	25	57	13	5
Comes promptly when asked	466	23	57	16	3
Offers good advice	472	20	60	17	3
Understands our foster child	473	22	51	23	4
Helps us handle difficult behaviour	437	18	46	30	6
Agrees with us about the way to handle child	467	23	60	14	4

Source: Foster carer questionnaire at Time 1. Alpha=0.93.
Note: the percentages may not add up to 100 across the rows due to rounding.

We used the mean rating for the various items to form two 'support scores', one for the family placement worker and one for the children's social worker.

The high degree of internal consistency found in the two support scores suggests a strong halo effect. Workers who respond promptly are not necessarily those who give excellent advice; nevertheless, perceptions of promptness were clearly associated with perceptions of wisdom in the foster carers' minds. This raises the question of whether other aspects of the social workers' or department's performance were associated with the support score, even though not apparently related to the aspects of the worker's behaviour listed above.

In exploring this issue, we looked at questions probing the foster carer's involvement in planning, the degree to which they considered they had been given adequate information, and whether they felt they had been involved in conflict with the department or social worker.

We defined four variables:

- *Information deficit* – the number of times the foster carer agreed that she had not been given adequate information on six areas: the child's health, potential problems or special needs, expected length of placement, expected contact with birth parents, plans for education/work, payments/boarding out allowances. More than half (57%) said they lacked adequate information in at least one of these areas, and a fifth (19%) that they lacked information on two or more. The most common need was for more information on length of placement (36%) and the least common concerned pay and boarding out allowances (12%).

- *Lack of planning involvement* – the number of times the foster carer said that she had not or hardly at all been consulted or involved over six areas: length of placement, contact with birth parents, going to nursery/play group/day care, schooling/work, plans for the future, discipline. Some of the areas (e.g. preschool placement) were only relevant to a minority of children. However, it was startling that in nearly half (47%) the cases, carers felt that they had not been consulted over five or six of the areas. The only area in which involvement was said to be at all common was preschool provision (66%). Nowhere else did it exceed a fifth (21%).

- *Disaffection* – the number of times the foster carer agreed that they were unhappy or very unhappy about one of the areas covered in the involvement score. Four out of ten were unhappy about one or more of these. The most common area of disquiet concerned contact with the child's birth family. Thirty per cent of the foster carers said they were unhappy about the plans (or lack of them) for this.

- *Disagreement* – the number of times the foster carer reported some or a great many conflicts with the social worker over the areas covered in the planning involvement score. A third (33%) described conflict in at least one of these areas. Again the most common area of conflict appeared to be contact with the child's birth family (20%).

We divided these scores as near as possible about their middle point and examined whether those who score high on (say) conflict scored 'worse' on the support score than those who scored low. In every case the differences were significant in the predicted direction at a level in excess of one in ten thousand (differences tested using one-way analysis of variance). The differences remain if we remove items from the support score which apparently overlap with the variables concerned (e.g. by removing 'He or she agrees with me/us about the way the child should be handled').

So the picture is that most carers approve of their social workers. This general approval is, however, compatible with quite high levels of specific dissatisfaction, notably over arrangements for contact with birth parents. The more the carer is dissatisfied with particular arrangements, the less overall approval they give to the child's social worker.

What determines perceived role performance

Carers were inclined to make excuses for social workers. Lack of reliability, for example, was sometimes seen as reflecting overwork. How far was there evidence for these excuses? More generally, what factors seemed to be associated with negative or positive perceptions of social workers?

One relevant factor seems to be the social worker's role. Despite minor changes of wording, it is apparent from Tables 13.1 and 13.2 that on all comparable questions family placement workers are more favourably seen than the child's social worker. We computed a score based on the comparable questions and examined how often the foster carer gave a 'better' rating to the family placement worker than to the child's social worker (or the average of scores given to the children's social workers where there were more than one). For statistical reasons, the analysis used the relative ranking of a score rather than the absolute value. In 52 cases the foster carers gave the children's social worker the same score, in 102 cases a better one, and in 223 cases a worse one (Wilcoxon test, z=8.54, $p<0.0001$).

The difference in the popularity of the child's social workers and the family placement workers is in keeping with other research (e.g. Triseliotis *et al.* 1998). It could occur for various reasons. Family placement workers could have been under less pressure than the children's social workers and thus able to visit more often and with greater reliability. The family placement workers may have been more experienced in or committed to foster care as they specialised in it. Alternatively, the differences could arise because of differences in role. The children's social workers had to balance the needs of the child, her or his family and the foster carer, and probably did so in that order. By contrast, the family placement social workers may have been more likely to give a higher priority to supporting the foster family. These possible explanations are based on hypotheses about what makes social workers more or less popular, and we test them below.

If one key to social workers' popularity is reliability we would expect that social workers who visited more regularly would be more popular than those who did not. As we have seen in our first book (Sinclair *et al.* 2004), this association appeared to hold for the family placement social workers. The same was true for the social workers. Those whom the carer rated highly were said to visit more frequently ($r=0.33$, $p<0.001$). These findings suggest that, for whatever reason, frequent visiting is associated with 'popularity'. However, the children's social workers visited more frequently than the family placement workers, so that frequency of visiting could not explain the greater popularity of the latter.

Nor was 'popularity' related to social worker reports that they were under pressure. Overall, 55 per cent of the workers responding said they were under heavy pressure, 44 per cent that they were under moderate pressure, and a sanguine 1 per cent that they were under little pressure. These reports were not related to frequency of visiting as reported by either social workers or foster carers.

What seemed to give with heavy pressure was the frequency of supervision. Social workers reporting moderate or little pressure reported significantly more frequent supervision at which they could discuss the case than those reporting heavy pressure. However, while frequent supervision may well have been reflected in the quality of the work, it was not related to foster carers' views.

There were similar negative findings on qualifications and experience. The very small number of unqualified workers in the study were, if anything, more favourably seen than those who were qualified. Nor were there any relationships with the number of fostering cases the worker had had in the past or the number they had in the present. The only other significant relationship we discovered suggested that some personality variable was involved. Social workers who returned their questionnaires were more favourably seen by the foster carers. Arguably, those who are obliging to researchers are obliging to foster carers as well. Alternatively, those who are involved with the foster child are both more likely to return a questionnaire and to be seen favourably by foster carers.

Overall, however, the key factor is probably role. Those whose primary role is to support the carer are not unsurprisingly seen as the most supportive, perhaps because they have fewer reasons for conflict. In keeping with this hypothesis, social workers who disapproved of the carers' performance (as evident in their low rating of carer qualities and their dissatisfaction with the placement) were themselves significantly less favourably rated by the carers. Conflict leads, perhaps, to mutual disapproval. If so, greater possibilities for conflict are likely to bring a greater chance that the child's social workers and the carers will fall out.

Perceived performance and outcome

We looked carefully for relationships between the perceived role performance of the social worker and our measures of outcome. In looking at role performance we used both global scores (e.g. overall measure of social work supportiveness) and individual measures (e.g. whether the carer felt she had been given a chance to say no to the placement). The results can be briefly stated. After allowing for adolescent deviancy and disturbance (as measured respectively by the social behaviour and the Goodman total scores) we found:

- no relationships between any measure of support from either the link worker or the child's social worker and disruption

- a significant association between the overall measure of support from the social worker and the first success rating ($p=0.018$) and almost with the second rating ($p=0.064$).

These results suggest that the link workers did not differ in their impact on the placement. Relationships with the link worker were generally good. Arguably, all had an equally benign impact. Alternatively, their impact may have been mainly on the morale of the carers and their willingness to continue fostering (here, as we have seen, they were effective).

The results for the social workers were more ambiguous. The association with success rating could suggest that good relationships produce success. Alternatively, good relationships could be an outcome of success rather than a reason for it. We have already seen that relationships are better when the social worker approves of the carer's performance – when things go well everyone feels on the same team. So the association could reflect a tendency for social workers to give favourable ratings to the placement when they and the carers got on well.

The fact that the relationship was not associated with the arguably more objective measure of disruption is a point against a causal explanation for the association between social work support and the success ratings. In addition, the association drops well below significance if we take account of the foster carer's parenting score. On balance, the most likely explanation is that good foster carers have good outcomes and, partly for this reason, get on well with their social workers.

Conclusion

Our findings reinforce the literature that exists on social work support for carers. More specifically, the research suggests that, in general, social workers and family placement workers are seen favourably, that the latter are seen more favourably than the former, and that these favourable perceptions often co-exist with some quite specific causes of complaint (see Berridge 1997; Triseliotis, Borland and Hill 2000). It also supports some earlier qualitative work in suggesting that carers do attribute some breakdowns to poor support from social workers. It is, however, decidedly less optimistic about the likelihood that an improvement in the supportiveness of social workers will bring an improvement in outcomes for the children.

We are not suggesting that social workers should retreat from the aim of supporting carers. Support is a moral requirement and, in any case, probably a prerequisite for help designed to increase effectiveness. So it is important that social workers are reliable, warm, efficient, considerate and respectful in their dealings with carers. To give some examples, they should generally:

- include foster carers in case discussion and planning
- avoid any impression they are manipulating them
- take what foster carers have to say seriously

- keep carers informed with up-to-date information
- give positive feedback when this is appropriate – but not in a patronising way
- be easy to contact and responsive when contacted
- be prepared to listen and offer encouragement
- take account of the family's circumstances and needs in fixing meetings
- get payments, complaints etc. processed as soon as possible.

All this, however, may be insufficient to produce better outcomes for foster children. The American work cited earlier does suggest that more specific interventions targeted at carer skills can be effective. What our research suggests is that generalised support on its own is not enough.

Note

1.   Some of the material in this chapter was first published in *Child and Family Social Work* (Fisher *et al.* 2000) and we are grateful to the journal for allowing us to reproduce this material here.

Chapter Fourteen

Other Forms of Support

Introduction

In this chapter we look at the association between outcomes and forms of support other than social work. We will examine three main groups of factors:

- support intended to benefit the carer and hence indirectly the child
- schooling and work, and
- special interventions such as psychotherapy which are specifically targeted at the child.

General support for carers

The effects of support on outcome could be more or less direct. One hypothesis is that its impact would operate by improving the mental health and morale of the carer. Carers who were supported would feel under less strain and thus be less likely to reject the child or handle her or him inappropriately. Even if the carer became stressed, one role of support would arguably be to prevent this stress turning into rejection and hence breakdown. In the first book we provided evidence that some forms of support could have an impact on carers' mental health and morale. Was this support translated into good outcomes for children?

Our data on the individual foster children showed that our general measures of foster carer morale were not related to outcomes. However, our mental health score, which was based on the *General Health Questionnaire*, was associated with breakdowns even after adolescent deviancy and the Goodman total score had been taken into account (for reasons explained in the last chapter, we checked this conclusion using a multi-level model and found that it still held).

This suggests that the measures we found associated with better mental health scores in the Time 1 survey should be associated with better outcomes in the Time 2 survey. Unfortunately, there was no evidence that this was the case. One reason for this may be the lack of specificity in our first set of measures. A general measure of satisfaction with support may have little to do with the specific forms of support needed when a placement gets into difficulties. For these reasons, we tried to look in detail at the relationship between specific supports and outcomes.

Breaks

In the first survey, carers reported that they had had a break from looking after the child in just under half the placements, either through respite care or through some form of care provided in their house. Opinions on its usefulness were divided. Just over a quarter (26%) said that they had not found the break or breaks at all helpful. However, around four in ten said they had found them very helpful. In keeping with these findings, we found in the General Questionnaire to foster carers that satisfaction with the provision of breaks was associated with reduced stress among carers. However, while breaks may be good for the carer they are not necessarily so for the child. For these reasons we were interested in any possible association between the experience of breaks and outcomes.

Somewhat to our disappointment we found no association between the provision of breaks at the time of the first survey and the judgement of placement success. Even more disturbingly, the experience of breaks was associated with disruption (see Table 14.1). Placements where there had been breaks were more likely to disrupt. Similarly they were also more likely to receive negative second success ratings.

Table 14.1 Association between breaks and disruption

Breaks	n	No disruption (%)	Disruption (%)
Yes	230	73	27
No	256	85	15
Total	486	78	22

Sources: Breaks and disruption from all questionnaires at Time 2.

This association, however, seemed to arise because breaks were more likely to be provided when the child was older, and more disturbed or more difficult. If we allowed for the Goodman total score and our social behaviour score, the association between breaks and disruption dropped a long way below significance.

These findings are based on breaks reported at the time of the first survey and delivered before that date. We also examined the relationship between breaks and outcomes if the breaks were delivered after the first survey. In this case, breaks were significantly associated with the absence of disruption. Only five (4.5%) out of 110 children who had had a short break disrupted. The comparable figure for the 394 without a break was 98 (25%). The provision of these breaks was also significantly associated with good success ratings at both the first and second survey.

This suggests that a break forestalled a disruption. However, there are other possible explanations. Children whose placements did not disrupt may have spent longer in a placement and therefore been more likely to receive a break than children who left shortly after the first survey. In addition foster carers who were determined that a placement should end may have refused short breaks on the grounds that they were an unacceptable palliative.

We examined these issues by looking at the success ratings of children who remained in the placement. Those who had had recent breaks in this group had significantly lower second success ratings. This was in keeping with the findings of the first survey. The explanation seemed to be that the children with breaks were much more likely to be 'rejected' by their carers. If we allowed for this fact children with breaks who remained with their carers were no more or less likely to have poor success ratings than others who also stayed in the same placement.

Overall our evidence on breaks is clear on some points and less clear on others. Breaks are more likely to be offered when the child is difficult and the carer is less committed to her or him. This explains the fact that at any one point in time children who have had breaks in the past are more likely to disrupt. So breaks do not in general cause disruptions. It is possible that they forestall or prevent disruptions. Our evidence on this is inconclusive. If they do, they do not improve the overall way the placement is going as measured by the success rating. The main argument for breaks is therefore that some carers want them and their well-being also has to be considered.

Back-up outside of working hours

Evidence from our General Questionnaire to foster carers suggested that the carer's satisfaction with response out of working hours was an important determinant of the degree to which they felt supported. We wanted to see if it had a similarly good impact on our measures of outcome. However, we found no evidence that it was associated with any of our measures, a disappointing result that persisted when we took account of the apparent difficulty of the children.

Financial support

Some of the evidence presented in our first book (Sinclair *et al.* 2004) suggested that finance might be an important inducement for carers to remain in foster care. However, we also suggested that it was likely to be most effective if it was seen as part of a 'package' which included more intensive training and the opportunity to meet with other foster carers and receive support and encouragement from them. We examined the relationship between these measures and our measures of outcome. The associations were in the predicted direction. Nevertheless, they were not significant, and fell well short of significance once we had taken into account the characteristics of the child.

These negative findings suggest that an approach to support which is purely designed to relieve strain on the carer is not likely to have much impact on the child. It may indeed be of value in its own right. However, unless it is accompanied by direct work with the child or by work with carers on the best approach to take with the child, it does not seem likely to have much impact on child outcomes. It may be a necessary condition for such further work, but it is not sufficient on its own.

Support from school

Children spend (or at least are supposed to spend) a large proportion of their lives in school. Not surprisingly, both social workers and foster carers mentioned school in their accounts of the reasons for which they thought a placement had gone well or otherwise. We therefore expected the support given by the school to the placement would be an important factor in the latter's success.

Two-thirds (64%) of the children were of school age and of these only five children (1% of the total sample) had no school to go to. Among this group of school-age children, just under half (45% of those of school age) were at the same school as they had attended prior to the placement. The remainder had just started school (6% of those of school age) or had gone to a new one (50% of those of school age and 32% of the total).

We asked nine questions about how the child was getting on at school. Of these, four were significantly related to disruption at a significance level of less than two in a hundred. These related to whether the carer felt they had encouraged the child at school, had conflicts with them over school, found that the child truanted from school, and felt that the child was happy at school. All but one of these associations dropped below significance once we took the adolescent deviance and disturbance (as measured respectively by the social behaviour and Goodman total scores) into account. 'Being happy at school' was, however, very strongly predictive of future success (see Table 14.2).

Table 14.2 Association between happiness at school and two outcome measures

Child is happy at school	n	Outcome 1: Placement gone very well (%)	Outcome 2: Placement disrupted (%)
Not at all true	23	26	29
To some extent true	117	42	24
To a large extent true	201	59	12
Total	341	49	17

Sources: Foster carer questionnaire at Time 1 and all questionnaires at Time 2. Chi square=8.58, df=1, p=0.0034.
Note: the percentages are based on row totals which vary slightly.

Work

Only 19 young people on whom the foster carers returned the first question-naire (3% of the sample) were of working age and in the 'job market'. Eleven of these were out of work, two were on a 'scheme' and six were in a paid job. Thirty-five or around 7 per cent of the sample were of working age but at school or some form of college. This did not necessarily mean that work was irrelevant to the remainder. Some will have had part-time jobs and others will have been thinking or worrying about what they might do in the future.

As a result, carers answered a rather higher proportion of questions about work than the numbers in the job market would lead one to expect. Disrup-tions were significantly more likely where the carer said they had not been able to encourage the young person over work and where they were unhappy about the effect of the work situation on the young person. These associations remained significant when we took account of the characteristics of the young people.

Leisure

Leisure time can be, like school and work, a source of support and gratification for the young people and their carers, or a source of disappointment and conflict. For this reason we asked a series of six questions about it, although some of these (e.g. about attending clubs) were not relevant to younger children.

The questions themselves related to the number of the child's hobbies and interests, the number of their friends, the groups and clubs the child attended, conflicts over leisure, effective encouragement of the child's interests and friends, and whether the child was enjoying his or her leisure time more than at the start of the placement. All of these questions were significantly related to disruption (see for example Table 14.3). However, the association was not significant if we took the child's characteristics into account. So positive leisure experiences are certainly a mark of a successful placement but they may not be a cause of it.

Table 14.3 Association between enjoying leisure and two outcome measures

Child enjoying leisure more than when s/he first came	n	Outcome 1: Placement gone very well (%)	Outcome 2: Placement disrupted (%)
Not at all true	23	14	30
To some extent true	127	34	32
To a large extent true	235	50	19
Total	385	43	24

Sources: Foster carer questionnaire at Time 1 and all questionnaires at Time 2. Chi square=16.37, df=2, $p<0.001$(col 1). Chi square=8.08, df=2, $p=0.018$ (col 2).
Note: the percentages are based on row totals which vary slightly.

Special help and interventions

According to the carers and social workers the children in the sample had received a variety of different forms of special help since the placement started. We provided them with a list. This covered extra educational help, life story book, play therapy, group therapy, behaviour therapy, psychotherapy, family therapy/meetings, other psychological help and speech therapy. Nearly two-thirds had received at least one of those mentioned. We then asked them which professionals had provided this help.

Table 14.4 Sources of special help

Type of professional	n	% receiving help
Educational psychologist	495	22
Other psychologist	495	12
Psychiatrist	495	7
Other professional	495	14
Psychotherapist	495	6
Play therapist	495	9
Social worker	495	32
Family centre worker	495	14
Speech therapist	495	10

Source: Foster carer questionnaire at Time 1.

We did not give the carers a definition of the terms involved. It is likely that a wide variety of different kinds of help of varying levels of sophistication were involved in, for example, play therapy. Moreover, the list did not cover other kinds of help, for example, physiotherapy, which might be available to disabled children.

Despite the limited nature of our information, the range of help provided is, on the face of it, impressive. A wide range of professionals were said by the carers to be involved – the most common being educational psychologists (in 22% of cases) and other psychologists (12%) or family centre workers (14%). Life story book work seems commonly to have been done by social workers – they were mentioned in 45 per cent of cases where this kind of help was given. Carers were apparently keen that the child should receive such help. In six out of ten cases where it was not already being given they thought that some additional help of this kind was needed. It is of interest to know if the help actually given had any obvious effects.

We asked the carers whether the help given had positive effects. On balance they felt that the outcomes had been good. They were, however, rather cautious in their assessments. In four out of ten cases where help had been given they felt there had been no change and in a small minority of cases (6%) they believed there had been a change for the worse. They only saw a very positive change in a fifth of cases. In just over a third of cases they either saw little change or change for better and worse.

There was some evidence that in the eyes of the carers those who had had contact with an educational psychologist (p=0.058), a psychologist (p=0.049) or a speech therapist (p=0.054) had gained more benefit than others. The social workers were asked a similar question. On this the only kinds of special help associated with particularly good outcomes were educational psychology (p=0.004), group therapy (p=0.075) and speech therapy (p=0.079). There was also some evidence that in the eyes of the carers the improvement associated with educational psychology was particularly impressive when they felt they had been fully involved. (Where they felt they had at best only been given some information, contact with an educational psychologist was associated with a poor outcome.)

We examined the association between these interventions and our measures of outcome. At first sight the only effects seemed negative or absent. Those who had received psychiatric help before the first survey were significantly more likely to disrupt. So too were those who were said to have received 'special educational help'. Fortunately these negative associations fell below significance once we had taken behaviour and disturbance into account. So the truth seems to be that special help of various kinds is targeted on the more difficult children rather than that it makes them more difficult. Nevertheless, with one exception discussed below, it did not seem to produce success.

The exception to this rule of no obvious effect was provided by contact with an educational psychologist. With one exception those who had such contact were all aged at least three. All subsequent analysis involving educational psychology will involve this group unless we point out otherwise. In this group those who had had such contact were less likely to disrupt (17% as against 25%). The difference was more marked when we took social behaviour and the Goodman total score into account. Once this was done, contact with such psychologists was significantly associated with the first success rating (p<0.05), and very significantly associated with the second success rating (p<0.005) and with avoidance of disruption (p<0.05) (see Table 14.5 for illustration).

Table 14.5 Association between disruption and contact with educational psychologist

| Goodman scores | Ed. psychologist | n | Whether placement disrupted (%) | |
			Yes	No
Low	No	134	18	82
	Yes	22	0	100
	Total	156	14	86
		Chi square=4.66, df=1, p=0.031		
High	No	105	37	63
	Yes	69	22	78
	Total	174	31	69
		Chi square=4.62, df=1, p=0.032		

Sources: Foster carer questionnaire at Time 1 and all questionnaires at Time 2.

The apparently good effects of the educational psychologist were not predicted. So it seemed important to explore possible reasons for it. On the face of it, the explanation was not related to the difficulty of the young people they saw. Those who scored high on the Goodman total score were more likely to have contact with an educational psychologist. So too were those who were considered by their social workers to have learning difficulties, to have other difficulties, or to have been abused. Those said by their carers to be 'disabled' were also more likely to have contact with an educational psychologist. These factors were either neutral in relation to outcomes or associated with worse outcomes.

A possible explanation is related to the greater amount of special help associated with contact with an educational psychologist. Children in touch with an educational psychologist were between two and four times more likely to receive all the kinds of special help we listed, with the exception of life story work. As a crude measure we counted the number of different kinds of help received. The list contained nine items given in Table 14.4 (special educational help, behavioural help etc.). The average for those said to have had contact with an educational psychologist was three as compared with just over one (1.1) for those who had not had contact with one. It appeared, however, that the effect of the psychologists could not simply be explained by their role as a conduit for various special kinds of help. After allowing for the characteristics of the children, there was no relationship between the amount of help received and outcome.

We examined a number of further hypotheses. These were to the effect that there was an interaction – for example, that behaviourally oriented help was beneficial when associated with an educational psychologist but otherwise harmful. There was no evidence for interactions of the kind we sought. Three interesting findings were, however, thrown up by this exploration.

First, contact with an educational psychologist was more likely when the carer was child-oriented and had a high parenting score.

Second, contact with an educational psychologist was associated with a relative being forbidden access, even after allowing for the existence or otherwise of suspected abuse.

Third, contact with an educational psychologist was most strongly associated with the avoidance of disruption when the child was, according to the carer, happy at school, next most strongly associated with outcome when the child was reasonably happy there and positively associated with disruption when the child was unhappy at school.

These findings provide the basis for a set of possible explanations. Child-oriented carers differ from others in their relationship with the child's school. They were more likely to say that they had encouraged the child there, thought it important to help with school work, had worked closely with the teachers, and were pleased with what the school was doing for the child. In terms of outcome they were also more likely to say that the child was happy at school and that the situation over the child's schooling had improved.

All these associations were statistically highly significant ($p<0.001$). It might be thought that they arose because it is easier to encourage 'easy' children. This is true. However, it does not seem to be the full explanation. Child-oriented carers were no more or less likely than others to say that they had had conflicts with the children over school or that their children had truanted from school. So their foster children do not seem to have been particularly 'easy' in this respect. Child-oriented carers were much more likely to say that they had been able to encourage the child even after her or his characteristics had been taken into account.

Encouragingly these findings strongly suggest that carers can influence how children get on at school. They see themselves as having been more successful in this respect. Their foster children are more likely to be happy at school even after their characteristics had been taken into account.

Child-oriented foster carers were also more likely to have children who had at least one relative forbidden contact. This, however, does not explain why those who had seen an educational psychologist were more likely to have a relative forbidden contact. This association remained significant even when other factors (abuse, being on a care order, having a child-oriented carer, and age) were taken into account. One possible (but to us unlikely) explanation would be that educational psychologists were more likely to recommend such restrictions.

Another possibility is that attention to the child's schooling and a willingness to restrict contact with relatives is a mark of a particular approach to foster care – one which gives a lower priority to the rights of families and a higher priority to the child's upbringing at the time. In keeping with this the lowest proportions with contact with an educational psychologist were found among those who had already left the placement or for whom there were plans for return to family or relatives. The highest proportion was for those for whom there were not yet plans or for whom the plan was long-term foster care.

The final hypotheses concerns the 'package' which is most likely to be effective in encouraging schooling and discouraging disruption. The pattern of findings strongly suggested that the effect of contact with the educational psychologist depended partly on the attitude of the child to school and partly on the attitude of the carers.

Where the child was said to be very unhappy at school, contact was associated with disruption – albeit not significantly. By contrast, as noted above, contact with an educational psychologist was strongly associated with absence of disruption when the child was happy at school. Where there was said to be considerable conflict with the carers over school, contact with the educational psychologist was again associated with disruption – albeit again not significantly (57% versus 28%, $p=0.09$). Where, however, there was only said to be conflict 'to some extent', contact with the educational psychologist was strongly associated with absence of disruption (4% v. 41%, $p<0.001$). There was a similar but non-significant trend when there was said to be no conflict (10% v. 19%, $p=0.16$).

In relation to the carers, contact with the educational psychologist was significantly or nearly significantly associated with the absence of disruption when according to the carer:

- the carer was happy with what the school was doing for the child ($p=0.007$)
- the situation over the child's schooling was better than at the start of placement ($p=0.007$)
- the carer thought it important to help with school work ($p=0.041$)
- the carer had worked closely with the school or college ($p=0.10$)
- the carer had been able to encourage the child over school ($p=0.07$).

Where the carer did not think these things – for example, where they had not been able to encourage the child over school – contact with the educational psychologist was associated with disruption, although the numbers were too small for the difference to reach significance. (The only exception was that in the few cases where the carer attributed no importance to help with school work no child had contact with an educational psychologist.)

Overall these findings suggest that contact with the educational psychologist has to be seen as part of 'a package'. The carer is 'child-oriented', values education and works closely with the school and the educational psychologist. Educational help is given a high priority and probably given at a relatively early stage and before the child becomes educationally disaffected.

Conclusion

Our exploration suggests three broad conclusions.

First, support designed to improve the morale and mental health of the carer is important. Indeed it could be regarded as a moral requirement. On its own, however, it probably does not have a major impact on the outcomes we have been examining. It may be a necessary condition for help designed to benefit the child. It is not sufficient on its own.

Second, there is a strong association between the children's leisure time activities, their school/work performance and our outcomes. The associations between leisure and outcome were explained by the characteristics of the child. The associations between happiness at school and outcomes were not explained in this way.

Third, there was an association between disruption and contact with an educational psychologist. This too could not be explained by the characteristics of those who saw the psychologist.

Further exploration suggested that contact with an educational psychologist was more likely when the carer was 'child-oriented'. In addition it was only associated with 'good outcomes' when the child was 'happy at school', the carer thought it important to help with school work and in other conditions which suggested that the school situation was comparatively favourable. Where there was minimal conflict between carer and child over school outcomes the apparently good effect of contact with the educational psychologist was particularly pronounced. Where there was a lot of conflict, contact with the psychologist was, if anything, associated with poor outcomes.

Overall the evidence strongly suggests that carers can influence success at school. Happiness and success at school can also influence success in the placement. Success in both settings probably requires three parties – school, carer and educational psychologist – to be working in harmony. It may also require early intervention if the child is not to become disenchanted with school – a situation in which the educational psychologist at least may find it difficult to work effectively.

These findings were not predicted. It is therefore important that they are tested in further work. In the meantime the safest assumption is probably that school is very important both in its own right and for its effect on the placement. Everything reasonable should be done to ensure that school and carer work closely together and that both are able to call on educational psychologists when they need them.

Fourth, most forms of special help (e.g. psychotherapy) had on their own no detectable effect on our outcomes. Their apparent association with poor outcomes was almost certainly explained by the fact that they tended to be given to children in difficulty. However, we found no evidence that they had a strong effect for good. This may, of course, reflect the resources available for them, the way they had to be delivered in the context of busy professional lives, or, perhaps, subtle interactions of the kind we seem to have found in the case of educational psychology. These issues again are matters for further research.

Chapter Fifteen

Change and Containment

Introduction

So far our study, like others before it, has been much concerned with disruption and hence with containment. Containment, however, is only enough if the child is either to remain for good in the protective environment or return to another which is equally supportive. Realistically, neither of these options is often on offer. So the question arises of whether the child can be helped (e.g. through education) to change so that he or she is better able to survive and flourish even in challenging environments.

This penultimate chapter focuses on change. How far and in what respects did the children change? How far are any changes explained by our statistical model? In particular, how far do they reflect the four key variables we have so far identified – the parenting, child orientation and rejection scores and contact with an educational psychologist?

In taking this focus on change we concentrate, for the most part, on children who were still in the foster placement at follow-up. In the case of these children we were able to compare scores at the Time 1 survey with scores at the Time 2 survey, examine how far there were differences and then try and explain them. As a complement to this approach, we also asked the carers in both surveys whether they thought the children had changed in certain respects. In the case of the survey at Time 1 we were able to examine their replies for all the children. We begin the chapter by considering the direct questions we asked about change. In the second part of the chapter we consider the change scores. As will be seen, the approach we adopt in these two sections is rather bald: we set down what we did and what we found. Unfortunately, what we found was rather complicated and confusing. In the third section of the chapter we report some further analysis intended to cast light on the results in the first two sections.

Changes between arrival in placement and first survey

We had no direct measures of how the child was at the time he or she arrived in the placement. We therefore relied on questions to the foster carer (and on one question to the social worker) asking how the child had changed. We asked the social workers:

> Thinking back to the start of the placement, has there been a change in how the child is doing relative to their age group? [A five-point scale – 'considerable improvement' to 'considerable deterioration'.]

We asked the foster carers:

> In relation to overall progress since arrival, which point best reflects the position of the child at the moment? [A four-point scale – 'good progress' to 'poor progress'.]

In addition, we asked the foster carer whether the child's situation at school had improved, whether he or she was less disturbed than on arrival, and whether the child 'fits in better than when first he or she came'. These five measures were all correlated with each other at a high level of significance ($p<0.001$) although the actual correlations were quite low (0.44 to 0.23).

The fact that the associations are significant suggests that some general measure improvement is being tapped by all the questions. The low value of the correlations suggests either that changes are quite specific in nature – so that improvement in, for example, school performance is not related to settling in – or alternatively that we are measuring overall improvement inaccurately so that our different measures of it are only weakly correlated.

Table 15.1 sets out the correlations between these measures and our main measures of the foster carer's parenting. As can be seen, all the correlations were significant except for one relating to the child's situation at school. Children whose foster carers were child-oriented and high scorers on our parenting scale did better as did those whose carers scored low on our rejection scale. According to their social workers they had on average improved more. According to their carers they had made on average better progress, fitted in better than when they came and had become less disturbed. Arguably, therefore, the children did change on arrival and they were more likely to change favourably in those families who did better on our main outcome measures.

Table 15.1 Measures of progress and parenting measures

Measures of progress	Scores		
	Child orientation	Rejection	Parenting
How far has there been a change in how child is doing relative to their age group?	0.284[1]	-0.296[1]	0.191[1]
Overall progress since arrival in the placement	0.181[1]	-0.531[1]	0.199[1]
Child seems less disturbed than when he/she first came	0.245[1]	-0.323[1]	0.252[1]
Fits in better than when he/she first came	0.221[1]	-0.435[1]	0.226[1]
The situation over the child's schooling is better than when he/she first came	0.210[1]	-0.189[1]	0.091 NS

Sources: Social worker questionnaire (question 1 only) and foster carer questionnaire at Time 1.
Notes: [1]$p<0.001$. NS= Not significant.

Our fourth main explanatory variable was 'contact with the educational psychologist'. Here the situation was more complicated. Our analysis was restricted to children aged five or over. On some variables there was improvement and on others no change, or deterioration.

Contact with the psychologist was associated with improvement in the eyes of the social workers ($p=0.033$). There was also a greater degree of improvement in these children's school situation as judged by their carers ($p=0.033$). In 68 per cent of these cases, there was said to have been considerable improvement in this respect and in only 15 per cent was there none. The comparable figures for those who had had no contact were 53 per cent and 19 per cent.

By contrast with this encouraging evidence, there was no evidence that children who had seen a psychologist had settled in better or become less disturbed. Moreover, the carers judged that those who had seen these psychologists were making poorer progress (only 36% of them were given the top rating for progress, as opposed to 53% of the others). So it seems likely that educational psychology was often provided for children who were not doing well – even if in certain respects they were seen as doing better than when they arrived. Its positive effects were probably quite specific.

Changes between Time 1 and Time 2 surveys

In those cases where a child remained with the same foster carer(s) we could explore the changes between measures at the Time 1 and Time 2 surveys. The main measures related to attachment problems, Goodman disturbance score, the 'looking after children' measures and the questions we asked about specific problems such as eating disorders or difficulties over drugs and alcohol.

Changes in problems related to attachment

As explained earlier, we computed two scores which related to attachment. One seemed to measure a kind of compulsive independence or stoicism. The second seemed to tap a kind of childlike or anxious attachment. On average, there was rather little change on either score. A third (32%) became more 'stoical', a third (30%) remained as stoical as before and a third (34%) became less stoical. The figures for childlike attachment were very similar – just over a third showed more of this behaviour, just under a third showed no change in this respect and around a third improved.

In keeping with this score, the rank order of the scores did not change much either. Those who scored relatively high on either score at the first survey tended to score relatively high at the second. Those who scored low similarly continued to score low. The correlations between the first and second scores was 0.64 (for stoicism) and 0.78 (for childlike attachment).

We examined whether our four key variables – rejection, child orientation, the parenting score and contact with an educational psychologist – were associated with changes on these scores. In carrying out these and similar analyses we faced the problem that change for the better was more likely when the child had scored particularly 'badly' during the first survey. If this happened, the child could not score much worse but could, in principle, score very well next time round. Moreover, bad scores are likely to represent chance downward fluctuations – for example, the carer may have filled in the questionnaire when the child had had a particularly difficult day. For similar reasons children who scored particularly well in the first survey were more likely to deteriorate.

In order to cope with these effects we fitted models of change that tried to predict the difference between the first and second state but allowed for the fact that this change measure was almost always highly correlated with state 1. For example, the model we tested for stoicism and rejection was:

change = (stoicism1 - stocism2)

change = a + $b_1$stoicism1 + $b_2$rejection

Unless we specifically state otherwise, all the models of change discussed in this chapter are of this kind and allow for the initial score. A second feature is that all focus on children aged four or over. Before this age the key variables – particularly the Goodman total score, child orientation and contact with the educational psychologist – are unreliable or inappropriate.

Using this analysis we found that rejection was associated with an increase in stoicism ($p=0.038$). In other words, children who were loved seemed to become less compulsively independent, while children who were not became more stoical. A similar finding is reported by Quinton and his colleagues (1998), who found that children who were loved by their new foster or adoptive parents became over time more attached to them. In keeping with this result we found that children who were rated by their carers as having relatively strong ties with at least one adult had lower childlike attachment scores by the second survey ($p=0.038$).

Rejection was not related to changes in anxious attachment and none of the other three variables were related to changes in stoicism or anxious attachment.

Disturbance

As others have also found (Beek and Schofield 2004; Farmer *et al.* 2004; Walker *et al.* 2002) our measure of disturbance (the Goodman total score) also showed, on average, little change. Overall 47 per cent improved on this measure and 47 per cent deteriorated (6% remained the same). The rank order of scores was also very little changed. The correlation between the first and second scores was 0.82 (i.e. children who scored well or badly relative to others in the first survey tended to do the same in the second).

Thus, strong association between the first and second scores suggests that differences between the children were not strongly reflected in greater improvement or deterioration among some than others. It was not, therefore, surprising that change on this score was not significantly related to any of our four major variables.

Extent of changes on the looked-after children scores

It will be remembered that in both surveys we asked the foster carers to rate the children on ten scales which related to their development. The dimensions we covered were taken from the 'looking after children' programme. The results are given below:

- *health* – 73 per cent of the children did not change at all, 8 per cent deteriorated and 19 per cent improved

- *education* – 51 per cent of the children did not change their position, 24 per cent deteriorated and 25 per cent improved

- *special skills and interests* – 53 per cent of the children did not change, 21 per cent deteriorated and 26 per cent improved

- *work* – this rating was only relevant to 15 children, a third of whom did not change their position, while 40 per cent deteriorated and 27 per cent improved

- *self-confidence* – 51 per cent of the children did not change, 22 per cent deteriorated and 26 per cent improved

- *emotional ties* – 53 per cent of the children did not change, 21 per cent deteriorated and 26 per cent improved

- *close friends* – 54 per cent did not change, 24 per cent deteriorated and 22 per cent improved

- *behaviour in social situations* – 55 per cent did not change, 22 per cent deteriorated and 23 per cent improved

- *emotional and behavioural development* – 55 per cent did not change, 23 per cent deteriorated and 22 per cent improved

- *self-care skills* – 52 per cent did not change, 20 per cent deteriorated, 28 per cent improved.

As can be seen it was only in relation to health that, on average, the foster carers reported a balance of improvement over deterioration.

Correlates of changes on looked-after children scores

Did our four main variables predict who improved and who deteriorated? As before, we calculated a change measure and its association with our four main variables, taking into account the initial starting point. This suggested that:

- child orientation and the parenting score were not associated with improvement or deterioration on any of the measures

- rejection was associated with deterioration in self-confidence ($p=0.063$), behaviour in social situations and emotional ties
- contact with an educational psychologist was significantly associated with *deterioration* in self-care skills, emotional and behavioural development, behaviour in social situations, special skills and interests, and education.

We calculated a crude overall measure of 'developmental improvement' by subtracting the total development scores at Time 1 from those at Time 2. (For this purpose we ignored the question on work since it applied to very few people.) This yields a score which is high when there is overall improvement.

As might be expected from the analysis of the individual scores, the results showed little average change. Forty-four per cent of the children had worse scores at the second survey and 44 per cent had better ones. The correlation between the total development scores at the first and second survey was high ($r=0.74$), showing that a child who scored high on the first survey was likely to do so on the second, and vice versa. None of our key variables were significantly related to this measure.

Changes in the specific problem scores

We asked the carers whether the children had problems in certain areas and, if so, whether these were improving, staying the same or getting worse. In the second survey we repeated the questions we had asked about this in the first. The survey questions at Time 1 referred to the time up to the survey itself. The questions at Time 2 referred to the time between the surveys.

Again, we wanted to see if changes among those who had a problem were related to the four main variables in which we were interested. For example, we explored whether those who were said to have problems with aggression were more likely to improve in households where they were 'accepted' as against those where they were 'rejected'.

The correlations in Table 15.2 (Kendall's tau) are low but reasonably consistent. As they only apply to those who displayed the problem, the numbers involved vary, a fact that explains why some apparently large correlations (e.g. the -0.68 between self-harm and contact with educational psychologist) are either not significant or only significant at a low level.

Table 15.2 Improvement and deterioration in specific areas related to key variables

	Parenting score		Child orientation		Rejection		Educational psychologist	
	Time 1	Time 2	Time 1	Time 2	Time 1	Time 2	Time 1	Time 2
Sexual behaviour	0.10	-0.08	0.14[1]	0.02	-0.26[2]	-0.19	-0.08	-0.09
Truancy	0.23[2]	-0.04	0.25[2]	-0.17	-0.17	-0.19	0.01	0.43[1]
Bedwetting	0.15	0.03	0.05	-0.06	-0.06	-0.17	-0.08	-0.05
Drink/drugs	-0.05	-0.18	-0.22	-0.21	-0.13	-0.13	0.16	-0.29
Self-harm	0.12	-0.07	-0.06	0.20	-0.19	-0.40	-0.01	-0.68[2]
Aggression	0.11	0.09	0.08	0.09	-0.35[2]	-0.03	0.06	-0.05
Run away	0.06	0.05	0.08	-0.01	-0.22	-0.12	0.15	0.43[1]
Obedience	0.22[3]	0.17	0.13*	0.08	-0.39[2]	-0.30[2]	0.06	0.04
Stealing	0.12	0.13[1]	0.11	0.04	-0.30[2]	-0.24[1]	0.03	0.00
Lying	0.17[2]	0.04	0.09	0.06	-0.34[2]	-0.12	-0.02	-0.05
Eating disorders	0.14[1]	-0.03	0.10[1]	0.14	-0.28[2]	-0.23[1]	-0.05	-0.12
Parent cont.	0.141	0.08	-0.03	0.10[1]	-0.18[2]	-0.04	0.05	0.05

Sources: All questionnaires at Time 1 and foster carer questionnaire at Time 2.
Note: [1]$p<0.05$ [2]$p<0.01$ [3]$p<0.001$. Negative correlations imply the variable is associated with deterioration.

As can be seen, the parenting score generally correlated positively with change, although only four of these correlations are significant. The child orientation score was associated with some change for the better, although only in relation to 'obedience' and truancy/school attendance were the correlations significant. The rejection score had the strongest associations with change, particularly in the first survey. Its association with increasing problems over aggression, sexual behaviour, discipline, stealing, lying and eating problems suggest a spiral of difficult behaviour leading to negative reactions and more difficult behaviour.

The pattern for contact with an educational psychologist was interesting. It was not significantly associated with changes on these variables in the first survey. However, it was significantly associated with improvements in truancy, and running away as reported in the second survey. It was also associated with self-harm at the second survey, although the numbers were very small (n=16).

We looked for other associations with special kinds of help and found only one. Those who were said to have received special help using behavioural methods were significantly more likely to have improved in relation to aggression/violence (see Table 15.3). There was a similarly significant association in the second survey between behavioural help in the next year and improvement in aggression ($p=0.039$).

Table 15.3 Changes in aggression and receiving behavioural help

	Behavioural help			
	Yes		No	
Change in aggression	n	%	n	%
Improved	36	82	87	62
No change	5	11	30	21
Deterioration	3	7	23	17
Total	44	100	140	100

Sources: Foster carer questionnaires at Time 1 and at Time 2 – table based on children said to have problems related to aggression. Kendall's tau=0.172, $p=0.016$.

Explaining the findings

The findings we have given so far in this chapter vary in their plausibility. Some seem straightforward and in keeping with earlier results. Others are paradoxical and confusing. The findings on contact with the educational psychologist seem particularly difficult to explain. In what follows we report further analyses designed to cast light on the explanation of these results.

Disturbance, attachment and deviance problems

Our measures of difficulty related to 'disturbance', attachment and 'social behaviour'. As we have seen, there was little evidence that, on average, children in foster care grew less disturbed or that their attachment scores improved.

There was also rather little change in the positions of children relative to each other on these scores. There was a very high level of correlation between the four scores at Time 1 and Time 2 (between 0.55 and 0.82 depending on the variable concerned). So it is not just that there is little change on average. There is not much evidence that some children are improving more than others.

Despite the relatively low level of change while we followed the children up, there was some evidence of earlier change. Parenting and child orientation scores were associated with improvements before the first survey as judged by the social worker and carer. They were also associated with improvement in some specific behaviours – again as judged by the carer. There was some evidence that the child orientation but not the parenting score was associated with a drop in the number of problems presented by the child over the time we knew them. Neither variable was associated with changes on the developmental scores.

In general, rejection was more strongly associated with these changes (in a negative direction) and it was also associated with deterioration on the stoicism or aloofness score.

Another exception to this rule of no change over the period of follow-up was that children who scored relatively high on the Goodman total score tended to deteriorate more than others. The more disturbed the child, the greater was the average deterioration on the looked-after children overall development scores ($p < 0.001$ after allowing for initial position).

A possible explanation for this phenomenon has to do with the connection between the Goodman total score and rejection. As we have seen, the Goodman total score was strongly associated with the rejection score. We suggested in the last chapter that it may produce disruption through this association (i.e. that where difficult behaviour did not lead to rejection it did not lead to disruption). This new finding suggests that, in practice, disturbance often leads to increasing rejection by the carer and that this then leads to negative change on the child's overall development and specific problem scores. In short, disturbed children are less easy to like, this lack of liking may lead to rejection and this in turn to more difficult behaviour. These findings recall the downward spirals identified in our case studies.

In order to explore this hypothesis further we created a second rejection score from the variables we had available from the second survey (a smaller number than those available for the first). The three questions we used were:

- There's no point in asking the child why he or she misbehaves.
- There's no point telling the child why I/we don't like her/his misbehaviour.
- I am not sure how long I/we can put up with the child.

These questions were answered on a three-point scale from 1 ('not at all true') to 3 ('true to a large extent'). We formed a score by adding them together.

As predicted, we found a significant correlation between evidence of 'rejection' at the time of the second survey and evidence of disturbance at the first (r=0.48, $p<0.001$). Those who had high Goodman total scores at the time of the first survey were more likely to be rejected at the second. This correlation dropped but remained highly significant if we took account of the fact that those who had high scores were more likely to be rejected at the time of the first interview. This suggests that children do tend to wear their carers down, gradually increasing the likelihood that the latter will come to see them as incorrigible and feel unable to put up with them.

The question of whether this rejection exacerbates difficult behaviour remains somewhat uncertain. As might be expected, the second rejection score was strongly associated with relatively poor developmental progress and with deterioration in the specific problem scores. The problem is that causation could, and almost certainly does, run both ways. Rejection can lead to lack of progress and lack of progress can lead to rejection. So the sensible conclusion may be that both apply. Help is needed for the carer's understandable distress, and also to reduce the extent of the child's difficulties.

Contact with an educational psychologist

The most puzzling set of findings related to contact with an educational psychologist. Why should something which, as we saw in the last chapter, predicts good success ratings and the avoidance of disruption also predict deterioration or lesser improvement in development scores? And if it does predict deterioration why should it be associated with some improvements in both the first and second survey? For as we have seen, it is associated with early improvement in the minds of social workers and also with carer reports that the child's situation at school had improved in the first survey. In the second survey it is associated with reports of less truancy, and running away.

The association with deterioration is in some ways not surprising. The receipt of most forms of help is associated with deterioration, presumably because it is prompted by it. Against this background, it is the association between educational psychologists and some good outcomes that calls for explanation. We argued in the last chapter that it may have reflected the focus of the psychologist on specific problems the child had. This focus is limited – hence in many respects the children may not improve. However, the changes achieved may be specific but crucial. As we have seen, there is some evidence that the psychologists help to reduce truancy and hence the amount of time a young person might be about the carer's house with too little to do. More importantly, they may improve a child's social situation at school and hence, conceivably, reduce the misery which leads to running away. In this respect they may play a crucial role, but one which needs to be exercised in collaboration with the school and the carer and which is by no means sufficient on its own.

Conclusion

We did not find major changes in the personalities and social performance of children over the year in which we followed them up. This evidence is in keeping with that of others who have been concerned with children over a longer period of time. Longitudinal studies in the 1960s and 1970s suggested that children were troubled before they entered the care system and remained troubled after they had done so (albeit in most cases only for a short period) (Lambert *et al.* 1977). Longitudinal studies of foster children and children who have been adopted have likewise shown remarkably little change on average (Heath, Colton and Aldgate 1994; Rowe *et al.* 1984; Rushton and Treseder 1995). Children's educational performance does not improve relative to that of their peers, there is little reduction in their disturbed behaviour, and even if they seem for a time calm, the propensity for disturbance is latent rather than absent.

Despite this rather depressing conclusion our results do suggest some more encouraging ones:

- There is probably improvement in quite a wide range of behaviour when the children are first placed.

- Committed foster care is subsequently associated with avoidance of breakdown and with an increase in the ability to attach even if it does not, of itself, improve global measures of behaviour.

- Specific changes are associated with both parenting and (to a much lesser extent) with specific interventions (behavioural help and help from an educational psychologist).

- The relationship between carer and child is probably (not certainly) a particularly important determinant of changes in the child, with each having an impact on the other.

Chapter Sixteen

Summary and Conclusions

Introduction

This book has been about foster placements. More specifically it has been about the purposes of placements, what foster children want from them and what helps them succeed. In reviewing our results we need to look at both purposes and means. Are the explicit or implicit purposes of placement appropriate? If they are, what changes might make them more likely to be realised?

Some basic issues

Our sample of foster children represented, as far as we could tell, a cross-section of foster children in the care system in England at a particular point in time. We have provided a picture of their characteristics and of what happened to them 14 months later. Carers, social workers and foster children told us why, in their view, the placements were more or less successful. We have tried to test their explanations statistically and compare our results with those of others.

Our findings are in many ways very encouraging. The great majority of foster children who answered our questionnaires said they were happy with their placements. These favourable opinions were probably shared by children not responding to the questionnaire, who were, after allowing for age, no more likely to experience placement breakdown. Moreover, the children's endorsement of foster care is in keeping with other evidence. Our case studies illustrated excellent practice. Our questionnaires gave ample evidence of the commitment of carers. Social workers judged that around seven out of ten placements were going or had gone very well, a proportion similar to those found by Rowe and her colleagues (1989) and Cliffe with Berridge (1991).

Despite these encouraging results our study identified a number of key problems. The most fundamental of these was the contrast between children's wish for a stable family life and the limited time most spent in placements. Foster care was not conceived as treatment designed to change the child. It was infrequently seen as a preparation for return home. It very rarely offered a long-term family for life. Essentially it provided, in a phrase used by Thoburn, Wilding and Watson (2000), 'a port in a storm'.

These problems are perhaps related to the fundamental approach to foster care. At bottom it is seen by many as a confession of failure. It is best if children remain with their parents. It is acceptable if they can be adopted. Parenting by the state is seen to be expensive and ineffective – something which should only be undertaken as a last resort and which should be as temporary as possible. Given such beliefs it is not surprising that so many of the foster children in our sample were repeatedly tried at home and that so few of them stayed on in foster care beyond the age of 18.

This set of beliefs does not easily provide a coherent framework for foster care. The old approach to foster care as a kind of quasi-adoption is no longer accepted. Yet if foster care is not a kind of upbringing what is it? In contrast to what was formerly true of residential care it does not claim to provide 'therapy'. Treatment if provided at all is given in the context of foster care. It is not seen as an intrinsic part of it.

So the concept of foster care as a port in a storm seems to be what is left. Foster care is certainly seen as benign. Its carers are commonly seen as 'the salt of the earth'. However, they are neither acknowledged as responsible parents nor treated as responsible professionals. What has our research to say that might help this to change?

We tackle these issues under three major headings:

1.   *Permanence.* The majority of the children replying to our questionnaire said they wanted to stay in their placements to 18 or beyond. Very few of them seemed likely to do so. What can be done about this?

2.   *The provision of durable and successful placements.* Although most placements were seen as successful the levels of success would have been higher and the rate of breakdown lower if all practice had been as good as the best. How can these lessons be applied?

3.   *Difficulty of enabling change to occur.* Children may change at the beginning of a placement. Thereafter we found little shift in either the absolute level of children's disturbance or social performance

or their position in these respects relative to others. Could foster care do more to help children change?

In what follows we will concentrate on these issues. In most cases we make recommendations. These are highlighted. This is to distinguish them from the rest of the text which is mainly summary and analysis. They are clearly not findings but we hope they encourage debate.

Permanence

Many of the children who enter foster care return home rapidly. Those who remain take up the bulk of foster care placements and figure largely in any cross-sectional survey of placements such as ours. These are children whose return is difficult to arrange. In our sample, return home had quite often been tried in the past. Six out of ten children had a previous experience of the care system. Optimism about the possibility of return had now faded. In only a fifth of the cases were social workers working for a return home at the first survey. Fewer than one in seven were at home or with relatives a year later.

The most common reason for entry to the care system was abuse. In the great majority of cases (around 90%) the social workers thought there was some evidence of abuse. In two-thirds of the cases the evidence was strong.

The relatively low rate of return home also reflected the children's wishes. According to the foster carers at the second survey more children (28%) wanted to be at home than actually were so. However, even more (44%) wanted to be with the foster carers. The children who replied to our questionnaire seemed to concur. Two-thirds of the children wanted to stay until they were at least 18, and nearly half wanted to stay longer than this.

These findings suggest that the care system needs to provide long-term stability. This, however, rarely seemed on offer. Very long stays in placements were uncommon. Fewer than one in eight had been in the same placement for longer than four years. Four out of ten children who had told us they wished to remain with their foster carers long-term were not with them a year later. Many experienced a kind of 'serial parenting' with different families – sometimes living with their own families and sometimes with different foster families.

The reasons for instability have to do with policies of community care, the strains on the foster care system, the difficulties surrounding adoption, and the difficulties of identifying long-term placements which would be suitable for a particular child. Further reasons have to do with the frequency with which placements break down and are dealt with in our next section.

Policies of community care

One reason for the instability of foster care lies in the policy of returning children to their parents wherever possible. Inevitably some returns will not work out (for relevant previous research see Packman, Randall and Jacques 1986; Rowe *et al.* 1989). So a policy which gives a majority of those entering the care system a chance of a permanent home with their parents must also produce a minority of children who return to the care system. On average those aged 16 or over when we first contacted them had had at least four episodes 'in care' punctuated by returns home. The number of times children had returned home was a very much stronger predictor of the number of foster placements they had experienced than either their disturbance or their age.

It is unlikely that this problem of 'serial parenting' can be removed entirely. There is a moral imperative to keep children in their homes or return them there if possible. Children and families may only accept long-stay care if every effort has been made to enable family care to work. So permanency depends in part on increasing the effectiveness of support in the community, on identifying more sharply those children for whom care in the community is not going to work, and on being willing on occasion to take decisive action where this is the case.

The issues are also easier to state than resolve. What seems decisive to some may seem insensitive and unjust to others.

> In our view, research is needed to identify the characteristics of children who have a high chance of returning to the care system if they return to their families, and to see if additional support would enable them to remain with their families.

These issues are outside the scope of the present book in part at least because they involve systems of family support in the community rather than foster care services themselves. These issues are by contrast a central concern of our third book on foster care.

Strains on the foster care system

A year after we first got information on them, four out of ten of the children were no longer fostered. Their destinations depended on age. The main ones were their family (all ages), adoption (for younger children), residential care (for teenagers) and independent living (for older teenagers). Without these 'exports' the system could not have managed the demands upon it. One authority was very reluctant to keep children over 16 with foster carers.

In our view, additional money, support adapted to the carers' situations, and more effective recruitment packages would increase the supply of carers and hence reduce these strains on the system. These issues are dealt with in our first book (Sinclair *et al.* 2004). They have to be tackled if longer-term foster care is to be offered.

A greater use of care by relatives and friends would also help tackle these problems. 'Kinship care' has particular problems of its own (both family disputes and the material problems are common among kin), is at present ill-supported and should not be regarded as a 'free lunch' (see Hunt 2001; Sinclair *et al.* 2004; Wilson *et al.* 2004). Nevertheless and despite low levels of support, foster care by friends and family is not recognisably 'worse' than foster care by others. It has potential major advantages in terms of continuity and the maintenance of family ties. It would allow longer stays in foster care without using up scarce existing sources of foster carers. It should also make easier the ethnic matching of children and foster carers.

Lack of appropriate long-stay foster placements

According to foster carers in the second survey, the children's most common wish would have been to remain with their foster carers either fostered (20%), adopted (15%) or on a residence order (8%). This proportion (43%) is close to the 44 per cent of children who told us they would like to stay on beyond 18.

In our first survey about one in six carers (17% of placements) would have liked to adopt their foster children or have them live with them on a residence order. The number had dropped by the time of the second survey – carers said they would like this in around 9 per cent of cases. American and British research suggests that breakdown rates are lower when short-term foster carers are confirmed as permanent foster or adoptive parents for children (Barth and Berry 1988; Borland *et al.* 1991; Lahti 1982).

In practice very few children stayed for long periods with their carers and hardly any stayed on for a long period and then remained after they were 18.

In our view, these findings imply a recognition by all authorities of the need for long-stay fostering (most of those who cannot return do not want to be adopted, and most are not going to be); encouragement for placements to continue after the child is 18; recognition and encouragement for the work carers do with children after they have left; a willingness to support rather than oppose adoption by foster carers including assistance with legal fees, adoption allowances, and subsequent support if necessary, equivalent to that offered to carers.[1]

> The development of a range of long-stay placements would include the encouragement of placements with family and friends but also small, low-staffed, quasi-children's homes for those who did not want the closeness of family life.

Lack of effective support for adoptive placements

Adoption reduces the strain on the system and potentially provides stability. It is not seen by foster carers as attracting support or finance equivalent to foster care.

> In our view, the criteria for allocating financial and social support to placements should be based on need, not legal status: adoptive placements should receive high support if needed.

Limits to professional discretion

There are quite widespread beliefs that children should be placed with their siblings; that placements in families where the carer has her own children are risky, particularly if the foster child is close in age; and that placements with relatives are to be preferred to placements with strangers. These beliefs can limit the number of placements available to a particular child.

In general none of these hypotheses were borne out in our study. We did *not* find that outcomes were *on average* better or worse in placements with relatives, where the child was placed with brothers or sisters, where there were other unrelated foster children or where the carer had resident children of her own.

This does not suggest that the carer's children are unimportant, that foster children can be moved at will, or that it does not matter whether foster children are placed with relatives or with their siblings. For example, if foster children did not get on with other children in the placement this was obviously very difficult. On average, however, these situations were balanced by others where they did get on with other children. Thus in each individual case the question of whether a child should be placed with others or on his or her own is very important. There is, however, no generalisation which says what the answer should be. So there are no substitutes for listening carefully to what those involved want and weighing the factors in each case.

> In our view, a greater reliance on social workers' professional discretion, rather than rules of thumb, is a prerequisite of good practice and should also increase placement choice.

Logistical difficulties in ensuring choice

Placements which are intended to be permanent should be carefully chosen. This implies that choice is possible. However, in most cases there was said to be no choice of placement at the moment it was made. Where they lacked choice, social workers made placements which in 40 per cent of such cases in our sample were said not to be fully satisfactory. These placements were more likely to disrupt in the short-term, although if they lasted they were as durable as others.

Placements which were intended to be long-term were, in the great majority of cases, seen as well-matched. However, this was apparently achieved by letting the child wait in a short-term placement until such time as a longer-term one became available. Children in our sample who were said to have been placed 'short-term while things were sorted out' or 'to help get parents and child back together' had already been in the placement for an average of over two years. Even those placed 'for assessment' had waited on average for 21 months.

The common expectation is that this problem of choice can be resolved by an increase in the number of foster carers. Our evidence suggests that this is unrealistic. An increase in foster carers would help. However, social workers match on a wide variety of factors (e.g age, ethnicity, expected length of stay, need for particular school, special skills of carer, geography). It is unlikely that, say, a long-stay placement, able to take siblings and with a carer skilled in working with sexually abused children, will be available close to a particular school the moment such a placement is needed. Immediate close matches can only be guaranteed by a massive pool of vacancies. Foster carers would then need to be paid a retaining fee in order to keep them while they waited for a match. The result would be very expensive and reduce the money available to attract more foster carers.

One solution to this problem might be to develop a version of a 'bridging placement' staffed by professional foster carers. Such carers would need to accept a wide variety of children. They would also need to accept that these children would stay with them for varying lengths of time.

They might also be required to take varying numbers of children. Our evidence suggests that the possibility of a placement being successful is not impaired by placing more than one child in the same placement. Other research has confusingly found that placement with others reduces risk of poor outcomes (Berridge and Cleaver 1987) or, by contrast, increases it (Quinton *et al.* 1998).

In our view, bridging placements should be developed as described above. There should be further research on the relationship between outcomes and numbers of foster children placed.

What made for durable and successful placements?

These suggestions made above are intended to encourage more permanent placements. They may not diminish breakdowns. If anything they may make them more painful, more visible and more likely. More is likely to be invested in placements which are seen as permanent so their breakdown will be more painful. The more definite the commitment to a placement the more it will be obvious if it does not last as long as planned. If the number of children in children's homes is decreased (the most plausible method of paying for more permanent placements) the number of difficult children who are fostered will increase. This in turn may increase the number of placement breakdowns. For these reasons, the reduction of placement breakdowns is a crucial issue for policies designed to increase permanence.

We defined a 'breakdown' as occurring when the foster carer, social worker or family social worker said that a placement had disrupted. On this definition between a fifth and a quarter (22%) of the placements 'broke down' over the year. Unfortunately, the likelihood of breakdown, while reducing over the first two years, thereafter remained reasonably constant. Long placements (four years or over) were therefore rare.

Our concentration on breakdown as a measure of outcome is partly justified by its importance. It is also justified by its relevance to 'placement success'. In our study we obtained ratings of success from social workers, carers and family placement workers. Our overall rating was equivalent to the least optimistic rating made by any of these three groups. Placements which broke down were rated as much less successful both before and after the disruption. Moreover factors which made breakdowns less likely also made it more likely that the placement would be judged a success.

Our model predicting placement durability is essentially the same as the model predicting success. Both focused on four broad groups of variables. These concern the child, the carer, the interaction between child and carer, the birth family, and outside interventions (special help and support from school).

Three points should be made about the model:

- It is a model of placement rather than case success. Placements can succeed in the sense that children and carers get on and the child flourishes but fail in their purpose (e.g. to prepare for adoption).

- It is not a tightly linked set of hypotheses. Rather, the model specifies the kinds of variables that are likely to be important in explaining success and provides hypotheses as to how they work.

- There is unequal support for different parts of the model. For example, the importance of responsive parenting is (in our view) underlined by evidence from all the qualitative material, the statistical analyses, and evidence from other studies (Farmer *et al.* 2004; Quinton *et al.* 1998). By contrast, our statistical findings on the educational psychologist come, as it were, from out of the blue. We are not aware of confirmatory evidence from our qualitative material or other research.

So much acknowledged, the model does, in our view, provide a useful way of holding our material together. Comparison between our statistical material on the list of 'conditions' at the end of Chapter 8 shows some statistical evidence for most of them and no statistical evidence against any of them. In addition, there is evidence for the usefulness of distinguishing between the 'prior condition' for responsive parenting (e.g. being a skilled carer) and responsive parenting itself (dealing with a particular child in a responsive way). In what follows we therefore follow the broad outline of the model.

The children's contribution

The majority of the children entered the placements because of abuse or, particularly if they were older, because of the breakdown of relationships with their families. Both sets of problems are either rooted in relationship difficulties or likely to lead to them. In addition there was some evidence that relationship difficulties were often antecedents to social difficulties such as problems at school which in turn led on to wider problems in handling social life.

These problems had consequences for the placements. Children who were 'difficult' were less likely to succeed in their placements. Conversely, those who showed attractive characteristics were more likely to do so. Thus children who appeared to have difficulties with attachment or to be disturbed, or whose social performance was poor, were more common in less successful placements. By contrast, children who helped others, saw tasks through to the end and showed other admirable traits were more common in successful ones.

The children's motivation was also important. Those who were seen by their carers as wanting to be in their placements were more likely to succeed in them. Some carers saw these children as making the placement succeed. The children's wants and needs also determined what they looked for in a placement and hence how they reacted to it. They did not all want the same things. However, they shared common needs.

One set of needs was for *a normal family life*. So they wanted the care, concern and encouragement others get from their families, to feel they belonged and were not the 'odd one out', fair treatment – not to be picked on or treated too strictly, to get on with all in the placement including other children, not to have their family or school turned into a branch office of social services, as much pocket money etc. as other children, and to be able to ask their foster carers rather than their social workers for permission to stay with friends.

A second set of needs arose from the insecurities and conflicts of their particular position. They were not true members of the family. They had their own families towards whom they often had complex emotions. They could be moved at short notice and at the behest of others. So they wanted *respect for their individuality, the kind of contact they wanted with particular members of their family*, and *some say over their careers in care*.

Implicitly, therefore, they wanted carers who would respect their culture and values, would listen to them, would not be competitive towards their families, and who would fight for their point of view in discussions with social services.

The ability to meet these needs and cope with the difficulties children present depends heavily on factors discussed below. However, three points should be made here:

The children's problems have to do with relationship difficulties commonly compounded by difficulties at school and associated with difficult social behaviour. An understanding of these difficulties and of the children's wishes for a normal family life, and a say in the arrangements for their placements and future, should be the bedrock of foster care policy, training and practice.

Some children complained they were not moved from placements where they were unhappy.[2] Such movements are likely to be discouraged by new performance indicators but should, in our view, be left to the professional discretion of social workers.

> Some children were able to chose placements (e.g. by arranging accommodation with a teacher or a family friend or by asking to remain in a short-stay placement). Anecdotally, these placements seemed to get off to a good start (a view for which other research provides statistical support – Beek and Schofield 2004) and were to be encouraged.

The carer's contribution

Some carers seem particularly committed to fostering and good at it. These carers were more likely to succeed with their current foster children and less likely to have breakdowns among their previous ones. Our research provided different but complementary accounts of what made a successful carer.

According to carers, success depended on loving or liking the child, and on commitment, persistence and 'stickability'. Carers had to be able to take difficult behaviour, something which was easier if they were able to interpret it as something other than an attack on themselves, and they had to provide appropriate expectations.

To this demanding list of qualities social workers added a need for a kind of dispassionate love. Carers had to care for the child while remaining able to give them up. They had to avoid competing with birth parents. The social workers added that this was easier if the carers had a sense of the limits of what they could do, were not under stress from other sources and were able to ask for help when needed.

Our case studies gave a more detailed picture of the skills and qualities needed by carers. They had to be comfortable with the way children expressed needs to be safe and loved – some children wanted closeness and warmth from their carer, others wanted something more distant. They had to encourage the children and help them to feel worthwhile. They had to handle difficult behaviour but not in a way that made the child feel insecure, unloved or worthless. They had to be able to deal with the child's birth family, avoiding, as far as possible, a conflict of loyalties. They had to elicit help from those from whom they needed it – their own family, the social workers, the school and so on. Finally, they had to be able to 'ride out' difficulties – not reacting to them in such a way as to make matters worse. Difficulties in one of these areas – for example, in handling behaviour – could lead to problems in others and hence to a downward spiral and breakdown.

Our statistical analysis suggested that success was linked to these parenting approaches. We asked the social workers to rate the carers in terms of whether they were caring, accepting, encouraging, clear in their expectations, not easily upset by the child's failure to respond and capable of seeing things from the child's point of view. In general, carers received very high ratings on these qualities, but those who received particularly high ratings had better success than others. So too did those whose replies to the questionnaire suggested they were 'child-oriented' and spent time with the child doing things which he or she might be expected to like. By contrast, years of experience and amount of training received were not linked to outcomes.

In our view, effective foster care depends on the quality of carers. This means that good carers are recruited, the small number of ineffective ones are counselled out, and the natural commitment of carers is enhanced by high quality training and supplemented by appropriate supervision/support. We saw in the first book that breakdowns were potent triggers for carers to cease fostering, and thus offer an opportunity either to change or prevent this.

> In our view, the overall quality of the 'carer workforce' should be monitored through routine statistics on breakdowns and allegations, and ratings of carer quality made by social workers.

Breakdowns and endings should be used as an opportunity to review lessons from placements that have lasted some time with a view to:

- counselling out the small number of poor carers
- ensuring that any lessons about the kind of child that fits the carer's family are learnt
- acknowledging and valuing the carer's contribution.

Training should:

- be based on an analysis of the precise skills carers need (as above)
- involve practice in using these skills
- involve experienced carers
- be evaluated.

Social work support should reinforce the same training – at present such support is not obviously associated with outcomes for children.

Matching, fit and interaction

Outcomes depend not only on the individual child and foster carer but also on how the two get on. Three rather different issues are involved. First, there is the question of *matching*. By this we mean the degree to which the child is, on the face of it, suitable for the foster family (e.g. the placement is close to the child's school and approved for the children of that age). Second, there is the question of *fit* – this means that the child adapts easily to the family's way of doing things and gets on with family members. Third, there is the question of *affinity* – 'some you bond with, some you don't'. Some children appealed to their carers because of their needs, others because they were a challenge, others because of their sense of humour, their resilience, or through pride in their achievements.

Our study produced evidence that matching, fit and affinity were all related to outcomes. Poor matching (or at least 'perceived unsuitability') was related to poor outcomes in the first year. Placements for children who were not liked by others in the household were likely to fail. Conversely, children to whom the carers were attached were likely to do well. Both our case studies and our statistics emphasised the importance of 'spirals of interaction'. Thus carers might react negatively to children's bad behaviour which in turn grew worse in response to the negative reaction.

The ease of matching should be enhanced by suggestions already made (increasing the number of carers, 'bridging placements').

The likelihood of a good 'fit' should be increased by paying attention to what the foster family say, providing them with good information about the prospective foster child, and paying attention to their views.

The likelihood of affinity should be increased by paying attention to child and carer choices.

The likelihood of negative spirals should be reduced by early intervention which:

- helps carers to tackle negative behaviour early on

- encourages them to respond to the good things the child may be doing

- reinterprets the child's behaviour so that it is less likely to be seen as a personal attack on the carer.

Birth families

Birth families were very important to the children. This did not necessarily mean that they wished to return to them, or that they wanted to have contact with all of them. They were able to distinguish between members of their family. They did not necessarily wish to have the same kind of contact with each member. At the same time, children's determination to see unreliable or otherwise fallible parents sometimes led to what seemed to us unproductive confrontations with foster carers.

Our study highlighted the diverse reasons for which social workers supported contacts with birth families, and the stress these sometimes involved for carers and children. Contrary to what some might expect, the placements of abused children were more likely to be successful if someone was forbidden access to them. These findings add to the evidence that although children generally want more contact with their families than they get, these contacts can nevertheless be detrimental to them (Farmer *et al.* 2004; Quinton *et al.* 1998).

So the study highlights the need for social workers to:

- pay attention to the differing views of children on contact and return

- work with carers and children on the kinds of support needed over contact

- distinguish between family members in thinking about contact – other research suggests that foster children often want contact with particular relatives, that social workers are often unaware of these wishes (Cleaver 2000) and that contact with grandmothers can be particularly helpful (Farmer *et al.* 2004)

- ensure children are not put at risk during contact

- be willing on occasion to forbid contact.

For their part carers need to:

- avoid confrontations with children over their views of their parents

- avoid conflicts of loyalty over parents

- encourage contact in a discriminating way.

Schools and special help

Carers sometimes mentioned the lack of special help such as psychotherapy as an explanation for why placements did not go well. They rarely, if ever, mentioned the presence of special help as an explanation for success. In keeping with this, our findings on 'special help' were discouraging. Except in the case of contact with the educational psychologist, it was associated with worse outcomes. The association was usually much reduced if we took account of the children's disturbance. However, with the exception of educational psychology, there was no evidence that these interventions were powerful forces for good.

These findings are depressing. In this area, effective policy depends on an effective method of intervention. There is, for example, little point in trying to increase liaison between social services and community mental health teams if the latter are in no better position than social workers to offer help to disturbed foster children.

In this rather gloomy context our positive findings are particularly important. First, contact with an educational psychologist was associated with good success ratings, the avoidance of disruption, and certain specific improvements (in truancy and running away) that may reflect an improvement in the child's situation at school. The apparently beneficial impact of these psychologists may be specific to particular behaviours. They may also depend on early intervention – contact when the child is already disaffected may be less effective – and on collaboration with both school and carer. Whatever the limitations, these findings need replicating. At present they are a ray of hope in a rather gloomy picture.

Second, help which used a behavioural approach was associated with a reduction in aggressive behaviour. Given the evidence that difficult behaviour can lead to rejection by carers, this too is a lead which deserves to be taken up.

Third, happiness at school predicted good outcomes even after other characteristics of the child had been taken into account.

> These findings suggest:
>
> - a need for an increased use of educational psychology
> - research into the applicability of a behavioural approach in foster care
> - a need for a wide view of the importance of school – it is not simply an arena for acquiring qualifications; it may also have a key impact on the child's quality of life and on her or his social skills and behaviour.

The difficulty of enabling change

The children in our study had, albeit to varying extents, difficulties relating to attachment, emotional and behavioural disturbance, and social performance. Some could not trust others and had few close emotional relationships. Some behaved in a disturbed way – for example, they might lie, steal, be overactive, or display inappropriate sexual behaviour. Some displayed difficulties outside the home – failing at school, truanting, staying out late, and becoming involved with delinquency or drugs. These characteristics do not provide them with much of a basis for success in later life.

We looked at whether children who remained in the same placement had improved on measures related to these difficulties. However, we found that psychological change was difficult to bring about. Encouragingly, disturbed behaviour did seem to improve at the beginning of a placement. Afterwards it was very persistent, changing little over the year the children were followed up. The same was true of problems over giving and receiving affection, and over social performance such as school attendance. Among those children who remained in the placement, our measures of disturbed attachment, overall disturbance and social performance were all on average almost exactly the same for the two surveys. Nor was there much evidence that some children were doing better than they had been and others doing worse. Why was this so and what might be done about it?

Reasons for lack of psychological change

The reasons for this lack of psychological change are unclear.[3]

One possibility is that placements reach a *modus vivendi*. When the child first arrives in the placement, he or she is likely to be in an upset state. Demands are placed on her or him. Either the placement breaks down, or the child changes, or the placement adapts. Usually, no doubt, there is some give and take on both sides. This, however, produces a situation where the need for change is less and no further change ensues.

Another possibility is that we are looking for more fundamental change than is likely. Disturbed attachments may reflect early traumas and be hard to change. Disturbance may reflect not only the abuse and deprivation the children have suffered but also their temperaments. Again change may be too much to expect. Educational performance builds up over time. Children commonly enter foster care when they have already fallen behind. Short of a massive programme of remedial education, their educational deficits may be hard to make up. And in these respects foster children may not be unusual. How often do any of us change fundamentally? Is it not more often the case that we learn tricks, skills, ways of managing our social performance? And in this way most of us get by, despite our flaws and original sin.

So much acknowledged, we can nevertheless put forward hypotheses about what might enable change to occur.

The importance of environment

Whatever the explanation one implication is that intervention must include the environment as well as the child.

> If the children are not going to change, their environments must adapt to them.

The implications of this depend on whether the children return home or not.

> If they are not to return to their parents, their foster homes have to be available to them as long as needed and beyond 18 if necessary.

If the children are to return home there is a need for work with the home environment. Many foster children are clearly very difficult even for self-confident, experienced foster carers. It is unlikely that their own parents, often troubled by poverty and other problems, find them any easier.

> If the children are to return home, there is a need to provide their families with at least as much support as is currently available to foster families.

(Again this is an issue we consider in more depth in our third book, where we show that the families of foster children often receive little support.)

The need for an appropriate theory

Foster children have generally experienced abuse, severe family conflict or both. This leaves many of them with difficulties in handling relationships. This in turn probably contributes to their difficulties at school. Difficult behaviour learnt at school or in other social settings can in turn exacerbate their relationship problems.

Attempts to reduce these problems should ideally be based on an appropriate theory. Our own view is that this theory should probably include an understanding of attachment (which is particularly relevant to relationships) and of social learning (which is particularly relevant to behaviour).

We would see attachment theory and social learning theory as complementary rather than competitive. For example, the identification of the antecedents of difficult behaviour and of the rewards which maintain it may often require an understanding of the relationship within which the behaviour takes place. Similarly a key difficulty in foster care lies in the need to confront unacceptable behaviour while enabling the child displaying the behaviour to feel secure. A key element, as we saw it, in Mrs Stanton's success lay in her ability to combine these apparently contradictory requirements.

Evidence for this view comes from three sources:

- It is logical in the light of what is known of the difficulties of foster children.

- It fits, in our view, the analysis of other researchers, although these typically emphasise one of the components or the other. See e.g. Downes (1992), Schofield et al. (2000), and Beek and Schofield (2004) for attachment theory; Chamberlain (1998) for social learning theory; Walker et al. (2002) for a general emphasis on relationships and on responsible social behaviour.

- It fits with our qualitative data on what makes for effective practice in foster care.

This evidence is indirect. It fits the data from this report. Other explanations might also fit the data. Even if they do not, the theory lacks proven applications. What is needed is a study of intervention. Is it true that training and support explicitly and consistently based on an understanding of attachment and social learning produces better outcomes? Without this evidence training lacks a solid basis.

> In our view, studies of the effects of theoretically based training and support need to be undertaken.

Need to value small gains

> A further implication may be that carers and social workers should concentrate on changes which can be achieved.

There was evidence that some children became less violent, others improved their attendance at school, others became less distressed over contact with their birth families and so on. Changes in specific behaviours may make it easier for a placement to last, and thus enable a supportive environment.

> Behavioural methods and contact with an educational psychologist seem on our evidence promising ways for achieving these results.

Need to emphasise education

Social workers and carers are rightly urged to emphasise education. The emphasis is partly on attendance and partly on success in examinations. We return to this subject in our next book, where we argue that success in examinations has to be accompanied by support to achieve the kind of work in which examination success counts. However, in both that book and this we produce evidence that importance of school is too narrowly viewed. Happiness at school is crucial.

> In our view, it is vital that social workers and carers take a wide view of schooling, are alert to bullying and other causes of unhappiness and also quick to spot opportunities offered by school for a wide range of positive experiences and achievements.

Need to develop a coherent approach

If children change on moving to the environment of a new foster home, it is likely that they will change again on returning to the old environment of their family. This at least seems to be the lesson of earlier research on residential care (Sinclair 1975). The maintenance of changes made in foster care may therefore depend on consistency between what occurs within the foster home and what occurs subsequently. More generally it is likely that children will find it easier to change if the 'messages' given by key individuals such as carers, parents and foster carers are consistent.

The research provides some evidence for these hypotheses. Foster carers complained that some parents undermined their messages while the child was still fostered. The apparently negative effect of contact in certain circumstances is evidence for the potential of the original environment to harm. The power of this environment would certainly be greater when the child returned to it. In our third book we will provide evidence that children returning home often did not do well.

The study also suggested that the good effect of the educational psychologist was not independent of the approach of the foster carers. Rather the psychologist was only likely to be effective if the carers were also keen on encouraging the child at school. It seems likely that a similar coincidence of approach may be necessary for the effectiveness of other forms of treatment, although we have provided no evidence of this.

All this suggests that interventions are most likely to succeed if they work with the key elements in the children's environment – in this case the foster carers and, sometimes, the birth parent(s) – and if they focus on specific behaviours or changes. This suggestion is in keeping with the two models of foster care that have been evaluated as successful in the United States (Chamberlain 1998; Clark *et al.* 1994). One in particular draws heavily on a behavioural approach to parent training. It teaches the relevant skills to foster carers and then if the child goes home to the child's parents. This approach is intended to ensure that changes which occur in the placement are reinforced when the child returns home. It seems to us logical.

> Given the lack of evidence for most kinds of special help in Britain we need to adapt this approach to British conditions and try it.

In this respect there is a problem. The research reported here is not experimental. Our conclusions are (to us) plausible but we cannot show that any practice recommendations would actually improve results. If research is to play its part in improving practice it needs to become more experimental. Unfortunately, the cost of an intervention is usually much greater than the cost of evaluating it. Strained research budgets cannot fund interventions. So there are few carefully designed experiments in social services departments. Practice suffers as a result.

> In our view, the Department for Education and Skills should fund a linked programme or programmes of research and development in the field of foster care.

Conclusion

Foster care is an impressive system to which both carers and children are committed. However, it has three key problems. It rarely offers permanence. Its placements are too liable to break down. It does not have proven ways for enabling its children to change.

Our research suggests that policy designed to provide permanence for young people should be more determined. Bridging placements should be deliberately developed to allow time for matches between child and placement to be made. The decisions between adoption, residence orders and long-term fostering should be based on rights, wishes and needs rather than finance. The possibility of some continuing contact between foster carer and child after the child has left should always be considered. Local authorities should never operate on the assumption that children should leave their long-term placements before their eighteenth birthday – they should have the option of staying on with their families as other children do. There should be more adoptions by foster carers and more support for stranger adoptions.

Practice also needs to develop. This implies self-confidence – a willingness to acknowledge that social workers are taking professional decisions and should not be bound by rules of thumb and inappropriate performance indicators. It implies the development and testing of effective ways of training foster carers in the skills they need. It implies attention to the relationship between what goes on in the foster placement and the child's subsequent environment.

On all these matters we have made suggestions. We may, of course, be wrong, as may others of equal good will and greater wisdom. For what is still needed is a readiness to acknowledge the difficulty of the problems to be tackled and the lack of sure knowledge on how to do so. Hence comes the requirement both to build on the expertise which carers have and to test the approaches which result.

Notes

1. Around 7 per cent of the sample were said to want adoption and to have carers who would have wished to adopt if additional support had been available (data from second survey).

2. It might be felt that this would increase disturbance. However, we did *not* find that children became more disturbed because they changed placements. It was rather that children who were already disturbed were more likely to have many placements.

3. Evidence of a similar kind comes from various longitudinal studies. The problem is not that foster care causes problems but that it fails to reverse them (Aldgate *et al.* 1992; Rushton and Treseder 1995).

Are Our Samples Representative?

Introduction

The samples discussed in this report represent the results of a complicated process of selection. Our samples were drawn from the foster children of carers who had responded to a questionnaire (the General Questionnaire) sent to all foster carers in the seven authorities and who agreed to answer a further questionnaire on at least one foster child. However, the questionnaire about a specific child was sent some six months after the General Questionnaire, and so the sample had to be selected from those who were still fostering and had a child at that date.

As can be seen, this process allows for a variety of sources of bias. The final sample is influenced by response rates to the General Questionnaire, the proportion agreeing to go forward to the next sample, the proportion of those who had an eligible foster child at the appropriate date, the proportion of those sent a questionnaire and so on. The sample will be biased if these processes depart from random selection – for example, if older carers were less likely to respond to the first questionnaire than younger ones. This appendix examines these possible sources of bias and their relevance to the questionnaires returned by foster carers, social workers and children.

Before discussing these issues we should point out that according to usual criteria our samples pass as highly representative. As has been seen (Chapter 2), they reflect almost exactly the national picture in terms of the age and sex of the children, the length of time they have been in the care system, and their legal status.

Sampling frame

We showed in Appendix 1 of our first book (Sinclair *et al.* 2004) that, as far as could be judged from national statistics, our local authorities were, taken as a whole, highly representative. They had almost exactly the right proportion of children looked after per 10,000 population, and the right proportions of these fostered, in children's homes or placed for adoption.

We showed in the same appendix that our sampling frame may have excluded some carers who were fostering relatives and were supported by area social workers rather than family placement social workers. We also showed that response rates to the first ('general') questionnaire were lower if the foster carer was in a London borough and, largely for this reason, if they came from a minority ethnic group. There were lower response rates from inactive carers and from carers who fostered 'specific' children (i.e. they were only registered to foster relatives or 'specific' children).

The effect of the low response rate from minority ethnic carers should be to reduce the proportion of minority ethnic children in the sample. This effect may have been mitigated by our deliberate policy of over-sampling authorities with relatively high proportions of minority ethnic groups in their population (we included three). As discussed in Chapter 2, our proportions of minority ethnic children seem similar to those found in other studies.

The effect of the lack of London children depends on how far these children differ from others. With the exception of minority ethnic groups we did not find that they did.

We have undoubtedly under-sampled children with relatives. We have also probably under-sampled children whose 'specific' foster families may have regarded the children as 'part of the family' and therefore been reluctant to answer a question-naire which implicitly regarded them as something different.

Response bias in foster carer replies at Time 1

In the General Questionnaire we asked whether carers would be willing to complete a further questionnaire on a specific child. Only 10 per cent said they would not. We found few differences between those who agreed to take part and those who refused. Carers aged 55 or over were more likely to say 'no' (18% did so, as against 9% of the remainder). Carers who had definite opinions on foster care on our fostering score either for or against were more likely to say 'yes' than those whose opinions fell in the middle group. Relative carers were slightly more likely to say 'no' but the difference from others was not significant (16% versus 9%). So too were carers from ethnic minorities (15% as against 9%), but again the difference was not statistically signifi-cant. Carers who were intending or contemplating leaving over the next two years were significantly more likely to refuse to take part.

We drew our sample six months later. The criteria were:

- the foster carer should not have said they did not wish to take part
- we had to have up-to-date information on whether carer was fostering
- the carer had to have a child at that time
- no carer should have more than two children in the sample.

Originally we had intended to exclude children who had been looked after for less than six months. We found that if we did this we could not achieve our target of 600 children. We therefore relaxed this restriction but we did not take children in respite care unless they had been looked after continuously for three months.

Differences between carers who were, and carers who were not, sent question-naires followed from these rules. After excluding the 10 per cent who had declined to take part, carers were less likely to be sent a questionnaire if:

- they had not been fostering at the time of the General Questionnaire (26%)
- they were respite carers (12%)
- they were under 35 (40%)
- they were relative carers (38%)
- they were definitely intending to leave over the next two years (31%)
- they had left by the time of the follow-up (30%).

The figures in brackets give the proportions of carers in these categories who were eligible for the study and therefore sent a questionnaire. The proportion of the whole sample included in the survey was 52 per cent.

We sent out 596 questionnaires on these eligible children to the foster carers and received back 495 – a response rate of 83 per cent. Eighty-seven per cent of those sent questionnaires returned at least one. We looked for differences between respond-ers and non-responders. The only ones we could find were slight:

- ethnic minority carers were less likely to respond than white carers (72%)
- lone carers were less likely to respond than couples (78%)
- carers the average age of whose foster children was high (in top quartile) were less likely to respond (78%).

Although these groups were less likely to respond, the response was nevertheless very good. Thus the main sources of bias, if any, do not reflect the response rate of those to whom we sent the questionnaire. Rather, they reflect responses to the original ques-tionnaire, and the decisions we made in drawing the sample from those who responded to the questionnaire and agreed to take part in a further study. Particularly important decisions were to draw the sample six months after the General Question-naire and to exclude respite carers who did not have a child fostered for more than three months.

We had three major sources of possible bias. These reflected the cumulative results of the processes discussed above.

First, the sample under-represented minority ethnic carers in the authorities where we did the study. This reflected the much lower response rate from the London boroughs to the General Questionnaire, the lower response from Asian carers outside London in the same survey, the slightly greater unwillingness of minority ethnic carers to agree to take part in the second survey which asked about a specific child, and their lower response rate if they did so. The cumulative effect of these biases may have been mitigated by our decision to go to three authorities with very high proportions of minority ethnic carers.

Second, the sample under-represented respite carers and relative carers. Respite carers were virtually excluded by our deliberate choice. We only included them if they had been caring for at least three months. Relative carers were less likely to be identified in the sampling frame than would have been expected from national evidence, less likely than others to respond to the General Questionnaire, and more likely to be excluded from the study because they had no child at the time.

Third, the sample under-represented recent or withdrawing carers. This effect reflected choice at the first stage when those who were not actively fostering were less likely to return questionnaires. It reflected choice at the second stage when those who were contemplating leaving were less likely to agree to take part. It reflected choice on our part since we delayed drawing the sample for six months after the first survey. We thus restricted it to those who were continuing to foster actively, in most cases intended to continue, and had been fostering for at least six months.

Differences between respondents and non-respondents

These effects will bias the sample if different kinds of children go to carers of these different kinds. It is particularly important to know if the characteristics which are over- or under-represented in the sample are associated with outcomes. If they are, this would affect the picture of how successful fostering is. It could also, although this is unlikely, distort the relationship between other variables and outcome.

There were too few children with relative and respite carers to say whether they tended to be different.

Children from minority ethnic groups were more likely to be with minority ethnic carers. They did not differ significantly from other children on the other variables which have been the focus of the report. In particular, they were no more or less likely to disrupt or have lower success or better success ratings.

We examined the outcomes of children whose carers had considered withdrawing. They were no more likely to disrupt than others. Those whose carers were merely contemplating withdrawal as opposed to having made a definite decision to withdraw were said to be doing somewhat worse at the time of the first survey. Difficulties at this time may have led to the carer's uncertainties.

We also examined the outcomes of children whose carers had joined relatively recently (within a year of the General Questionnaire). They were no different from the outcomes of anyone else.

Sources of bias in the other questionnaires

The key processes that could affect the representativeness of the foster carer returns on the sample occurred before the questionnaires were sent to them. After that, the response rate was high. Similar processes affected the social worker returns and family placement social worker questionnaire at Time 1 and the response rate from all three sources at Time 2.

- In the case of the family placement social workers, the response rate was again very high (83% at Time 1 and 78% at Time 2).

- In the case of the social workers the response rate was lower (53% for full information and 70% for information on key variables at Time 1, 57% at Time 2).

- The response rate from foster carers was uniformly high (83% at Time 1 and 85% at Time 2).

As indicated above, we increased the response rate for the first social work question-naire by sending a much briefer questionnaire to those social workers who had not responded. This ensured that we had information on certain key variables (e.g. whether child had previously been abused) for 70 per cent of the sample.

Comparing children described in different questionnaires

We could check for additional bias by focusing on children covered by one question-naire (say the Time 1 foster carer questionnaire) and comparing those included in say the social worker questionnaire with those who were not. Such checks are a great deal more sensitive than the usual checks for response bias which can only examine such things as age and ethnicity.

We compared those who were returned or not returned in the different question-naires on the following variables:

- first and second success variables, disruption, fostering score (all questionnaires)

- child orientation score, rejection score, length of time in placement, social behaviour score, Goodman score Time 1, contact with educational psychologist, happiness at school (all questionnaires except that for foster carers at Time 1)

- abuse (all questionnaires except that for social workers at Time 1).

We used chi square tests, tests for trend and t tests as appropriate. Obviously we could not use this kind of approach for questionnaires which were the only source of a par-ticular variable. We found that:

- those who had a returned fostering questionnaire at Time 1 did not differ from those without one on any of the variables tested

- those who had a returned fostering questionnaire at Time 2 were more likely to have remained with their foster carer

- those who had a returned social work questionnaire at Time 1 were more likely to have a disruption at Time 2, and had worse success scores and lower parenting scores at Time 1

- those who had a returned social work questionnaire at Time 2 were more likely to be male and more likely to have a disruption (just).

As can be seen, children who were the subject of a social worker questionnaire were more likely to have low first success ratings. This was an artefact of the way we defined the rating. Because most children were successful we based the rating on the lowest of three which could be made on each individual child. If three ratings were available (one from foster carer, one from social worker and one from family placement social worker) it was obviously more likely that one of the three would be relatively low.

Sources of bias in the children's questionnaires

As with the social worker replies we checked the representativeness of the children's replies by using information from the foster carer's questionnaire. In this case we restricted the analysis to children who were aged five or over.

Response rates were higher when:

- the child did not come from an minority ethnic group (37% as against 20%)
- the child remained in the foster placement (41% as against 28%)
- the child was ten or over (38% as against 28%)
- the child was female (39% as against 29%).

There were no associations with the degree of the child's disturbance (as measured by the Goodman total score), the measures of their foster carers, or their outcome measures.

The most likely explanation for the pattern of responses is that it was strongly influenced by ability to read and, since the questionnaire was sent some time after the one to foster carers, by whether the child remained in the placement. The response rate among children who were aged between 11 and 17 inclusive and who remained in the placement was 52 per cent and thus comparable with the 54 per cent achieved by social workers.

Conclusion

Our sample under-represents minority ethnic children in the authorities we studied, children related to their carers and children in respite care. By including three authorities with large minority ethnic populations we may have compensated for our failure to recruit a high proportion of those contacted. The proportion of minority ethnic children does not seem low relative to that in other studies.

These biases do not seem to affect the representativeness of our sample in terms of age, length of stay and so on (see Chapter 2). It is very unlikely that they influence our findings on the relationship between background variables and outcome.

The response rate among children does suggest a high degree of bias towards older children who could read and who remained in the same placements. Among these, the response rate was higher than expected. Their comments are therefore more likely to give insight into the situation of this older, longer-staying group of children than into those who stay briefly in foster care. This, however, is equally true of the study as a whole.

Selection of Placements for Interview

We selected 24 placements from four local authorities. We carried out:

- 24 face-to-face interviews with foster carers.
- 23 telephone interviews with child's social worker or link worker (2).

Criteria for selection
We selected 12 successful placements on the grounds that:

- foster carer rated a success for child and foster family
- child's problems said by foster carer to have improved on more counts than deteriorated.

We also selected 12 'less successful' placements on the grounds that:

- foster carer rated 'had gone as well as could be expected' or 'not very well'
- child's problems said to have deteriorated on more counts than improved.

We tried to match each case by:

- age
- sex
- time in placement.

In practice we ended by selecting 13 'successful cases' and 11 less successful ones. It was also the case as described in the book that some cases turned out better or worse than expected. Table A2.1 gives some basic details of the cases involved.

Table A2.1 Interviews

Name	Successful Age (years)	Time in placement (months)	Name	Less successful Age (years)	Time in placement (months)
James	9	24	Giles	10	34
Robert	11	40	Timothy	13	34
Oliver	4	12	Terri	5	20
Sally	12	14	Susan	14	14
Ashley	8	17	Daniel	8	6
Tobias*	18 mths	14	Liam	2	14
Paul	12	32	Gemma	13	36
Gareth	5	6	Leon	6	6
Donald*	20	96	Lindsay*	17	23
Helen	10	120	Carole	12	96
Kieran	10	7	Christine	15	15
Sophie	9	19			
Isobel	5	24			

*Foster child from minority ethnic group.

References

Aldgate, J. (1980) 'Identification of factors influencing children's length of stay in care.' In J. Triseliotis (ed) *New Developments in Foster Care and Adoption*. London: Routledge and Kegan Paul.

Aldgate, J., Colton, M., Ghate, D. and Heath, A. (1992) 'Educational attainment and stability in long-term foster care.' *Children and Society 6*, 2, 91–103.

Aldgate, J. and Hawley, D. (1986) *Foster Home Breakdown*. London: British Agencies for Adoption and Fostering.

Arden, N. (1977) *Child of a System*. London: Quartet Books.

Barn, R. (1993) *Black Children in the Public Care System*. London: Batsford.

Barth, R. and Berry, M. (1988) *Adoption and Disruption: Rates, Risks and Responses*. New York: Aldine de Gruyter.

Bebbington, A. and Miles, J. (1990) 'The supply of foster families for children in care.' *British Journal of Social Work 20*, 4, 283–307.

Beek, M. and Schofield, G. (2004) *Providing a Secure Base in Long-Term Foster Care*. London: British Agencies for Adoption and Fostering.

Berridge, D. (1997) *Foster Care: A Research Review*. London: The Stationery Office.

Berridge, D. and Cleaver, H. (1987) *Foster Home Breakdown*. Oxford: Blackwell.

Biehal, N., Clayden, J., Stein, M. and Wade, J. (1992) *Prepared for Living*. London: National Children's Bureau.

Biehal, N., Clayden, J., Stein, M. and Wade, J. (1995) *Moving On: Young People and Leaving Care Schemes*. London: HMSO.

Bilson, A. and Barker, R. (1992) 'Siblings of children in care or accommodation: a neglected area of practice.' *Practice 6*, 4, 307–318.

Borland, M., O'Hara, G. and Triseliotis, J. (1991) 'Placement outcomes for children with special needs.' *Adoption and Fostering 15*, 2,18–28.

Bowlby, J. (1971) *Attachment and Loss* (3 vols). Harmondsworth: Penguin Books.

British Agencies for Adoption and Fostering Adoption Statistics Project (1997) *Focus on Adoption: A Snapshot of Adoption Patterns in England in 1995*. London: British Agencies for Adoption and Fostering.

Broad, B. (1999) 'Kinship care: enabling and supporting child placements with relatives and friends.' In British Agencies for Adoption and Fostering (ed) *Assessment, Preparation and Support*. London: British Agencies for Adoption and Fostering.

Bullock, R., Little, M. and Millham, S. (1993) *Going Home: The Return of Children Separated from their Families*. Aldershot: Dartmouth.

Chamberlain, P. (1990) 'Comparative evaluation of specialized foster care for seriously delinquent youths: a first step.' *Community Alternatives: International Journal of Family Care 2*, 21–36.

Chamberlain, P. (1998) *Blueprints for Violence Prevention. Book 8: Multidimensional Treatment Foster Care*. Colorado: University of Colorado Center for Study and Prevention of Violence.

Chamberlain, P. and Reid, J. (1991) 'Using specialized foster care community treatment model for children and adolescents leaving the state mental hospital.' *Journal of Community Psychology 19*, 266–276.

Clark, H., Prange, M., Lee, B., Boyd, L., McDonald, B. and Stewart, E. (1994) 'Improving adjustment outcomes for foster children with emotional and behavioral disorders: early findings from a controlled study on individualized services.' *Journal of Emotional and Behavioral Disorders 2*, 207–218.

Cleaver, H. (2000) *Fostering Family Contact*. London: HMSO.

Cliffe, D. with Berridge, D. (1991) *Closing Children's Homes: An End to Residential Childcare?* London: National Children's Bureau.

Department of Health (1989) *An Introduction to the Children Act*. London: HMSO.

Department of Health (1999) *Children Looked After by Local Authorities: Year Ending March 1998*. London: Government Statistical Service.

Downes, C. (1992) *Separation Revisited: Adolescents in Foster Family Care*. Aldershot: Gower.

Farmer, E., Moyers, S. and Lipscombe, J. (2004) *Fostering Adolescents*. London: Jessica Kingsley Publishers.

Farmer, E. and Pollock, S. (1998) *Sexually Abused and Abusing Children in Substitute Care*. Chichester: Wiley.

Fever, F. (1994) *Who Cares? Memories of a Childhood in Barnado's*. London: Warner Books.

Fisher, M., Marsh, P., Phillips, D. and Sainsbury, E. (1986) *In and Out of Care: The Experiences of Children, Parents and Social Workers*. London: Batsford.

Fisher, T., Gibbs, I., Sinclair, I. and Wilson, K. (2000) 'Sharing the care: the qualities sought of social workers by foster carers.' *Child and Family Social Work 5*, 225–233.

Fratter, J., Rowe, J., Sapsford, D. and Thoburn, J. (1991) *Permanent Family Placement*. London: British Agencies for Adoption and Fostering.

Fry, E. (1992) *After Care: Making the Most of Foster Care*. London: National Foster Care Association.

Garnett, L. (1992) *Leaving Care and After*. London: National Children's Bureau.

George, V. (1970) *Foster Care: Theory and Practice*. London: Routledge and Kegan Paul.

Gibbons, J., Conroy, S. and Bell, C. (1995) *Operating the Child Protection System*. London: HMSO.

Glaser, B. and Strauss, A. (1967) *The Discovery of Grounded Theory: Strategies for Qualitative Research*. New York: Aldine de Gruyter.

Goldstein, H. (1973) *Social Work Practice*. Columbia: University of South Carolina Press.

Goldstein, H., Rasbash, J., Plewis, I., Draper, D., Browne, W., Yang, M., Woodhouse, G. and Healy, M. (1998) *A User's Guide to MLWIN*. London: University of London.

Goodman, R. and Scott, S. (1997) *Child Psychiatry*. Oxford: Blackwell Science.

Heath, A., Colton, M. and Aldgate, J. (1994) 'Failure to escape: a longitudinal study of foster children's educational attainment.' *British Journal of Social Work 19*, 6, 447–460.

Hensey, D., Williams, J. and Rosenbloom, L. (1983) 'Intervention in child abuse: experience in Liverpool.' *Developmental Medicine and Child Neurology 25*, 606–611.

Hill, M., Lambert, L. and Triseliotis, J. (1989) *Achieving Adoption with Love and Money*. London: National Children's Bureau.

Hunt, J. (2001) *Friends and Family*. Scoping paper prepared for the DoH (available on www.qualityprotects.doh.gov.uk/familycarerscoping.pdf).

Kahan, B. (1979) *Growing Up In Care*. Oxford: Basil Blackwell.

King, J. and Taitz, L. (1985) 'Catch-up growth following abuse.' *Archives of Disease in Childhood 60*, 12, 1152–1154.

Lahti, J. (1982) 'A follow up study of foster children in permanent placements.' *Social Service Review 56*, 4, 556–571.

Lambert, J., Essen, J. and Head, J. (1977) 'Variations in behavioural ratings of children who have been in care.' *Journal of Child Psychology and Psychiatry 18*, 335–346.

Loveday, S. (1985) *Reflections on Care.* London: The Children's Society.

Maclean, K. (1999) 'Meeting the needs of sibling groups.' In M. Hill (ed) *Signposts in Fostering: Policy Practice and Research Issues.* London: British Agencies for Adoption and Fostering.

Maluccio, A., Fein, E. and Olmstead, K. (1986) *Permanency Planning for Children.* London/New York: Tavistock.

Marsh, P. and Triseliotis, J. (1993) *Prevention and Reunification.* London: Batsford.

Millham, S., Bullock, R., Hosie, K. and Haak, M. (1986) *Lost in Care: The Problems of Maintaining Links Between Children in Care and Their Families.* Aldershot: Gower.

Minty, B. (1999) 'Outcomes in long-term foster family care: annotation.' *Journal of Child Psychology and Psychiatry and Allied Disciplines 40*, 991–999.

Minty, B. and Ashcroft, C. (1987) *Child Care and Adult Crime.* Manchester: Manchester University Press.

Packman, J., Randall, J. and Jacques, N. (1986) *Who Needs Care: Social Work Decisions About Children.* London: Basil Blackwell.

Parker, R. (1966) *Decisions on Child Care: A Study of Prediction in Fostering.* London: Allen and Unwin.

Parker, R., Loughran, F. and Gordon, D. (1992) *Children with Disabilities in Communal Establishments; A Further Analysis and Interpretation of the Office of Population, Censuses and Surveys' Investigation.* Bristol: University of Bristol.

Quinton, D., Rushton, A., Dance, C. and Mayes, D. (1997) 'Contact between children placed away from home and their birth parents: research issues and evidence'. *Clinical Child Psychology and Psychiatry 2*, 3, 393–413.

Quinton, D., Rushton, A., Dance, C. and Mayes, D. (1998) *Joining New Families – A Study of Adoption and Fostering in Middle Childhood.* Chichester: John Wiley.

Quinton, D. and Rutter, M. (1988) *Parenting Breakdown.* Aldershot: Avebury.

Rowe, J., Cain, H., Hundleby, M. and Keane, A. (1984) *Long Term Foster Care.* London: Batsford.

Rowe, J., Hundleby, M. and Garnett, L. (1989) *Child Care Now.* London: British Agencies for Adoption and Fostering.

Rowe, J. and Lambert, L. (1973) *Children Who Wait.* London: Association of British Adoption Agencies.

Rushton, A., Dance, C., Quinton, D. and Mayes, D. (2001) *Siblings in Late Permanent Placements.* London: British Agencies for Adoption and Fostering.

Rushton, A. and Treseder, J. (1995) 'An eight-year prospective study of older boys placed in permanent substitute families.' *Journal of Child Psychology and Psychiatry and Allied Disciplines 36*, 687–695.

The Scottish Office (1991) *Adoption Services in Scotland: Recent Research Findings and Their Implications.* Edinburgh: The Scottish Office.

Schofield, G., Beek, M. and Sargent, K. with Thoburn, J. (2000) *Growing Up in Foster Care.* London: British Agencies for Adoption and Fostering.

Sellick, C. and Thoburn, J. (1996) *What Works in Family Placement?* Ilford: Barnado's.

Sinclair, I. (1975) 'The influence of wardens and matrons on probation hostels.' In J. Tizard, I. Sinclair and R. Clarke (eds) *Varieties of Residential Experience.* London: Routledge.

Sinclair, I. and Gibbs, I. (1998) *Children's Homes: A Study in Diversity.* Chichester: Wiley.

Sinclair, I., Gibbs. I. and Wilson, K. (2004) *Foster Carers: Why They Stay and Why They Leave.* London: Jessica Kingsley Publishers.

Sinclair, I. and Wilson, K. (2003) 'Matches and mismatches: the contribution of carers and children to the success of foster placements.' *British Journal of Social Work 33*, 871–884.

Sinclair, I. Wilson, K. and Gibbs, I. (2001) 'A life more ordinary: what children want from foster placements.' *Adoption and Fostering 25*, 4, 17–26.

Stein, M. and Carey, K. (1986) *Leaving Care.* Oxford: Basil Blackwell.

Sykes, J., Sinclair, I., Gibbs, I. and Wilson, K. (2002) 'Kinship and stranger foster carers: how do they compare?' *Adoption and Fostering 26*, 2, 38–48.

Thoburn, J. (1994) *Child Placement.* Aldershot: Arena.

Thoburn, J., Norford L. and Rashid, S. (2000) *Permanent Family Placement for Children of Minority Ethnic Origin.* London: Jessica Kingsley Publishers.

Thoburn, J., Wilding, J. and Watson, J. (2000) *Family Support.* London: The Stationery Office.

Thorpe, R. (1974) 'Mum and Mrs So and So.' *Social Work Today 22*, 691–695.

Trasler, G. (1960) *In Place of Parents.* London: Routledge and Kegan Paul.

Triseliotis, J. (1973) *In Search of Origins.* London: Routledge and Kegan Paul.

Triseliotis, J. (ed) (1980) *New Developments in Foster Care and Adoption.* London: Routledge and Kegan Paul.

Triseliotis, J. (1989) 'Foster care outcomes – a review of key research findings.' *Adoption and Fostering 13*, 5–17.

Triseliotis, J., Borland, M. and Hill, M. (1998) *Fostering Good Relations: A Study of Foster Care and Foster Carers in Scotland.* Edinburgh: Scottish Executive Research Unit.

Triseliotis, J., Borland, M. and Hill, M. (2000) *Delivering Foster Care.* London: British Agencies for Adoption and Fostering.

Triseliotis, J., Borland, M., Hill, M. and Lambert, L. (1995) *Teenagers and the Social Work Services.* London: HMSO.

Triseliotis, J. and Russell, J. (1984) *Hard to Place – The Outcome of Adoption and Residential Care.* London: Heinemann Educational.

Wade, J. (1997) 'Developing leaving care services: tapping the potential of foster carers.' *Adoption and Fostering 21*, 3, 40–49.

Walker, M., Hill, M. and Triseliotis, J. (2002) *Testing the Limits of Foster Care: Fostering as an Alternative to Secure Accommodation.* London: British Agencies for Adoption and Fostering.

Ward, H. (1998) 'Using a child development model to assess outcomes of social work intervention with families.' *Children and Society* (Special Edition: Assessing Outcomes in Child Care, An International Perspective) *12*, 3, 202–211.

Waterhouse, S. (1997) *The Organisation of Fostering Services: A Study of the Arrangements for Delivery of Fostering Services in England.* London: National Foster Care Association.

Wedge, P. and Mantle, G. (1991) *Sibling Groups and Social Work.* Aldershot: Avebury.

Wedge, P. and Phelan, J. (1986) *Essex Child Care Survey (1981–1985).* Norwich: Social Work Development Unit, University of East Anglia.

Weinstein, E. (1960) *The Self-Image of the Foster Child.* New York: Russell Sage Foundation.

Whitaker, D. (1985) *Using Groups to Help People.* London: Routledge and Kegan Paul.

Wilson, K., Petrie, S. and Sinclair, I. (2003) 'A kind of loving: a model of effective foster care.' *British Journal of Social Work 33*, 991–1003.

Wilson, K., Sinclair, I., Taylor, C., Pithouse, A. and Sellick, C. (2004) *Fostering Success: An Exploration of the Research Literature in Foster Care.* London: Social Care Institute for Excellence.

Wolkind, S. (1977) 'A child's relationships after admission to residential care.' *Child: Care, Health and Development 3*, 357–362.

Zimmerman, R. (1982) 'Foster care in retrospect.' *Tulane Studies in Social Welfare 14*, 1–119.

Subject Index

The letter n refers to notes at the end of a chapter

Author Index

The letter n refers to notes at the end of a chapter